ULYSSES

AND JUSTICE

ULYSSES

AND JUSTICE

JAMES MCMICHAEL

PRINCETON UNIVERSITY PRESS

PRINCETON, NEW JERSEY

Copyright © 1991 by Princeton University Press
Published by Princeton University Press, 41 William Street,
Princeton, New Jersey 08540
In the United Kingdom: Princeton University Press, Oxford

Library of Congress Cataloging-in-Publication Data

McMichael, James, 1939–
Ulysses and justice / James McMichael.
p.   cm.
Includes bibliographical references and index.
ISBN 0-691-06547-0 (cloth : acid-free paper)
1. Joyce, James, 1882–1941. Ulysses. 2. Justice in literature.
I. Title.
PR6019.09U6837   1991
823'.912—dc20   90-42596

This book has been composed in Goudy with Futura display

Princeton University Press books are printed on acid-free
paper, and meet the guidelines for permanence and durability of the
Committee on Production Guidelines for Book Longevity of the
Council on Library Resources

Printed in the United States of America by
Princeton University Press,
Princeton, New Jersey

1   2   3   4   5   6   7   8   9   10

FOR BW

CONTENTS

ACKNOWLEDGMENTS

For their responses to different portions of this book at different times, I want to thank Mary Bartholemy, Michael Blaine, Eduardo Cadava, James L. Calderwood, Killarney Clary, Richard Ford, Alexander Gelley, Jesse Gellrich, Michelle Gellrich, Linda Georgianna, Louise Glück, Robert Harbison, Brenda Hillman, Rhoda Huffey, T. R. Hummer, Aletha Irby, Timothy Peltason, Robert Pinsky, Mark C. Taylor, Brook Thomas, Linda Wallace, Charles Wright, Barbara Wuest, and Joanne Zitelli. I am very grateful to Jane Lincoln Taylor, who copyedited the manuscript. To Michael Clark and Margot Norris I owe special thanks.

ULYSSES

AND JUSTICE

he began," the old 78 recording begins: "Mr chairman, ladies and gentlemen: Great was my admiration in listening to the remarks addressed to the youth of Ireland a moment since by my learned friend." And for just under four minutes—deliberately, solemnly, even with pride—James Joyce reads from *Ulysses* the only part of it he ever bothered to record.[1] It is a curious selection. With a hundred likelier and more welcome passages available to him, why did Joyce choose a minor character's reconstruction of a speech that someone named John F. Taylor gave in 1901 at a meeting of the Law Students' Debating Society?

An answer may be that it is one of the few passages in *Ulysses* whose scope is one thing when read as written, quite another when heard in the writer's voice. I am suggesting something different than that the spoken word is more forceful than the written, that any other passage Joyce had chosen to record would be comparably enlarged by that recording. Before I can explain how this particular passage is of greater range for Joyce's still-audible recording of it, I must therefore consider the passage itself in some detail.

It is the passage in which Professor MacHugh does his best to remember word for word Taylor's analogy between Israel and Ireland, two nations in bondage to the laws of their oppressors, each nearly paralyzed with need.[2] Just as Moses's had been, Taylor had told his Irish listeners, yours is "the language of the outlaw": against all odds, use it toward your deliverance.

Though Taylor had been urging first that Ireland use the Irish and not the English language, the chance to put English to work for Ireland is there at hand in the offices of the *Weekly Freeman and National Press* even as MacHugh speaks. However small and seemingly negligible, there are things to be done with the *Freeman*, things consonant with Taylor's words. Even the lowly canvasser for ads has hit upon a way to use that "GREAT DAILY ORGAN" (7: 84) as Taylor's outlaw would. Leopold Bloom is not there for the speech, is busy selling to a merchant named Keyes an ad he'll run with "two crossed keys" (7: 142), the

Part of this chapter was first published in *The Kenyon Review*—New Series, summer 1989, vol. xi, no. 3. Copyright© 1989 Kenyon College.

emblem a reminder to the *Freeman* readers that even the Isle of Man has its own Parliament while Ireland does not.

With its "innuendo of home rule," the pun on "KEY(E)s" (7: 150, 141) may have pleased Bloom when it dawned on him and whenever he thought about it later. But rather than settle for his pleasure in it, he is now doing the tiresome work of getting the idea into print. MacHugh and his listeners (the *Freeman*'s editor among them) work differently. They have become almost perfect at taking what pleases them in language and stopping there. As their own needs have, so have the needs of their people become too much for them. Doing as little as possible to meet those needs, they exhibit the symptoms of a disease that Joyce identifies again and again: sentimentality. Like many other characters in *Dubliners*, *A Portrait of the Artist as a Young Man*, and *Ulysses*, MacHugh and his listeners sentimentalize language by detaching the pleasure they take in it from the needs it obliges them to address.

"*The sentimentalist,*" it says in *Ulysses*, "*is he who would enjoy without incurring the immense debtorship for a thing done*" (9: 550–51). "Cribbed out of Meredith" (14: 1486), the definition is a useful index to motive in Joyce's world. Its last phrase, though, is taxingly vague. Is it someone else who does "a thing" that the sentimentalist then sentimentalizes, or is it "a thing done" by the sentimentalist himself? In Meredith's *The Ordeal of Richard Feverel*, it would seem to be the second if only by the narrowest of appeals to grammar. " 'My wound has healed,' " Sir Austin said to Lady Blandish. " 'How?' she asked. 'At the fountain of your eyes,' he replied, and drew the joy of new life from her blushes, without incurring further debtorship for a thing done."[3] Because her blushes are plural, the one "thing done" would seem to be the tribute that has prompted them. In having paid that tribute, in having done that "thing," Sir Austin sentimentalizes insofar as he enjoys the corresponding blushes but shuts down all "further debtorship" to the blusher. There are responses Lady Blandish might subsequently need from him now that he has fueled her romantic interest in him. He *owes* her these responses because of the "thing" that he has done. But rather than be guided by his new debtorship to her in such a way that he sooner or later offers her these responses, he sentimentally refuses to acknowledge his debt by substituting for it his sheer joy.

When I translate the scene from Meredith back into the seventh chapter of *Ulysses*, Professor MacHugh's reconstruction of the speech is the "thing done." Unlike Sir Austin, though, MacHugh is not the lone sentimentalist. Pleased by the speech because they sense that it is very much the kind of thing the Irish need to hear if they are ever going to make their world more adequate, MacHugh's listeners incur along with him a debtorship not only to Taylor but also to the Irish people as a whole. Rather than acknowledge that debtorship as they collectively do the "thing" of hearing it, MacHugh's listeners sentimentalize the speech by not questioning at all the manner in which he presents it.[4] Instead of offering it as a model for how to move people to act in their own and one another's best interests, MacHugh sentimentally domesticates the speech, he makes it more comfortable for his listeners and for himself by introducing it as "the finest display of oratory" (7: 792) he had ever heard. As "display," the speech need only please. Pleasant to feel one's "blood wooed by grace of language" (7: 776). Much less pleasant to be pointed by it toward unfinished business. MacHugh and his friends are forever ready to defer that business. Language, for them, responds to one need only: the need to be pleased by language.

The passage is largely ironic: here is a handful of characters whose sentimental irresponsibility with words is measured by the very words that please them. Now readers who are pleased to identify the irony incur a debt they must not sentimentalize if they themselves are to avoid becoming objects of that same irony. Joyce's recording of it emphasizes that the passage must not be sentimentalized. With the recording, the words MacHugh speaks are no longer quite as simply the words of a character. They are also, for the time they take to hear, the words of their writer. While in the written passage by itself MacHugh sentimentally eludes responsibility for what he says, James Joyce implicitly asks with his recording of it that those who hear him hold him answerable for what they hear. And more insistently than does the written passage by itself, Joyce's recording eases us into the places of MacHugh's listeners. That done, it charges us with the responsibility of doing better by Taylor's speech than MacHugh and his friends do.

But just how broad is that charge? Narrow enough if all we have to do is not get caught sentimentalizing political language. Our debtorship might have been limited to that if Joyce had excerpted from the passage as a whole only Taylor's speech. Had Joyce recorded only the speech, we could conclude that his indebtedness stops at the borders of the speech and that ours does too. We might conclude that whereas it is surely the province of political language to appeal to our indebtedness to other persons so that we will respond to their needs as justice demands, nothing comparable happens when we read a work of fiction. We might conclude that writers of fiction do not make that appeal since to make it is to abandon fiction for politics. Had Joyce recorded only the speech, we could hear it that he had momentarily transformed a small bit of fiction into politics but that it returned to its proper place soon after that and now exacts no debt from those who read *Ulysses*.

It turns out, though, that while the speech is central to the recording, Joyce also reads the omniscient narrator's introduction to the speech, the narrator's accompanying sentences in the past tense, the narrator's interjected headline "FROM THE FATHERS," and Stephen Dedalus's unexpressed thoughts in the present tense, as well as a sentence he remembers from Saint Augustine. Far from separating the languages of politics and fiction as if they had no business together, Joyce's recording of the passage mixes them, thereby complicating for listeners and readers alike the debtorship he feels is theirs if they find *Ulysses* pleasing. By recording the passage as a whole and not just Taylor's speech, James Joyce implies that persons who are pleased by *Ulysses* incur no less a debt than do those whom political oratory pleases. If it is sentimentalized, Joyce implies, *all* talk is cheap, even his own. He implies that it is not just Taylor's speech but also *Ulysses* that its readers must do better by than MacHugh and his friends do by Taylor's speech.

Sorting out how to do that is no simple matter, and I will begin cautiously, limiting my consideration to the passage Joyce recorded. The questions I will begin by asking are informed by the definition of the sentimentalist above. Do I enjoy the passage? If so, what is it about it that I enjoy? At the same time that I enjoy it, am I resisting a debt that would otherwise be mine? What is that debt, and what would it take for me to incur it so that my response to the passage might not be sentimental?

I enjoy the passage. I am "wooed" by the speech itself, as the characters are. But unlike them, of course, I am privy to the other words in the passage, words without which there would be no irony directed at their sentimental pleasure in the speech, since there would be no *Ulysses*. Were I to miss the irony, the passage would please me less than it does. My pleasure in it therefore turns at least in part on my knowing something about the characters that they seem not to know about themselves: that they are being sentimental. If they were persons about whom I knew as much as the passage allows me to know about these characters, what would my responsibility toward them be? Would I be obliged to call them on their myopia in the hope that they might correct it? Maybe they are better off seeing no more than they do. Unless they need to, persons do not insulate themselves so effectively from their responsibilities as these characters do. MacHugh and his friends have been so numbed by personal and national reversals that *not* to indict them for what they fail to see might be the course that responds most justly to their needs. Although passive, even that course would be taking me a step beyond sentimentality, for my response to their need would not have stopped as soon as I had had the pleasure of identifying the irony of their situation. But if that were the course I settled on, I would nonetheless have to answer for allowing them to move just that much further into helplessness.

Pleasant not to have to decide. As parts of speech that merely sub- stitute for the persons they would be but are not, MacHugh and his friends oblige me to do nothing other than to read and enjoy. Joyce having seen to it that they need nothing more than these specific words which render them the chacracters they are, there is nothing further to be done for them, and nothing to answer for in doing nothing further. As far as anyone's responsibility toward them goes, they are freebies. "No blame attached to anyone" if it pleases me to catch within the passage an irony the characters themselves would miss if they could read.⁵ Whereas persons are born subject to their needs and call to one another for justice, characters merely substitute for such persons. The characters in *Ulysses* are not the wretched of the earth. They are noth- ing more than parts of speech, words on the page. Since it is persons and not characters who need my unsentimental response and since the passage seems to implicate me with characters only, I can argue with some reason that I am not sentimentalizing if I simply enjoy it.

And yet while the character named Stephen Dedalus merely substi- tutes for a person who was born, his character connects discernibly with the person whose recorded voice I hear reading Stephen's thoughts. From inside Stephen's mind as he waits for the next installment of Tay- lor's speech, James Joyce says "Noble words coming. Look out. Could you try your hand at it yourself?" Stephen substitutes for a person who wants to try his hand at writing. Less than an hour before, on the strand, he had scribbled some lines of verse and then wondered "Who ever anywhere will read these written words?" (3: 414). When I read that question, I obviously become one answer to it: *I* am someone, somewhere, sometime, who has now read those written words. As an answer to it, though, I am implicated more immediately with the per- son who has written *Ulysses* than with the character named Stephen Dedalus, for I can be that answer only if I misunderstand what Stephen means by the word "these." Whereas I understand that Stephen means for it to refer back to the written words of his poem, I nonetheless allow it to take no antecedent, I allow it to signify "these written words" that form the question to which I am one answer. The connection between what Stephen means by the word and what I let it signify is the con- nection between character-as-would-be-writer-of-*Ulysses* and the per- son who wrote *Ulysses*. I say that it is a "discernible" connection be- cause I feel *Ulysses* encourages me to think of Stephen as a character who substitutes for James Joyce at age twenty-two. "Ten Years," Mul- ligan tells Haines about one of Stephen's few unguarded statements to him. "He is going to write something in ten years" (10: 1089–90).

Ulysses concludes with the dates "1914–1921." For all the differences
between Stephen Dedalus and James Joyce, Stephen can be read as a
portrait of that particular young artist who began to write *Ulysses* ten
years after 1904. Especially when it is reinforced by Joyce's recording,
Stephen's connection with Joyce is one that implicates me with the
person to whom I am indebted for the pleasure I take in *Ulysses*. Reading *Ulysses* is a "thing" I do. If I am not to sentimentalize when I read
it, I must incur my debtorship to James Joyce.

My understanding of that debtorship begins when I recognize *Ulysses*
as the testament of a person who wants justice, as most persons do.
Justice, as I understand it, is a situation in which every person has a
case with all persons. A person *is* a case in the sense that he calls for
help in meeting his needs. Help can come, though, only if he *has* a
case, only if another person hears his call and responds to it unsenti-
mentally. *Ulysses* is such a call. Joyce's case with me in *Ulysses* is that
he wants to be "with any as any with any" (17: 68), which he can be
only if every person has a case with all persons.[6] It is in this way that
Ulysses is as political as Taylor's speech. Aware that the Irish were pro-
foundly in need of help, Taylor was aware of his debtorship to them, a
debtorship he sought to offset at least a little by the thing he did in
giving his speech. More or less accurately remembered by MacHugh,
the speech passes Taylor's debtorship along to those who "enjoy" the
speech while at the same time sentimentally refusing to incur the debt.
As aware as Taylor was that there were Irish cases to be heard, Joyce
wrote *Ulysses*. Its characters are Joyce's answer to the question put to
him continuingly by persons in need: "What do you make of me, what
kind of case do I have with you?"[7] Other persons' cases having no less
to do with justice than his own, Joyce's case includes their cases, it is
integral to his own case that the cases of others be heard, his wanting
their cases to be heard is itself his own case and so he tells them as his
own.[8]

I will be distinguishing between a wider and narrower sense in describing James Joyce's case. In the wider sense, his case is that, wanting
them to be heard, he told the cases of his people. His case in the narrower sense is whatever he told that largely excludes the cases of others
in its focus on himself. Stephen Dedalus is a telling of Joyce's narrower
case. Rather than not tell it, Joyce told his case in this narrower sense,
I believe, so that his own would be one case among others, not indifferently above being told along with all the rest. It is the intolerable
discord between Stephen's narrower and wider concerns that holds him
back from beginning to write: for Stephen, being an Irish writer is a
contradiction in terms. It will of course have to become less contradic-
tory if *Ulysses* is to be the book he will begin to write "in ten years."

Though there are signs that it *is* that book, they must be read critically so that they are not mistaken as evidence that Stephen in 1904 is a portrait of the artist as a mature and not a young man.

One of the larger costs to Stephen in what seems to him his endless apprenticeship is the too-persistent fear that the words he tries his hand at will be lost. "—That is oratory, the professor said uncontradicted" (7: 879) after bringing Taylor's speech to its impressive end. In the respectful silence that follows, Stephen has time to reflect that his own writing will not win him the love and praise accorded to the great orators. Nor will even their words last. "Gone with the wind," Stephen thinks about any political speech. Then his thoughts focus on Daniel O'Connell. "Hosts at Mullaghmast and Tara of the kings. Miles of ears of porches. The tribune's words, howled and scattered to the four winds. A people sheltered within his voice. Dead noise. Akasic records of all that ever anywhere wherever was. Love and laud him: me no more" (7: 880–83). O'Connell's speeches in 1843 had drawn hundreds of thousands. He had called himself "the tribune," an officer whose job it is to protect plebian interests against the patricians. Four days after his speech at the Hill of Tara, the *Nation* reported O'Connell as saying that he felt himself at one with "the People of Ireland . . . in their wishes and wants." He said he was "speaking their sentiments and [seeking] to procure them relief."[9] It was because of O'Connell's unmistakable debtorship to them that the Irish were, in Stephen's terms, "a people sheltered within his voice."

But by 1904, the relief O'Connell had sought for the Irish had not come. The voice that had been their shelter was now "scattered to the four winds." After he thinks of O'Connell's words as no longer anything but "dead noise," Stephen makes one of those allusive leaps of his to "Akasic records of all that ever anywhere wherever was." Just minutes before, J. J. O'Molloy had mentioned "that Blavatsky woman" (7: 784) to Stephen. Stephen obviously has none of Madame Blavatsky's high-toned belief in the theosophical, but he has read in *Isis Unveiled* her description of the Akasa as "a vast repository where the records of every man's life as well as every pulsation of the visible cosmos are stored up for all Eternity!"[10] Minutes after thinking of O'Connell's voice as "dead noise" and being reminded of the Akasa, Stephen is again reminded of it by thinking of an encounter with a whore. "Damp night reeking of hungry dough. Against the wall. Face glistering tallow under her fustian shawl. Frantic hearts. Akasic records. Quicker, darlint!" (7: 927–29). Within the Akasa, which records all that ever anywhere wherever was, what's to choose between the noblest use of language and an illiterate prostitute's anxious plea for haste? How frantic must any heart be—hers, O'Connell's, Taylor's, Stephen's own—if the words that spill from it are to escape the fate of being "scattered to the four winds" along with everything else in the Akasic records? For Stephen, the Akasa is the consummate leveller of everything that matters to any person. Whereas frantic hearts are hearts in need of something that makes a difference to them, no one thing registers with the Akasa as more or less important than any one other thing. Its omniscience, Stephen thinks, is a standard for remembering. What it takes to meet that standard is perfect indifference to what is remembered, an indifference so thoroughly impersonal that it precludes that sense of debtorship to persons on which justice depends.

Because it goes on recording knowledge indiscriminately and for its own sake, the Akasa outlasts all other entrants in the contest for longevity that Stephen wants the words he writes to win. Despite his deep admiration for them, Stephen believes that O'Connell's and Taylor's words fare no better than they do because they are not for their own sake (though MacHugh and his friends sentimentally make them just that) but for persons in need. Wanting to be sure his own writing will avoid the trap of care for persons into which O'Connell and Taylor have fallen, Stephen may begin to see a writing modelled on the Akasa as the most promising alternative. It is a sentimental alternative. Rather than apply himself to a use of language that is just insofar as it issues from his debtorship to persons, Stephen covets the pleasures of authoring a deathless artifact. I imagine Stephen's casual "if you can't beat 'em, join 'em" attitude toward the "Akasic records" beginning to take form ten years later in the narrative structure of *Ulysses*.

A rather unlikely scenario, I admit. Throughout the day, Stephen's thoughts about theosophy are consistently derisive. Madame Blavatsky is ample proof to him that it is possible for some people to believe almost anything. And yet since what Stephen wants most is to author writing that will not die, he might well begin to consider writing a narrative that reads as if it issues from an all-knowing intelligence perfectly indifferent to what it knows. What might an intelligence like the Akasic records disclose about certain precincts in Dublin on a single day? About certain characters within those precincts? There is plenty of time for Stephen to ask himself those and related questions, since it is 1904 and the writing of *Ulysses* will have to wait. Immediately before remembering the prostitute, Stephen thinks the isolated word "Dubliners" (7: 922), unconsciously supplying himself with the title of the first of two books he will have to write before he can write *Ulysses*. By 1914, Stephen may have begun to imagine *Ulysses* as a tiny fraction of the "Akasic records," for *Ulysses* reads as if it might be the disclosures of an intelligence that goes on storing up "every pulsation of the visible cosmos."

But many other more conventionally omniscient narratives read that way as well. *Ulysses* is by all accounts an *un*conventional book. Stephen's interest in the peculiar indifference of the Akasa is useful to the degree that it lends focus to what is least conventional in *Ulysses'* omniscience. In the passage Joyce recorded, most of what the narrative discloses is conventional: that Professor MacHugh "began" to speak, the words he spoke, that "his listeners held their cigarettes poised to hear." Less conventionally, it discloses the unspoken thoughts of one of those listeners. But so unconventional is one of its disclosures that it and others like it within the chapter have with good cause been regarded by many readers as pivotal within *Ulysses* as a whole. Centered and in caps, "FROM THE FATHERS" is neither third-person disclosure of what was said and done in the offices of the *Freeman* between the hours of noon and one nor the first-person thoughts of a character in those offices at that time. It is instead one of the chapter's more than sixty headlines (or, more properly, "kickers"). Each headline is enough like all the rest that it can easily be gotten used to. But getting used to something obviously requires a shift away from something else. Most accounts of this shift describe it as one within which the narrative takes a peculiarly impersonal direction, a direction I read as being peculiarly compatible with Stephen's interest in the Akasa.

For Hugh Kenner, the first six chapters of *Ulysses* are at least partially controlled by conventions that a twentieth-century reader expects to find in any novel. The shift occurs when a second narrator emerges in the seventh chapter. Kenner describes this narrator as an "ironic, malicious figure."[11] Regardless of how malicious or ironic, a narrator remains personal to the degree that the term "narrator" always includes among its other possible referents "a person who narrates." While still just personal enough to be called a narrator, Kenner's second narrator prefigures within the narrative as a whole a "principle of pervasive indifference" that Kenner reads as dominating subsequent chapters.[12] His understanding of this principle may owe at least a little to David Hayman, whose designation of an "arranger" controlling the narrative is one that Kenner admires. The "arranger" of *Ulysses*, Hayman wrote in 1970, is a "figure or a presence that can be identified neither with the author nor with his narrators, but that exercises an increasing degree of overt control over increasingly challenging materials."[13] Ten years later, Hayman revised the definition. "Perhaps it would be best to see the arranger as a significant, felt absence in the text, an unstated but inescapable source of control."[14] Like "narrator," the word "arranger" can imply "a figure or a presence," in this case a presence who arranges, who cares to arrange. In Stephen's "Akasic records," thorough control of knowledge depends on there being no figure or presence who cares one way or the other about narrating or arranging, much less about the things known. Hayman's revision interests me in this light because while "figure" or "presence" is revised to "a felt absence," the arranger's control remains intact, almost as if there were a necessary relationship between absence and control, a relationship between them that *Ulysses* may be peculiar in exposing.

Karen Lawrence writes that the headlines in chapter 7 come from "a power outside that of the initial third-person narrator which has claimed authority for the establishment of the empirical world of the novel."[15] When the headlines intrude into that "world" from somewhere "outside," the illusion of the initial narrator's omniscience is punctured since there can be no knowledge "outside" everything that is known. In retrospect from chapter 7, the initial narrator has the look of a figure or presence who either knows less than everything or is concerned enough about preserving the illusion of his omniscience that he suppresses all "outside" knowledge about how to puncture it. Unconcerned, the "power outside" the initial power is like Hayman's revised arranger in that it is firmly in control of what is disclosed and in control because the "power" is felt in what is not there. Lawrence writes that the more conventional language of the first six chapters is displaced in chapter 7 "by a language not its own, as if the pen received automatic writing" from "the text of received ideas."[16] As do all the other headlines, "FROM THE FATHERS" reads as if it issues from an intelligence empowered by its receptive absence and its unconcern.

But however boldly these headlines announce a shift toward a narrating intelligence more unconventionally omniscient because more impersonal and indifferent, they are nonetheless the product of a person to whom they obviously make a difference. If Joyce is to have a case with me by way of *Ulysses*, I must follow each of three separable but commingled lines within its narrative.[17] One of these lines is the peculiarly omniscient because peculiarly impersonal narrating intelligence. Another is Stephen, who imagines writing a narrative as impersonal as the "Akasic records." "In a retrospective sort of arrangement" (11: 798) made possible by *Ulysses*, Stephen may be read as having written *Ulysses*. To read it this way, though, is to ignore the radical discrepancy between what Stephen imagines he will write and what Joyce wrote. A third line must therefore be pursued so that Stephen's immaturity may be read in retrospect for what it is. As separable as this third line is from the second, it remains as distinct from the first as a person who writes is distinct from a peculiarly impersonal narrating intelligence. The first and second lines are essential to my hearing Joyce's case, but it is this third that brings me closest to Joyce insofar as it is very much the most personal of the three.

Setting Stephen aside for the moment, I want to show that the lines of narrator and writer cannot be isolated without considerable and sometimes even strained effort. Does the headline "ONLY ONCE MORE THAT SOAP" (7: 221) issue exclusively from the impersonal narrator or is it infiltrated by the writer? Because it discloses knowledge of each of the soap's earlier appearances and discloses it as if from a point outside the time and space within which persons move, it can be said to come from the impersonal narrator alone. But does the agent of the headline not seem to take some pleasure in it? While it may be that the joy inherent in the headline is rooted in the narrator's debt-free omniscience, it may also come from the writer's satisfaction that he will share the humor of the headline with persons who find it funny. Once I identify even so small an opening for the writer in what is otherwise a peculiarly impersonal narration, larger openings present themselves as well. Because they collect "every pulsation," the "Akasic records" would surely be much less interesting to persons than *Ulysses* is. It can be said that the narrating intelligence behind *Ulysses* is personal to the degree that its disclosures are no less selective than James Joyce himself has made them.

And yet while it must be remembered that the three lines of narrating intelligence, would-be writer, and writer merge within *Ulysses*, my debtorship to Joyce requires that I not confuse them. For the purposes of recognizing what it has to do with Joyce's case, I will isolate the first by saying that the narrating intelligence behind *Ulysses* is *not* selective. According to the line I will follow on it, that intelligence's impersonal omniscience is not compromised when it discloses the headline insofar as what it discloses is its knowledge that readers are tiring of the pesky soap and will be amused to have had their minds read on this point. And I will say more generally that it is not the narrating intelligence's selectivity but rather its knowledge of readers that accounts for all disclosures in the book. Knowing that readers can take only so much of Tom Kernan and will require at least so much of Bloom, the narrator condescendingly discloses less of Kernan, more of Bloom, neither character mattering to it one whit, the readers themselves not mattering to it either except as things it knows. If anything can be said to matter to the narrating intelligence behind *Ulysses* it is its own omniscience, an omniscience that requires complete immunity from concern. When I speak of this intelligence, therefore, I am referring to a boundless store of knowledge about characters *and persons*, a store of knowledge perfectly consistent with what Kenner sees in *Ulysses* as "the principle of pervasive indifference."

"The intelligence behind *Ulysses*" is a cumbersome phrase and I will replace it with a word that may at first seem confusing. The word is

"Jamesy." It is a word that Molly Bloom may or may not be using to address the intelligence behind *Ulysses*. Thirteen characters in *Ulysses* are granted interior monologue. However short or long, monologues by each of the first twelve of these interrupt the omniscient narrative but are then absorbed back into it as it predictably and unfailingly resumes. It is only the last of the thirteen, Molly, whose thoughts are not stapled to the narrating intelligence. Just as that intelligence discloses in the earlier interior monologues its complete knowledge of the other twelve characters' thoughts, it discloses in Molly's that it knows hers too. For once and at last, though, it does not bracket its knowledge of a character's thoughts between third-person sentences in the past tense. Molly would have the last chapter of *Ulysses* all to herself if it were not for her suspicion that a narrating intelligence is there in every word as her monologue proceeds. Virtually immobile in bed, she is not sure she can as much as move without its leave. "I want to get up a minute if Im let" (18: 1104), she thinks as she feels her period coming on. Of those imagined people whose unspoken thoughts are written in *Ulysses*, it is Molly alone who acknowledges dependence on the narrating intelligence.

It is therefore she alone who seems to know it by name. "O Jamesy," she implores, "let me up out of this pooh" (18: 1128–29). It may be the case that these words are not addressed to the narrative, as I am claiming they are. "O Jamesy" may itself be simply another of Molly's "O, rocks"-like oaths (4: 343). Nor is "pooh" necessarily a noun and not an interjection. But the phrase can also be read as Molly's shot in the dark at what might be a narrator in the narrative. Her imprecation comes from the feeling that if there is such a beast as a narrator in *Ulysses*, then he has incurred a debt to her. While she has to grant that she depends for her very life as a character on this Jamesy's narrative, she has at least some claim on him since his narrative depends in turn on her very life. Since he can narrate her menstruating only because it is she who menstruates, the least he can do is bend the narrative enough to let her get up out of the "bloody pest of a thing" (18: 1534) he has left her with. I read "O Jamesy let me up out of this pooh" as Molly's exasperated but faintly hopeful call for justice.

Just as any character would be, Molly is of course only substituting for a person who might make such a call. Characters only play at enacting their wills. "Tom Kernan, harking back in a retrospective sort of arrangement talked to listening Father Cowley, who played a voluntary, who nodded as he played" (11: 797–99). The puns have it that Father Cowley plays two voluntaries at the same time. One of the two things he plays is a musical improvisation: the other is a person who does things on his own volition, a person, in Cowley's case, who improvises at the piano, who listens, nods and plays. Characters in fiction do nothing except play as if they have wills of their own out of which they act, the details of their play having been written for them letter by letter. Slaves to the narrative, they are almost always so without playing that they know it. Along with Molly, one possible exception is the lunatic Cashel Boyle O'Connor Fitzmaurice Tisdall Farrell, whose only words, spoken fiercely and with "ratsteeth bared," are "—*Coactus volui*" (10: 1111, 1113), I willed it under compulsion. It may be that Farrell has been driven mad because he has lost the innocence that preserves most characters' sanity. If he were innocent of the knowledge that he is a character in a narrative and therefore merely playing "a voluntary," Farrell would be spared the perhaps maddening awareness that the narrative compels him to function like a person with a will while seeing to it that he is not. Knowing that he is the property of narrative alone, Farrell may be parading his string of names in a vain attempt to establish as proper to himself at least that much.

Rather than having lost her reason because she knows that she is a character and nothing more, Molly challenges Jamesy to suspend the narrative for something they might both prefer. She challenges him to determine for himself if he would rather deal with her always as narrator to character or, if only this peevish once, as one person to another. Once would be enough to invoke justice. And justice, once invoked, would undermine the rules of completed narrative, rules, that is, which allow completed characters to substitute for persons who either do or do not deal justly with one another and for whom justice is therefore possible. Molly wants the impossible. She wants to be a person. Though she understands that she is at least substituting for a person, though she should perhaps count her blessings and abide unquestioningly by the rules that let her be such a substitute, she is momentarily unruly: she lets her narrator know that she thinks justice is better than the rules by which they are playing. And in no one other phrase does she come so close to being what she wants to be.

But at the same time that the narrative enclosure of *Ulysses* stretches its farthest toward allowing Molly to be a person subject to needs and calling for justice, it contracts to show that she is not a person at all but only narrated parts of speech in a book that is written and done with. Because he plays by the rules of completed narrative, Jamesy incurs no debt for the "thing" he does in disclosing Molly as a substitute for a person who needs to get up and go to the chamberpot. That she subsequently gets up and goes does not mean that Jamesy has responded to her out of his debtorship for a thing done. Responses take time. *Ulysses'* writtenness is its transport out of the time it takes to respond. "O Jamesy let me up out of this pooh" plays with the possibility of responsive, responsible, uncompleted give-and-take between character and narrator, almost as if "pooh" were not only the displeasing effects of Molly's period but the completed and therefore paralyzed narrative as well. Jamesy does not respond to Molly. If he can be said to mean anything, he means all along to narrate even her unruliness. Jamesy does not so much let Molly challenge him as force her to. Through his narrative, she summons him to give up his supremacy as narrator, to enter a world in which he would be "with any as any with any." But that summons is already too late since it arrives at all only because of the narrative it asks him to give up.

So it is of course only in play that Molly can be said to summon the narrator out of her need. She could not so much as play at knowing the narrator's name if she were not also playing that she knows the writer's. The word "Jamesy" hardly comes to her as a lucky guess. It comes instead with all the intimacy of a name she has used for years. By calling the narrator "Jamesy," Molly hints that she and a person named James Joyce have been familiar for at least as long as it took to write *Ulysses*. The tone of "O Jamesy let me up out of this pooh" is something like "Give it up, slyboots! We've been at this too long for you to be pretending that you don't know what I'm going through."

Jamesy is not pretending. Nor is there anything that Molly is going through. For her to be going through something, she would have to have time. She would have to have been born in Gibraltar on September 8, 1870, and to have lived a life commensurate at all points with the life narrated for Molly Bloom in *Ulysses*. Nor is that all. She would also have to have a time the anachronism of which can be resolved only in play. In 1921, when her "O Jamesy" assumes its timeless place in the completed narrative, the living being named Molly Bloom would have to be, not fifty, but an eternally-young thirty-three. Molly *is* thirty-three in 1921. But only because she is merely playing at being thirty-three in 1904, merely playing at having time.

James Joyce was born in Dublin on February 2, 1882. On his fortieth birthday, Sylvia Beach of Shakespeare and Company handed him one of the first printed copies of *Ulysses*. By calling the narrator "Jamesy," Molly plays at jostling him out of his imperious presence and back into the writer's time. Jamesy does not budge. There is not time for him to move since what is past is past. The writer's time was over when James Joyce abandoned the characters of *Ulysses* to the rules of completed narrative according to which characters no longer subject to change are substituted for persons. After that, Joyce did not give them any of his time.

Or could not give it, rather. Those are the rules. At some moment in his life, James Joyce stopped writing *Ulysses*. If there had been at least one more thing he meant to fuss with or fix, one more thing he meant to do to the book, he never did it.[18] *Ulysses* was at that moment complete. While *Ulysses* is Joyce's considered response to persons in need, its justice as response is compromised because by completing it he removed it from time. Time is essential to the sequence within which debtorship is incurred as persons again and again call for justice out of their needs. For the many persons who called to him for justice, Joyce substituted the phrases that are *Ulysses*. Each phrase was simultaneously a part of his response and his tacit question "Am I doing this person justice in this phrase?" When he stopped asking himself that question, as he obviously had to when he stopped writing the book, the case of each person was closed. In a case that is closed, a person who might otherwise have had a case has been removed. Because it is unjust to remove persons, there is a measure of injustice in closing a case. In *Ulysses*, Joyce is asking to be held answerable for the justice with which he has substituted completed characters for persons.

"A thing done," *Ulysses* as an artifact is a succession of words only if "succession" is an all-at-once. "Stately" does not precede "plump" as a first thing in time precedes a second: instead, it appears to the left of "plump" in the same line of type. Neither word is restless to connect with the noun it modifies further to its right, nor is that noun restless to connect with its verb. Syntax is not restless: it is the people who use it who are. Like that of any other completed, written thing, *Ulysses'* return to time depends on its being put to responsible use. Joyce was restless for it to make that return. I sense some of his restlessness in his recording, each of his spoken words falling on my ears before the ones to their right or further down the page.

But I sense Joyce's restlessness in the recording only because it is there for me throughout *Ulysses as written*. If there is in the narrative itself a narrator named "Jamesy," he is at once the least personal and most knowing of narrators—so knowing that it could be Jamesy himself who from all eternity inscribes the "Akasic records," only a minuscule fragment of which is disclosed in *Ulysses*. The fragment is enough to make it clear that Jamesy knows every need, debt, and response of every person, its readers included. If Jamesy's vast knowledge of persons were all *Ulysses* passed along to us, we could rest with what we ourselves can manage to know about *Ulysses*. That is not all it passes along. *Ulysses* is for us, but not in the sense that Joyce learned a great deal about persons in need, made what he learned available in *Ulysses*, and thereby absolved its readers of any debts for their reading beyond those that oblige them to be interpreters. There can of course be no response to *Ulysses* without interpretation. But interpretation alone cannot ensure the unsentimental response that justice demands. Because it passes along to us not only Jamesy's knowledge but also Joyce's restlessness, *Ulysses* nags at us to do justice by what we know.

I want to underscore this point because it will be central to my purposes throughout. By "Joyce's restlessness" I mean something that includes but does not stop at what Fritz Senn describes as "a restless Joycean strain that works against premature interpretation."[19] For Senn, the "highly different narrative programs" in *Ulysses* encourage a reader to acknowledge that "no single perspective is privileged" and that "Joyce allows each of them to correct the others."[20] As a compendium of all possible perspectives, the narrating intelligence that I call Jamesy contains the "correct" answers to every possible interpretive question. My project differs from Senn's and from that of many other Joyceans, I think, insofar as it assumes that *Ulysses* obliges me to interpret it with as much skeptical care as I can bring to it but also to do more.

Jamesy is strategic within my project, and for this reason I am superimposing him briefly on Senn's account of Joyce's restlessness. If in responding to Joyce's restlessness within *Ulysses* I myself were restless only to have the correct answers, I would want to be Jamesy, who has them all. Jamesy is Joyce's way of making it easy for me to feel whether or not that is what I want. Jamesy dramatizes the power I would enjoy if from a point outside myself I knew "all that ever anywhere wherever was." Joyce himself is of course much closer to that Archimedean point than I, closer to it by virtue of his having written both Jamesy and Stephen, a character on his way toward writing Jamesy. So close does *Ulysses* bring James Joyce to that perfectly restful point of all-knowing that his attendant restlessness in *Ulysses* is all the more unsettling. Instead of letting me read it as the case of a person who settled for the success with which he had promoted the illusion of unlimited cognitive reach, *Ulysses* makes me restless to apply whatever I learn about it to my dealings with persons who call to me for justice out of their needs. Much of the force with which it does this turns paradoxically on that grossly impersonal aspect of the book I am calling Jamesy. As an important first phase of my responding justly to *Ulysses*, I will identify Jamesy as Joyce's acknowledgment that his having completed a "thing" as successful as *Ulysses* does not acquit him of his ongoing and immense debtorship to persons in need.

II

I cannot recognize Jamesy as the intelligence behind *Ulysses* unless I distinguish him from James Joyce, a man of some intelligence. The distinction presupposes that James Joyce, a mere person, knows less

than the impersonal Jamesy does and that *Ulysses'* parts of speech disclose at least a little of what Jamesy knows. Molly's monologue prompting him to ask if Joyce knew what it means to be a woman, Patrick
McGee answers "Of course not." "Did Joyce know that he did not
know?" McGee goes on to ask. "Let's say that his writing knew."²¹ The
writing's knowledge exceeds the writer's, McGee implies, because it
somehow manages to slip beyond the limits of what a person of one sex
can know he does not know about a person of the other. When Julia
Kristeva describes *Ulysses* as "halting at no one identity—whether personal, ideological, or sexual—but knowing them all," she implies an
equation within which knowledge increases as it loosens its bonds with
any person who might be thought of as its agent.²² Jamesy is a name for
this equation. As Jamesy's knowledge about everything under the sun
accumulates, he himself becomes more and more impersonal, each side
of the equation augmenting the other, both sides in concert heighten-
ing the sense that *Ulysses* is absolutely authoritative because unau-
thored in any personal sense of the term.

Kenner's, Hayman's, and Lawrence's differing but related views imply that *Ulysses'* narrator is what Jean-Michel Rabaté says an author is,
"an essential absence which nevertheless ensures its transcendence in
immanence."²³ For me, Jamesy's authoritative "transcendence" depends on the "absence" of anything within his disclosures that would
allow me to mistake him as an even faintly personal intelligence.

I am aware that I have been asking the word "person" to carry a good
deal of weight. Its disjunctive relation to the word "author" is basic to
my use of it, and I can best say how I understand that relation by invoking the word "subject." While persons are themselves *subject* to a
host of conditions—the body and face that one is born with, one's own
untransferable mortality, the determinants imposed on one by one's
culture, one's limited as opposed to unlimited knowledge, one's debtorship to other persons—a person who authors is a person who sub-
jects. Each person is an author in the sense that she again and again
puts herself in the position of the grammatical subject "I" which in
stated and unstated phrases subjects other parts of speech to its assumed
authority. But from person to person and from time to time, the person
who authors is more or less personal, more or less authorial. The more
authorial I am when I think or speak or write, the less likely I will be
to acknowledge that I am subject to conditions including those imposed
on me by the structure and history of my language, and the more I will
be inclined to think of my words as having issued from a source whose
authority cannot be questioned insofar as it is a source prior to all conditions. As my urge to be this source increases, as there is less and less
evidence in my words that I remain subject to conditions nevertheless,

I pursue a course the goal of which is Jamesy. Jamesy's authority within *Ulysses* is simultaneously the greater and the more impersonal to the degree that he appears to be above or before conditions and therefore subject to none.

Such authority can be peculiarly disturbing. While readers seek an authorial power that subjects the written materials to its control, there is an obvious payoff when that power is at least personal enough so that they can identify with it. "We learn to abstract the author," Vicki Mahaffey writes, "honoring him or her as the operator of language and not as someone upon whom language operates, an exemption that we can then extend to ourselves as readers."[24] By assuming the authority implicit in the grammatical subject, an author extends to his reader by way of the transferability of that subject the very exemption he has assumed for himself: as author and not merely a person who writes, "I" supply you with a controlling perspective that you yourself then take on as an "I"-who-now-reads-what-you-authored. But if the cumulative effect of my phrases leaves you feeling that I myself am as thoroughly impersonal as Jamesy, there will be no such exemption—as Mahaffey insists there is none in *Ulysses*. What happens instead, she writes, is that the narrative's "willful opacity compels the reader to look *at* language" as at a condition that does some formidable subjecting of its own.[25]

When Fredric Jameson looks at *Ulysses'* language, he finds "a form of discourse from which the subject—sender or receiver—is radically excluded" insofar as any unifying, personally authorial perspective has been removed.[26] Jameson explains that removal as Joyce's response to the "increasing social fragmentation and monadisation of late capitalist society, the intensifying privatisation and isolation of its subjects."[27] Those who would themselves subject are instead subject to linguistic forms imposed on them by capitalism's deep investment in separating private from public and personal from political, a process that reduces its subjects to ineffective monads. Joyce's success in pointing toward a remedy for this subjection, Jameson claims, is to make us ask "why we should be interested in stories about private individuals any longer."[28] All Joyce gives us to care about in his protagonist is whether or not Bloom will reassert "his authority in what can therefore once again become a vital family unit," Joyce making it plain to Jameson that the political cost of such a unit is "monadisation," an unacceptable cost.[29]

Bloom's story as a political subject is a good bit more complicated than that for me. In my reading of it, which I work out in detail toward the end of this book, Bloom's problem with Molly is not that he has been exercising too little authority within the family but rather far too much. He has been authoring for more than ten years since Rudy's

death a story in which Molly agrees to his substituting domestic favors
and small sums of cash for the unrestrained attentions he knows she
craves from him. It is a story he tells himself daily and daily imposes on
his wife. He does this because the story forestalls indefinitely his being
subject to Molly's call. Bloom is afraid to answer her still unuttered call
because he fears that the "complete carnal intercourse" she desires with
him might result in the death of another child. Rather than having
authored her own story of the marriage, a story within which she allows
herself to call to her husband for what she wants most, Molly has been
conforming to the character that he has authored for her. As Shari
Benstock writes, "storytelling is a male province" in *Ulysses*.[30] Sexual
politics have worked their way so effectively into the goings-on at 7
Eccles Street that the implications of Molly's reticence reach well beyond the family unit. It is one of her responsibilities as a political subject not only to hear the case Bloom's tacit story tells her about his fear
but to tell her case as well. It is Bloom's long-overdue responsibility not
to be the only author in the house.

His situation with Molly is of course only part of Bloom's story as a
political subject. While for his own private purposes he subjects Molly
to his controlling perspective within the family, outside the house he
is something of a model among public men. His good offices to the
blind, the widowed, and the orphaned may strike Jameson as politically
trivial since they address nothing grander than individual needs, but
"it was Bloom gave the ideas for Sinn Fein to Griffith to put in his paper
all kinds of jerrymandering, packed juries and swindling the taxes off of
the government and appointing consuls all over the world to walk
about selling Irish industries" (12: 1574–77), "it was he drew up all the
plans according to the Hungarian system" (12: 1635–36). My reading
of *Ulysses* differs from Jameson's at least in part because I understand
differently than he the relation between persons and politics. With
Jameson, I feel that a person is a political subject when, along with
other persons who share his general needs, he acts toward the end of
becoming the author of his own political fortunes. Unlike Jameson,
though, I feel that a person is also a political subject when she responds
with some measure of justice to other persons whose very particular
needs she may or may not share. Whereas Jameson is convinced that
we must give over any lingering interest in persons since it only subjects
us all the more to the repressive forces we must act collectively to reverse, I am convinced that we cannot give up such interest without
also giving up the languages in which we think, speak, hear, read, and
write.

Jamesy's indifference to persons takes him a long way toward fulfilling Jameson's requirements for the political subject, Jameson attribut-

ing that indifference not to the narrator of *Ulysses* but rather (and mistakenly, I think) to its writer. For reasons antithetical to Jameson's, Joyce goes a long way toward fulfilling my requirements for the political subject. Through his writing of *Ulysses*-Jamesy, Joyce acknowledges and takes responsibility for what is necessarily impersonal and unjust in even the most personal of authorial perspectives. How he does this is not quickly told, and I offer here only a rough sketch of it.

Jamesy is Joyce's parody of the imperious author that lurks in all persons. As parody, it underscores the difference between *an author* and *a person who thinks, speaks, or writes phrases*. While "author" and "phrase-making person" are never altogether separable in any *person*, persons being both subject and subjecting, Jamesy is altogether *im*personal, altogether authorial and subjecting—and this despite the incontrovertible fact that he has been written by a person named James Joyce. Jamesy's omniscient disclosures throughout *Ulysses* are such pure examples of the authorial impulse to subject that they isolate that impulse and hold it up to view. Any person might understandably aspire to be Jamesy, Joyce's parody implies, because Jamesy's authority transcends the discomforting and ultimately fatal conditions to which all mere persons are subject. But the critique inherent in the parody also implies that Jamesy transcends these conditions only because his omniscience is so unmixed with traits that a more personal author would exhibit that it is hideously impersonal and as alien to justice as an intelligence could be.

Joyce does not exclude himself from the critique. To the degree that *Ulysses* creates the illusion of a narrator whose authority over his materials is absolute, it implies that James Joyce, the writer of the narrative, has managed to transcend the conditions to which he was subjected with his birth: but to the degree that Jamesy can be read as Joyce's critique of authorial power and its injustices, *Ulysses* is Joyce's acknowledgment that his own dominance as a writer is not at all the blessing that it may appear to be. *Ulysses* persuades me that the last thing Joyce wanted was to be mistaken for an intelligence which, like Jamesy's, is above justice—it persuades me that what Joyce wanted most was to be recognized less as an author than as a person who writes.

Among those things to which a person who writes is subject are the things he signs for when he writes. Jacques Derrida describes a "subjectivity" in Joyce, one that "delegates itself to the word" not so that it might subject what remains other for it, but rather in subjection to that other: "A, E, I, O, U, *I owe you*, with the *I* constituting itself in the very debt."[31] For Derrida, "any writing in the widest sense of the word pledges a *yes*."[32] This pledge is the "signature" that any writing bears, a signature that "assumes the irreversible commitment of the person con-

firming, who *says* or *does* yes, the token of some mark left behind."³³
The *yes* "always inaugurates a scene of call and request."³⁴ As "the pri-
mary telephonic 'Hello,' " it "asks only for another *yes*, the *yes* of the
Other," "it begins by responding."³⁵ The position of the grammatical
subject "remains derivative with regard to this *yes*" because the "I" itself remains subject to the Other's *yes*.³⁶ "The *Ich* in *Ich bin* poses itself
. . . not as *ego* . . . but as a pre-performative force which . . . marks
that 'I' as addressing itself to the Other, however undetermined he or
she is."³⁷

Whereas for Jameson the wholly impersonal and unresponsive discourse that I call Jamesy is all there is to *Ulysses*, Derrida recognizes in
that same discourse a person whose "I" is the "aye" as yes-to-the-Other,
a yes that "begins by responding" to the Other out of its "very debt."
The person who writes and publishes cannot determine in advance the
identities of those persons she addresses. But that indeterminacy in no
way absolves her of her debtorship to them. As she is, though as Jamesy
is not, they are persons in need, persons whose needs cannot so much
as begin to be met until they are responded to by other persons in some
just measure. Jamesy's perfectly authorial and impersonal "I" discloses
that it knows everything there is to know about persons in need: while
Jamesy's unresponsiveness to those needs avoids the charge of sentimentality insofar as Jamesy is above enjoyment as he is above all other
personal things, a person is sentimental if he enjoys Jamesy's knowledge
without at the same time following James Joyce's lead as an "I" who
"begins by responding."

Joyce lived far enough into an age of mechanical reproduction that
he can still speak to us from the dead as O'Connell cannot, "Have a
gramophone in every grave or keep it in the house. After dinner on a
Sunday. Put on poor old greatgrandfather. Kraahraark! Hellohellohello
amawfullyglad kraark awfullygladaseeagain hellohello amawf krpthsth"
(6: 963–66). Joyce may have had moments in which he felt that what
he was leaving us in *Ulysses* was no likelier to elicit the Other's *yes* than
was poor old greatgrandfather's final garble. Derrida writes that Joyce
was "hardly ignorant of the fact that the book of all books . . . is still
fairly inconsequential among the millions and millions of others in the
Library of Congress."³⁸ When Joyce called *Ulysses* "his usylessly unreadable Blue Book of Eccles," his play on the words "Ulysses" and "useless"
was amused but also wistful, maybe even slightly self-pitying, as in
"Why couldn't the book have come to more?"³⁹ It comes to so much
for so many of us that it is easy to play down Joyce's own restlessness
with it even when that restlessness is there to be read in *Ulysses* itself.
As modifiers of his "Book," "usylessly" and "unreadable" may be unconnected, readability and usefulness each boycotting *Ulysses* indepen-

dently. I am going to be treating the two as if they are connected, though, as if to be able to read *Ulysses* requires that it be put to use beyond the uses of pleasure. For me, *Ulysses* is a do-it-yourself kit to ward off sentimentalizing. My task here is to say how I read its accompanying instructions.[40]

III

The use to which I put *Ulysses* begins with my letting Joyce have a case with me. As I have already said, letting him have that case requires that I follow each of the three lines of Jamesy, Stephen, and James Joyce. I will be following these lines so that I can be as clear as possible on how the person who wrote *Ulysses* differs both from the peculiarly impersonal and authorial *Ulysses* and from the character who may mature to write *Ulysses*. When I follow these three lines, Joyce's case with me is that he wants justice for all. In asking for my *yes*, in asking to have a case with me, Joyce asks that I hold him answerable for the justice with which he has told the cases of others. I can do what he asks only if I use *Ulysses* against him, only if I scrutinize it for its injustices, some but not all of which Joyce may himself acknowledge in *Ulysses*.

But since it is justice for *all* that Joyce wants my *yes* to and not only justice for himself, I cannot allow his case with me to be circumscribed by my dealings with *Ulysses*. What I must do instead is to put those dealings to use in my encounters with persons. If I am not to sentimentalize *Ulysses*, if I am to do its writer justice, I must do more than let it instruct me in how to do justice by all persons: I must also be coerced by it into getting justice done. The "thing" I do in reading *Ulysses* is sentimental unless I apply its instructiveness to matters other than itself, matters that impinge however slightly on a plurality of people and are political to that degree. Beyond the help it gives me in holding James Joyce answerable for the justice with which he has told the cases of others, *Ulysses* is useful insofar as it helps me do what I must in responding to persons. Because it is no more than speculative, of course, this book is *not* my response to persons: to say how I put *Ulysses* to use is not to put it to use.[41]

I said above that the characters in *Ulysses* are Joyce's response to persons in need, persons who wanted to know what he made of them. Far more often than not, understandably, the person Joyce responded to had not come right out and asked to have a case with Joyce but had only and quite inadvertently summoned his attention. Persons tacitly ask to be noticed simply by appearing where other persons can see them. What Joyce made of the person he noticed least was no less that person's case with him than if he or she had commanded Joyce to tender his appraisal on the spot. Joyce's response to them by way of *Ulysses'* characters was also tacit in that many of those persons never read *Ulysses*, and some among those who did read it failed to recognize their cases between its covers. Tacit as well is Joyce's request that I let him have a case with me. What I am setting out to do in this book is to be as explicit as I can about the ways *Ulysses* impresses its political imperatives upon me. If I am to do that, I must first give some account of what I understand to be the mostly tacit way in which persons call to one another and respond. [42]

Suppose that you and I are friends. When I answer your greeting by asking how you are, I am tacitly asking that at some point in our conversation you ask me how things are with me. Suppose that you do. There is a tacit interrogative in the declarative mood I use to tell you about my recent run-in with X. It asks you what you make of me, asks you, in the terms I want to apply, to let me have a case with you. I will have that case only if you hear what I say and judge it worthy of response. Suppose that your response is one that falls between your taking my side against X and your thinking that I have once again behaved like a fool. I may need very much for you to take my side and to tell me so. But what I need even more is for you to respond in whatever way you do, which will include the degree to which you tell me how you respond. Even if your response is tacit, it is something you do for me since anything else you do or say for me will be influenced by it in however small a way.

There are many reasons that I tend to be more tacit in asking you to hear my case than in asking you to pass the salt. I may not know you well enough to trust you with an explicit telling of my case. If I want to impress you as having great aplomb, I will probably keep to myself a request that might betray me. I may be taciturn about my needs because you are a friend I do not want to worry. I may be too unclear about whether I ought to have a case to trouble either of us with my confusion. Or I may think I am clear when I am not and thus proceed to tell you things explicit in themselves but so confused that they leave my case tacit for you. I may be manipulatively coy, may deflect what I am asking you by seeming to ask nothing at all. My case may have to remain tacit for less immediately personal reasons if you are not my friend but rather someone I do not know. It may have to remain tacit until it reaches you in an another part of the world or until it is translated into a language you speak. It may have to remain tacit until you distinguish it, from among others it resembles, as one person's case. My case may have to remain tacit until another person tells it for me since I myself am forcibly stopped from telling it or because I am dead. [43]

A case may remain tacit too because I, the person asked to hear it, allow it to remain that way. I am slow to question your politeness by demanding "Now exactly what is it that you're asking of me?" Just as manners dictate that I ask you about yourself if I need you to ask me about me, they also protect me from what would otherwise be an un-manageable flood of appeals to hear one or another person's case. The legal system offers me related protection by supplying persons with a place identifiably separate from me where they may contest their differ-ences. Persons who work together for a cause also allow cases to remain tacit for me. Because they are out to improve the lot of the persons for whom they speak and because they have settled on what that improve-ment must be, they tell a single case only and it is the case of no one person. Because each person they serve is for them a representative victim of the same injustice, whatever else there may be to his or her case remains tacit for me until I have heard it and judged it worthy of response.

But manners, laws, and responsible collective efforts do not absolve me of my obligation to let each person have a case with me even when that case is tacit only and not expressed. Because there is much in your case that remains tacit for me, I must assume enough but not too much to do it justice. It can be so unpleasant to answer for my unjust assump-tions that I am sometimes tempted to assume nothing whatever about your case. I wait for the least presumptuous time to ask you for clarifi-cation of what remains tacit in it for me. That time never seems to come and I wait longer, I tell myself that I can wait until you tell your case explicitly and expressly for me. The waiting itself is anything but pleasant, though, for I am answerable throughout it to what you are asking tacitly of me, which is to do your case justice. Because I cannot postpone my obligation to you, I often want nothing so much as to forget the obligation itself.

I forget it from time to time but it is always there. It is always there because there is always more to your case, to which I have not yet done justice. Unable to postpone my obligation to you or to forget it in a way that lasts, I am nonetheless free to excuse myself from it simply by being reasonable. I come up with reasons to forget what I owe.

Some of these are very good reasons, some not so good. Each of them, though, is a reason not to be *for* another person, a reason not to do for him what his need obliges me to do.[44] These reasons are elitist, the debt itself egalitarian in the extreme. I invariably have my reasons for doing more for this person than for that, reasons that protect me from the acknowledgment that my debt to each is unaltered by the discriminations I make between them. Since there are as many reasons to forget my debtorship as there are persons to whom I am indebted, the sampling below is as incomplete as it is impersonal. I offer it only for whatever it may suggest about the ways my reasons empower me to forget to do what I must. While one reason leads to the next at some points in the list, I am not implying stages in a chronology. In my dealings with a person, I pass from one of these reasons to another only as the circumstance tempts me to. Each item in the list is separate and self-sufficient. When I appeal to any one or to any combination of them, I have the temporary assurance that reason is on my side.

(1) What I offer another person only seems to be of help. Because it increases his dependence on me, my so-called help increases rather than lessens his need. If I am to be *for* him I must offer him no help.

(2) I either cannot or do not stop myself from resenting that I have to help him. He knows I resent it and wisely refuses to be helped by me. If I am to be *for* him I must forget my debt *to* him and stay out of his way.

(3) It is clear to me that I must help him *and* that I have helped him all I can. There are limits to how much I can bring myself to do for him. I have reached my limit.

(4) Even if I have exceeded my limit with him, there is more to be done. Since I suspect that I simply will not do it, it is therefore best to put the person out of my mind.

(5) It turns out that I do not put him out of my mind. By thinking intensely enough about how remiss I am in meeting my debt to him, I shift my attention away from his need and onto my guilt. The guilt proceeds from an awareness of his need, an awareness so acute that it should move me to do what I must. But that is not the way my guilt works. Posing as something between me and him, my guilt is instead and solely between me and me. This arrangement has its comfort. My debt to him discomforts because it remains outstanding for as long as he is in need: as a debt to myself that poses as a debt to him, on the other hand, guilt is a debt I can acquit again and again by repeatedly feeling guilty. Guilt lets me adjust to knowing that I am failing him in some way, it lets me meet my debt to him with feelings that do not move me toward him but rather and more imperviously back into the feelings themselves. Indebtedness, by contrast, is a prod. It is the feeling that I must say or do for him something I have not yet said or done, something that remains to be said or done because I have not yet managed to let him have a case with me. Having come to understand that guilt is a trap, I now have another reason to put the other person out of my mind: since guilt takes me away from my duties and into myself, I must

avoid all response to the other person who prompts that guilt in me.

(6) I insist, if only to myself, that duty is a two-way street. What, after all, has he been doing for me? Debts between persons, I reason, are reciprocal. If he is doing no more to meet my needs than I am to meet his, then I am not in his debt.

(7) As I am not in his debt if I submit my understanding of debt to the following critique. What I am describing as debt is a ridiculous exaggeration of what any person expects from me. Debt, as I describe it, is almost comically unreasonable. If I were to be led by it, I would spend most of my time going around like a lunatic asking people what they need. I come up with as many sound reasons to forget my debt because so torqued a view of debt *should* be forgotten. I tell myself that what I'm calling debt is mere hyperbole, a figure that dramatizes and renders absurd whatever I do not like about having to deal with persons. The other person's need simply is not my unconditional duty. I must therefore drop what I have understood debt to be and start over with a less histrionic, more reasonable version of it, a version I would be likelier to be guided by toward a debt I would be likelier to meet.

This last reason is of course the subtlest and most comprehensive. I would like to be persuaded by it. Failing that, I would like to feel that what stops me from being persuaded by it is my uncommon moral integrity, I would like to feel that in spite of all the reasons not to hold to it, I hold to my understanding of debt because I am good.

But what I feel instead is this: I do not hold to my understanding of debt: debt holds to me. It is not at all a feeling I champion. Neither is it one that I am glad to have. It is a feeling I am no abler to decline than the feeling that I will die. As a person in a world with other persons living and dead, I feel that I am subject to my indebtedness to persons, subject to it no less than to other unpleasant conditions about which I was not consulted before I was born.[45] The feeling of indebtedness that duty springs from has less to do with ethics than with the way another person's need adheres to me. Since I am subject to my side only in my dealings with him, since from my side of them those dealings begin with me, I am a first person to his second. Implicit in his call is the call of every person other than myself.[46] Because another person calls to me from within a polis that entangles each person with every person, his call reminds me of my debt not only to him, a second person, but to all third persons as well, to all persons any one of whom becomes a second person as soon as I am faced with him. Whether tacit only or loud and clear, the other person's call is as discomfortingly adhesive as there is a world of second and third persons who are in need.

When I respond justly to his call I am not being good but only doing my political best to loosen its hold. It pleases me, of course, if I can think I have had a part in helping him. What I get back most when I respond justly, though, is the always temporary sense that his need sticks less to me. While it does not acquit the debt, which remains outstanding for as long as he is in need, my responding justly to him allows me to sense that I am entangled with him exactly that much less by duty, exactly that much more by the pleasure he brings me insofar as he responds to my needs. Only if I sense this lessening can I also sense that within a world filled with persons there is room for my being pleased.

As a person with needs, I am a case to be judged by other persons. My needs are considered, though, only if I have a case, only if another person lets me have a case with him by hearing my tacit or explicit call and judging it worthy of response. Wanting my needs to be judged worthy of response, I may want to hold the other person responsible for hearing my case. But I have no right to what I need from him. Neither is there anything I can do to earn such a right, though I can pretend that there is. I can pretend that debt's adhesiveness is a feeling that operates in the other person and not just in me. By pretending that I can look at my dealings with him from a point outside myself, I can insist that my responding to his call obliges him to respond to mine. But no such point is available to me since I am subject to my side only in my dealings with him and can do nothing to alter that subjection this side of death.[47] He may say the same about himself from his side of our dealings, but that is up to him. From my side, from the only side to which I am subject, he owes me nothing.

I can know he owes me nothing and still expect some consideration from him, still be disappointed when it does not come. And yet what I must do for him is unpleasant not because I am sometimes disappointed in what I get back when I do it but only because I do not always do it, do not always do what I must. If I always did what I must I would be living justly. That is not how I live. The other person calls to me in his need. What I must do is respond to his call, as I will invariably do once I have let him have a case with me. Not letting him have that case is therefore my last line of defense against doing what I must. It is a defense I unjustly resort to again and again. Distracted, self-absorbed, put off by knowing how unstinting need is and that I will never be acquitted of my debts, I do not let the other person have a case with me, I fail to do what I must if there is to be justice, that impossible situation in which each person has a case with every person.

Justice is impossible if only because there is too little time for me to hear every person's case, each case needing to be heard anew with each change in the person's need. It would spare me much displeasure if I could quietly wish for justice as for utopia: but justice is more than utopian for the person who wants it since wanting it is a restlessness for which there can be no time at that end of political history that any utopia presupposes.[48] Although impossible, justice is what I want. And yet just as knowing what I must do does not keep me from forgetting or refusing to do it, neither is it enough for me to want justice, the impossibility of which keeps me restless. Restless to do what I must and displeased that I forget or refuse to do it, I come up with yet another reason not to meet my debts: I tell myself that what I want more than justice is to be debt-free. Understanding that I can be debt-free only if the other person is need-free and understanding that he will not be need-free until he dies, I stop myself from wanting him dead only by controlling how his obliging need affects me, I keep him at a safe distance by not letting him have a case with me.

If I am to be for justice by letting another person have a case with me, I must do more than give his sometimes only tacit case a hearing: I must tell it as well. Like James Joyce and, I suspect, like almost everyone, I am a teller of persons' cases.[49] A person *is* a case. A character is the case a given person has with me when I tell his case either to myself or to someone else. For me even to think about a person is to make a character of him by substituting thought for person. Though it can seem to be, the character I make is not the person it substitutes for.[50] It is instead something that is mine, something I am quite free to make of what I will.

But whatever I make of it I am answerable for according to how justly it is made. Relying on assumptions, any one of which may be unjust, I tell your case to myself by thinking about you, I substitute for your person a character that is nothing other than my series of phrases, each of which I must answer for. Each phrase is accompanied by a question I must but possibly will not ask: "Am I doing this person justice in this phrase?" The question refers to you in the third person rather than in the second because while I am answerable to you for the way I tell your case, I am answerable for it as well to every person. By my obligation to do you justice I do not mean that I must get down to the truth about you. Neither do I mean that I am answerable for it only if I tell it to you or to someone else. Even when it remains tacit because I tell it only to myself, the way I tell your case is something I must answer for not to the truth nor to God nor to humanitarian principles but rather and more unpleasantly to you as to all persons.

Subject to my unpleasant debt to you, I am understandably restless to be acquitted of it. It is when my restlessness with it gets the better of me that I may be sentimental. Not enjoying in the slightest my immense debtorship to you, I do something that lets me think that I am responding justly to you though I am not: I make a character of you that I enjoy in direct proportion to how little debt I incur in making it. This character is no less sentimental if I make it sinister and not saccharine. Under what passes with me as an abundance of feeling either for or against you, a feeling that makes me tell your case in just this way, I sentimentalize by forgetting that the way I tell it is something I must answer for. Because it is more enjoyable to forget what I must answer for to you as to all persons, I let myself think that I am answerable for the way I tell your case not to you or to anyone else but rather and only to the character that I have made of you.

If I could rest with what I am calling sentimentality, your case would be closed. My debt to you obliges me to keep your case open so that I may respond to you in a way that promotes your well-being in time.[51] When I sentimentalize, though, I revise my phrases about you not so that I can keep up with my debt but rather to the end of getting your character right once and for all. Restless to acquit my debt and sentimental, I indulge myself with the illusion that I am at last right about you, that I am in the right, with nothing owed. For the question "Does this character do the person justice?" I substitute the assertion "It will always be thus for me with that person," an assertion that follows from my having substituted one unchanging character for you and another for myself. Having gotten that fix on both characters and holding to it, letting myself have much the more compelling case, I have a sentimental defense against any debt-incurring surprises that would otherwise be coming my way from you if I were instead to do your case justice.

My feeling of indebtedness to you does not let me stop there, though, because you do not. Your tacit request that I let you have a case with me reminds me again and again not to be sentimental. I must not rest with either character, you remind me tacitly, but must keep revising each so that surprises between us are still possible. You remind me that the enjoyment I take in the two fixed characters is not a sign that I have acquitted my debt to you or even decreased it. The more pleased I am to have substituted finished characters for the always unfinished business of the debt, the less I keep up with my duty because the less I have to do with you. You remind me that any pleasure I take in the substitution renders me increasingly derelict. Because of that pleasure I have all the more to answer for to you, as to all persons.

This is to say that I have much to answer for if I turn you into a character in a book. Imagine that I have committed to writing at least some of the phrases I had been telling myself about your case. Once that writing is complete, once it is "a thing done," it is out of time. Between the timelessness of what I have written and the time of my accumulating debt to you there is a difference I must answer for. I do not answer for it if I am sentimental. What I do instead is to think of time spent having written your character as time spent having paid off my debt to you. Sentimentally thinking of those two times as if they were the same, I tell myself that I have substituted for your person a character to whom I owe nothing now that the writing itself is complete. For my person, the person whose debt to you increases in proportion to my sentimental pleasure in the writing, I substitute a character who is pleased with what he has written, pleased with it, that is, if only to the degree that he does not destroy all extant copies of it and so consents tacitly to its being read.

I am free to substitute a comparably sentimental character for myself when I read *Ulysses*. As those of the persons to whom I am in debt are not, the cases of *Ulysses*' characters are closed. I am free to forget the temporal difference between those characters and persons because I am free to accept the disclaimer implicit in works that are normally called fiction: "Any resemblance between these characters and persons living or dead is purely coincidental." As any writer can about his or her work of fiction, James Joyce can reasonably imply that he is doing something other than telling persons' cases in *Ulysses*. Since most of his characters are products of what he noticed not about any one person but rather about more than one or even many, those characters can reasonably be thought of more as an imagining than as the telling of a case. I am free to believe that because Joyce has imagined within one character the traits (some of which may of course themselves be imaginary) of many persons, he is not answerable for that character in the same way that I am answerable for what I think, say, or write about a person. If Joyce is not answerable for one or more of his characters, then neither am I. It pleases me to be dealing with the closed cases of *Ulysses*' characters without at the same time having to answer for those closures myself or to hold the writer answerable for them. Behind what passes as an abundance of feeling for the persons for whom *Ulysses*' characters substitute, I sentimentalize what I read by regarding it as off-duty time, time out, a time removed from what is owed to persons because a time removed from persons.

But however "purely coincidental" their connections with persons, the characters I read in *Ulysses* substitute nonetheless for persons. It is a curious thing about a character that it can substitute for a person even when it does not connect discernibly with any one person who was born. Because persons are continuingly telling the cases of persons to themselves and one another, characters in books are not like the persons we tell the cases of, but more of the same kind of telling. Whether or not it connects discernibly with any one person, a character in a book substitutes for a person because its writer is himself someone who continuingly substitutes phrases for persons in his response to them. When he writes a character whose connections with any one person may be claimed to be purely coincidental, he is supplying neither himself nor his reader with time out. For such a character is itself a part of the writer's continuing response to persons.

Leopold Bloom is *Ulysses'* most prominent example of a character substituting for more than one person. Richard Ellmann has identified three persons for whom at least some of the phrases that make up Bloom substitute.[52] Since Joyce has combined phrases that he substituted for one person with phrases that he substituted for other persons still, he has removed no one person in having closed Bloom's case. And yet while he therefore might not have to answer for any injustice in his writing of Bloom, Bloom substitutes nonetheless for a person whose imminent removal Joyce boasted of in August 1921. He had been telling himself at least something of Bloom's case for fifteen years, had spent much of the past seven making it available to anyone who might be interested. Enough is enough. "Bloom and all the Blooms will soon be dead, thank God," he wrote to Harriet Shaw Weaver just after beginning to write the final chapter of *Ulysses*.[53] Three weeks later he wrote to her to say "I have been in training for a Marathon race by walking 12 or 14 kilometres a day and looking carefully in the Seine to see if there is any place I could throw Bloom in with a 50 lb. weight tied to his feet."[54]

The sentence is more fun than it would be if Bloom were a person Joyce was dying to kill. It is fun to recognize that substitutes for persons cannot be murdered while persons can be. But if in reading Bloom's character I reason that a person has been removed only figuratively and that Joyce therefore does not have to answer for having closed a case, I respond neither to Bloom's case nor to Joyce's but only to the fun. *Ulysses* persuades me that there is an undercurrent of seriousness to Joyce's playful malice aforethought as he is about to finish Bloom off. Tacitly, throughout *Ulysses*, Joyce asks that I let him have a case with me by holding him answerable for the cases he has closed, holding him answerable for them not as if he were a murderer but because there are unjust consequences when someone closes a case.

As I have said, I would not hear Joyce's case if it were not for Jamesy. A figure for *Ulysses'* authorial, all-knowing completedness, Jamesy is Joyce's acknowledgment that *Ulysses* leaves its writer subject to the charge of having closed a multitude of cases—more cases, as I will explain, than those of the persons for whom its characters substitute.

1.

J A M E S Y

Dublin at One Remove

I read *Ulysses* as the testament of James Joyce, a person who wants justice. The book's most notable paradox for me is that those peculiarly *im*personal elements I refer to as "Jamesy" are basic to what I find most personal about it. Under Jamesy's name, I will be identifying these elements and describing how they render *Ulysses* more personal.

Jamesy is an illusion constructed by James Joyce. It is the illusion of an impersonal, omniscient, debt-free intelligence that is thoroughly indifferent to what it knows. While I do not forget that a person has constructed the impersonal Jamesy (the name "Jamesy" is itself a personalizing), what Joyce has constructed in *Ulysses'* peculiar narrator is at once so impersonal and so pervasive that it compels me to suspend my disbelief and think of the narrative as *Jamesy's* and not the writer's. Jamesy is the name I assign to my thinking that *Ulysses* issues wholly from an impersonal intelligence and not from the person who constructed him.

When I think of *Ulysses* as Jamesy's and not Joyce's doing, I pretend that Joyce is not answerable for any unjust elements of *Ulysses*: because I am fully aware that I am pretending, though, I am holding Joyce answerable all the while. What I am pretending is that Joyce has constructed in Jamesy a scapegoat for one simple but insoluble problem Joyce was stuck with as a writer: no matter how devoted to justice, no matter how personal, phrasemaking is never personal nor just enough. I cannot respond justly to a person until I assign certain (possibly silent) phrases to his needs. Such phrases are the hearing that I give his case. But however much my phrases enable me to *know* about his needs, they are at most preliminary to justice insofar as I may *do* nothing with the knowledge beyond sentimentally deriving from it what pleasure I can. And if I am James Joyce and my phrases are written and done with, as Joyce's phrases are in *Ulysses*, I have removed them from the time in which persons respond to one another and are answerable for the justice of their responses. Jamesy is a blame-absorbing construct for Joyce's self-reproach as the writer of *Ulysses*, a book that Joyce wanted to be more personal and more just than he could make it be.

However simple Joyce's motive for constructing Jamesy as *Ulysses'* narrating intelligence, the construct itself is quite elaborate. When I attend to Jamesy, Joyce asks me to do at least two things at the same time: (1) to take Jamesy on Jamesy's own terms by acceding to the possibility that Jamesy's omniscience is the only thing that matters, and (2) to be so repelled by the injustice of such a possibility that I myself begin to act justly. By temporarily setting aside the second of those two things, I must now focus on the first. As neutrally as I can, I will describe those elements that force me to identify Jamesy in the book as a whole. These are some of the matters I will be considering. How might I, a mere person, conceive of so impersonal and vast an intelligence as Jamesy's? How do his disclosures manage to register with me as singularly omniscient? What would it cost me if I were to imitate him in all ways? To what extremes does he go in his godlike isolation from persons? I should warn in passing that Jamesy's knowledge of all things, including persons and justice, may occasionally cause him to be mistaken as my model for how to read *Ulysses*. Jamesy could not be less of a model for me, though before I leave him and move on to Stephen, the second of the three lines I will be following, I will say what Jamesy contributes to such a model by default.

"A SUPERIOR INTELLIGENCE"

"It had better be stated here and now at the outset" (14: 1223) that the narrating intelligence behind *Ulysses* is a "a superior intelligence" (17: 1008). Persons and characters who substitute for persons think less than everything. Their intelligences are inferior to Jamesy's. As the narrating intelligence behind *Ulysses*, Jamesy thinks everything.

Describing what that might mean is the more difficult because the normal ways for talking about thinking are inhibited by their applicability to the inferior intelligences of mere persons. When he was nine, Stephen Dedalus had wondered at the enormity of all there was to think.

> What was after the universe? Nothing. But was there anything round the universe to show where it stopped before the nothing place began? It could not be a wall but there could be a thin thin line there all round everything. It was very big to think about everything and everywhere. Only God could do that. He tried to think what a big thought that must be but he could think only of God.[1]

A line around everything would make everything more thinkable by cutting it down to a size a person could think. But even the thinnest of lines is cheating since it excludes what must not be excluded if "everything" is to be thought. Substituting for a person, Stephen lacks the intelligence to think everything and not just one delimited thing and another. Stephen acknowledges that the thought of everything is too big for a person to think. Then he gives up trying to think *what* God thinks and thinks only of God.

When he thinks only of God and not also about what God thinks, Stephen thinks God's substance, he accepts that within God's substance there can be no line between the things God thinks. All delimitable things God might be said to think about are substantially one and the same: there is nothing other for God's substance, nothing of another substance than God in the way another person or thing can seem to be substantially other than oneself. As the omniscient intelligence behind *Ulysses*, Jamesy gives nothing away to God. Just as God's knowledge is not limited to those things the Bible discloses, Jamesy's is not limited to those things disclosed in *Ulysses*: instead, Jamesy's knowledge, like God's, extends to what is happening right now on the moons of Neptune and in Great Slave Lake. If God's and Jamesy's names are not interchangeable names for the most superior of intelligences, it is not because God alone thinks everything while Jamesy merely thinks delimited things. Though I will pursue the comparison only casually and only in the sense that Jamesy's omniscience is *godlike*, the differences between Jamesy and God do not involve differences in what they may be said to think: Jamesy, like God, thinks everything, everything he thinks therefore being of one substance with Jamesy himself.

"TO SUBSTITUTE OTHER MORE ACCEPTABLE PHENOMENA"

For mere persons who read it, *Ulysses'* tiny sampling of all that Jamesy thinks may seem to connect with Dublin on June 16, 1904. It does not. Filling everything, ethereal, the substance that is Jamesy's thinking does not admit connections. A connection requires the same gap in substance that Stephen seeks so that he might insert his "thin thin line." For there to be a connection, there must be a gap between the things connected, a gap between the connection and the delimited things it connects. Jamesy's thinking does not admit a gap. As a mere person, I assume that Dublin on June 16, 1904, was its welter of phenomena for persons. What persons tended to regard as the "real" Dublin on that day, I assume, was what persons knowing less than everything took it to be. If persons knew everything, if they could think what

Jamesy thinks, they would not only know what is real but would them-selves have substance or being: they would be real. Instead, persons are what Stephen thinks of them as: "Beingless beings" (10: 822). From the perspective that accords godlike omniscience to Jamesy, Jamesy alone is real. A person in any place on any day is subject to the sensi-bilities that are peculiarly his or her own. Since for any sensibility the thought of everything is too big to think, substance (or being, or real-ity) is closed to persons. Subject to thinking one delimited thing and another, subject to making connections, sensibilities offer only woe-fully imperfect approximations of all there is to think.

Jamesy, by contrast, is unencumbered by sensibility. Because he thinks everything, his thinking is the one true substance, a substance that fills what persons are subject to regard as gaps between delimited things. Because he discloses at least something of his substance in *Ulys-ses*, each person who reads *Ulysses* is privileged to deal not with a place and time as each merely takes it to be but rather with *Ulysses* as it most substantially is. No two persons will read *Ulysses* the same way. Its parts of speech are therefore merely phenomena and not reality. But because these parts of speech disclose something of Jamesy's superior intelli-gence, they are more acceptable phenomena than phenomena of the "real" Dublin or the "real" Anywhere Else. "Because it was a task for a superior intelligence to substitute other more acceptable phenomena in place of the less acceptable phenomena to be removed" (17: 1008–10), I pretend that Jamesy has removed "real" place and time and has sub-stituted for them the phenomena you and I encounter in *Ulysses'* parts of speech.

ALMOST SEEING IT

Bloom is admiring binoculars at Yeates and Son in Grafton Street when he thinks, "There's a little watch up there on the roof of the bank to test those glasses by" (8: 560–61). Was there "really"? Dubliners interviewed in 1969 could not remember having heard of it.[2] A little watch was either "there" on the Bank of Ireland's roof in 1904 or it was not. If it was not, it is the more acceptable as substance insofar as it was never seen. "Can't see it," Bloom decides as he tries to make it out with the naked eye. "If you imagine it's there you can almost see it. Can't see it" (8: 562–63). Seeing it is less acceptable, less pure than almost seeing it. Seeing it implicates sensibility, and sensibility taints by delimiting. Sensibility fractures the pure selfsameness of Jamesy's substance. Into portions a mere person can think, sensibility separates the undelimitable "everything" that Jamesy thinks and is. Almost but not seen, the watch remains forever the purer insofar as its substance and Jamesy's are not separable by as little as "a thin thin line," the line by which the person who "really" saw it would necessarily have distinguished the watch from "everything" that it was not. Almost but not seen, the "watch" is Jamesy's watchfulness over both the Dublin of *Ulysses* and the reader of *Ulysses*. It is a vigil at which Jamesy succeeds perfectly because of his superior, perfectly indifferent intelligence.

TESTABLE CONNECTIONS

Without compromising his superiority, Jamesy might have seen to it that there are only the most arbitrary of resemblances between the "real" Dublin and the Dublin of *Ulysses*. And yet while it is what he does disclose that constitutes as much substantial reality as mere persons are privileged to receive, is it not too much to ask of them that they receive his disclosures as if they were the divine truth concerning what is real? Though *Ulysses'* parts of speech are "more acceptable phenomena" than other phenomena against which they might be tested for their truth, mere persons are subject to their respective sensibilities and cannot accept that Jamesy knows what Dublin truly was on that day until they submit *Ulysses* to some tests. Just as the binoculars could be tested by the little watch, Jamesy's knowledge of the "real" Dublin on June 16, 1904, may be tested by newspapers, maps, schedules, directories, and the way specific buildings deflected the light. Such tests are a handy means for understanding how connectable Jamesy's substitutions are. When Lenehan tells M'Coy to "come over in the sun" (10: 530–31), Jamesy has replaced that part of Dublin with the knowledge that two people would indeed be moving from shade to sun if, under a clear sky, they were to cross to the north side of Wellington Quay at just that time of day and year. When Nurse Callan is so startled by a flash of lightning in "Ireland's westward welkin" (14: 82) that she is compelled to cross herself, Jamesy has replaced another part of Dublin with the knowledge that the front door of the National Maternity Hospital faces west. He has replaced a certain part of the bay with the knowledge that it is "five fathoms" (1: 673) deep, that its current tends toward the northwest, and that the second high tide in Dublin on June 16, 1904, occurred "about one" in the afternoon.

And Jamesy's knowledge may be found to connect with the "real" Dublin even when that knowledge is implicit only, not manifest in *Ulysses'* parts of speech. [3] Between the first and second chapters of *Ulysses*—which is to say within *Ulysses* but *in no words*—Jamesy has replaced the distance between Sandycove and Dalkey with the knowledge that a young man setting out around 9:30 in the morning would have time to walk that mile and not be inordinately late for the class he was to teach at 10:00. Between the second and third chapters, Jamesy has replaced the distance between Dalkey and Irishtown with the knowledge that even a young man would have to go by tram back north again past Sandycove, Kingstown, Blackrock, and Merrion if he is to be spotted by another man just after 11:00 near Watery Lane.[4]

It is admittedly no proof of superior intelligence that Jamesy knows one distance is greater than another. Nor is there anything extraordinary about the kinds of things he knows. Though he knows everything on his own and has no need to supplement his knowledge, what he knows is so commonplace that he might seem to have cribbed it from intelligences inferior to his own, from persons whose sensibilities subjected them to the "less acceptable phenomena" of "real" Dublin on one day. On that day, of course, there were persons in Dublin who offered descriptions of how things went and were likely to go. Many of their offerings are still available. Tide tables and nautical charts can be consulted in many good libraries, and a contemporary map of Dublin bears the letters "Hosp." in a west-facing square off Holles Street. Since Jamesy might have come by it in the most mundane of ways, any one thing he seems to know about Dublin is unimpressive as knowledge. And yet what clearer evidence could there be that Jamesy thinks everything? For the more common and expendable each thing he thinks, the less it seems that there were things too common and too expendable for him to think.

Not that a looked-for connection between the "real" Dublin and Jamesy's knowledge does not sometimes reveal him to be "in error." Clive Hart has catalogued a number of discrepancies between *Ulysses* and the "real" Dublin: what Jamesy calls the "Royal Canal" was instead the Grand, Grattan's statue was not "stone" but bronze, "Mac-Connell's corner" was not a corner, the Merrion and "Metropolitan" Halls have been confused.[5] While Jamesy has it that the Earl of Dudley's "cavalcade" made its way through Dublin on "16 June, 1904," Robert Martin Adams discovered that it "really" did so more than two weeks earlier and with a very different cast of characters.[6]

Hart and Adams do not defer to Jamesy's superior intelligence. They proceed as if "*less* acceptable phenomena" were commensurate with "*more*," as if the "real" Dublin as persons took it to be was not riffled with impurities but was instead the measure of what Jamesy does and does not know.[7] Jamesy has easier going with me—or at least so I am pretending. I have already shown a willingness to grant that his intelligence is of a different, higher order and that persons simply cannot test it. For there to be something Jamesy does not know, something tests might catch him not knowing, he would have to be separate from that thing. Because what he knows is unconnected, its testable connections with the "real" Dublin prove nothing about its truth but are instead mere exercises of inferior intelligence. Whether the phenomena of *Ulysses* pass these tests is incidental to their status as knowledge. Unlike Hart and Adams, and despite much sympathy for their resistance, I will be granting Jamesy whatever superiority it would take (1) to remove the separate, gross bodies of the "real" world as persons take their world to be, and (2) to replace that world with the subtle, selfsame, uninterrupted substance that is his omniscience. To the end of seeing what Jamesy's substance yields, I am going to consider *Ulysses* as his completion of a "task"—the task of substituting pure and certain knowledge for the impure, uncertain efforts at sense making that occupy mere persons during their waking hours. Before I do that, I should say explicitly that my use of terms that make it sound as if I am celebrating Jamesy's omniscience is more than a little ironic. Terms like "pure and certain" would be positive for me only if I held that knowledge for its own sake is more important than persons, which I do not: whatever such terms may imply out of context, therefore, they are decidedly negative for me insofar as they point toward qualities of Jamesy's knowledge that render it wholly impersonal.

SENTENCES AND FRAGMENTS

Jamesy's task would have been simpler if he had had to replace only the bodies that were the "real" Dublin, and not also how persons took them to be. "Real" Dublin on June 16, 1904, was more than the configurations of its iron, wood, masonry, glass, macadam, dirt, water, vegetation, and beasts. It was as well the collective, inferior intelligence of "real" Dubliners and the "less acceptable phenomena" that Dublin was for them. Jamesy's pure and certain knowledge replaces these "less acceptable phenomena" with phenomena *Ulysses'* characters play at experiencing for themselves. Though Bloom "can't see" the little watch, he can and does play at seeing and thinking about a "most farraginous" (14: 1412) profusion of things. Each of these things discloses Jamesy's knowledge not only of *what* Bloom perceives—this much is given since it is Jamesy who discloses it so that it might be perceived—but also of *how* Bloom perceives it. Through interior monologue, Jamesy's knowledge of the way Bloom perceives one thing or another passes as if it were unmediated by Jamesy himself. Though he reserves interior monologue most of all for Bloom, for Stephen, and for Molly, Jamesy also allows brief stints of it to Father Conmee, Blazes Boylan, Miss Dunne, M'Coy, Dilly Dedalus, Tom Kernan, Master Patrick Aloysius Dignam, Miss Kennedy, Miss Douce, and Gerty MacDowell.

Jamesy may seem to make these various and repeated allowances at no little risk to his selfsameness. He himself is *Ulysses* in its entirety, remember, not just those untainted parts of it that no one character plays at having perceived. How does he manage to substitute for the sensibilities of "real" Dubliners without at the same time forfeiting or at least compromising the omniscience without which he is something other than his real self? What is there in Jamesy's disclosures that allows him to remain his imperious self as he descends into the less-than-all knowing perspectives of his characters?

Whenever he descends, Jamesy remains himself because of the simple difference between fragments and complete sentences. Except when it occurs in direct discourse (a mode that he retains as his own), a fragment invariably signals that Jamesy has temporarily given way to what one of his characters plays at perceiving. The first such fragment turns up on *Ulysses'* first page. With Stephen as witness to the burlesque, Mulligan is translating his shaving-lather into the body and blood of Christ.

—For this, O dearly beloved, is the genuine christine: body and soul and blood and ouns. Slow music, please. Shut your eyes, gents. One moment. A little trouble about those white corpuscles. Silence, all.

He peered sideways up and gave a long slow whistle of call, then paused awhile in rapt attention, his even white teeth glistening here and there with gold points. Chrysostomos. Two strong shrill whistles answered through the calm.

—Thanks, old chap, he cried briskly. That will do nicely. Switch off the current, will you? (1: 21–29)

Because Stephen plays at being a person and because it substitutes for a connection that Stephen alone makes, the fragment "Chrysostomos" is a personal word. The rest of the passage seems to be impersonal: its direct discourse and complete sentences seem to substitute for what anyone might have but no one has perceived. Jamesy does not play at being "there" at the top of Martello Tower for the carryings-on. What Mulligan says and does, how he looks, his whistle, and the double, shrill antiphon from somewhere in the morning—all of this seems to be as distinct from what any one person plays at perceiving as sentences are distinct from fragments. Had you or I looked into Mulligan's frequently open mouth, either of us might have noticed "his even white teeth glistening here and there with gold points." Jamesy did not look. He did not have to look to know what I, a mere person, might have noticed. All Jamesy had to do was to be the phrases that disclose his pure and certain knowledge of Mulligan's molars, bicuspids, and incisors.

JAMESY'S DEFERENCE

Curious, then, that the seemingly impersonal words "gold points" should mix with Stephen's fragment. Despite the fact that Mulligan's teeth are described in one of those complete sentences through which Jamesy preserves his omniscience, the description itself is something *Stephen* plays at perceiving. Only if it is Stephen who notices the "gold points" can Stephen then go on, as he does, to connect those points with "Chrysostomos," the goldenmouthed saint of the early Church. Nor is this sentence an isolated accident. Just as it is the gold points on Mulligan's teeth that prompt Stephen to think of Chrysostomos, so too is it to Stephen and not to Jamesy that Mulligan's "plump shadowed face . . . recalled a prelate, patron of arts in the middle ages" (1: 31–33). While the diction and tone of this last phrase do not sound at all like Stephen, it is Stephen who would welcome a patron for his own art, whose education with its scholastic bent has led him to learn that prelates were patrons of art. As he does again and again throughout the first three chapters of *Ulysses*, the Jamesy who is at once every character and no one of them has deferred his protectable onmiscience for something that Stephen alone perceives.

There is a more acute example of this deference only one page further on. After calling Stephen over to look down on Dublin Bay as if at "our great sweet mother" (1: 77–78), Mulligan announces "—The aunt thinks you killed your mother" (1: 88). As Mulligan expects him to be, Stephen is extremely vulnerable to this jibe. Two of Jamesy's sentences substitute for what Stephen sees and thinks as he looks at the bay. The first of these seems to be the less personal. It substitutes for what anyone might perceive if, under the same purely physical conditions, she found herself looking down at what Stephen plays at seeing. "The ring of bay and skyline held a dull green mass of liquid" (1: 107–8). These words become peculiarly Stephen's, though, as soon as the second sentence has registered. "A bowl of white china had stood beside her deathbed holding the green sluggish bile which she had torn up from her rotting liver by fits of loud groaning vomiting" (1: 108–10). Because Stephen is subject to the indelible evidence of his mother's death-agony as well as to his own guilt for having refused her dying wish that he pray for her soul, he transforms Jamesy's pure knowledge.[8] Within words that would otherwise indicate Jamesy's omniscience insofar as they form complete sentences in the past tense, the horizon of Howth Peninsula becomes a bowl of white china, the water of the bay green sluggish bile.

REMOVAL OF PERSONS

Why has Jamesy rejected the grammatical device that distinguishes him from one of his characters? Is he weakening and becoming personal only three pages into the book? No. Jamesy is not throwing in with his characters except in the sense that he knows the products of intelligences inferior to and subsumed by his own. Even with his guard down, his superior intelligence withstands the incursions into it of whatever his characters perceive. Because *Ulysses'* parts of speech disclose nothing that Jamesy does not know, they proffer a reality against which Stephen's or any other character's most heated perceptions may be coolly gauged for their deformities.[9] Just as he knows what Stephen perceives, Jamesy knows that the ridge of a peninsula is what it is and not the rim of a bowl, he knows that the water in the bay is not green bile but many particles of simple composition moving here and there at appointed depths and times. Jamesy is never less personal than in those sentences in which the intensely personal perception of a character is exhibited simply as a mistake.

And Jamesy's characters are mistaken, after all, only in play. "Because it was a task for a superior intelligence to substitute other more acceptable phenomena in place of the less acceptable phenomena to be removed," Jamesy has substituted the mistaken perceptions that characters only play at having for those that persons outright have. The "real" phenomena to which a person is subject simply do not lend themselves to certain knowledge. As from Jamesy's unimpeachable overview it is more acceptable only to play at being subject to "real" phenomena, so too is a character who does such playing more acceptable than a person. A character who plays at perceiving is at one remove from a person and is therefore (from Jamesy's view of it, at least) the more acceptable. This "one remove" is more accuratly a removal: remove perceptions and you remove persons who perceive.

Jamesy has performed the "task" of this removal by having substituted the characters of *Ulysses* for persons who were born. Birth in the strictly biological sense is what distinguishes a person from a character. Whatever purely phrased "birth" they are given by their authors, characters are not born biologically, as all persons are. By substituting for persons who were born, characters exemplify the removal of persons from the conditions to which persons are subject because of their births, a removal that installs them as phrases only and not as persons in exactly that series of phrases their author assigns.

It is no accident that Jamesy's one oath and his one reference to

Ulysses turn up in a passage that makes an issue of biological birth, for it is precisely the biological that Jamesy's disclosures remove. "By heaven, Theodore Purefoy," Jamesy declaims just after Purefoy's wife has given birth to their ninth child, "thou hast done a doughty deed and no botch! Thou art, I vow, the remarkablest progenitor barring none in this chaffering allincluding most farraginous chronicle" (14: 1410–12). No matter how many children he is phrased as having sired, Theodore Purefoy is of course no more a biological progenitor than Jamesy is but is instead, like every character in *Ulysses*, yet one more of Jamesy's phrased "progeny." But despite their having been removed from biology into the abiological and pure phrases of *Ulysses*, characters that substitute for persons who are born are stained by the personal as Jamesy is not. In the passage above, Jamesy is not a character insofar as he is not substituting for a person who writes "I vow": what he is instead is the "chronicle" *Ulysses*. Jamesy is empowered to disclose his Dublin at one remove only because his use of the first-person pronoun has been cleansed of any personal stain.

So that I might have some notion of what such cleansing requires, I am going to imagine a ladder to the wholly impersonal purity of the "chronicle." Jamesy is stationed at the top of this ladder: to ascend it is to remove the personal with every step. These, in descending order, are the rungs:

> CHRONICLER
> NARRATOR
> CHARACTER
> WRITER
> PERSON

Beginning at the bottom, it is only by removing the biological PERSON from the WRITER that there can be any movement toward the top. (CHARACTER is the most eccentric of the five terms and I will pass over it for now.) Less personal than WRITER because potentially as impersonal as Jamesy, NARRATOR is still more personal than CHRONICLER, who chronicles this and that, dies, then has his entries followed by those of another chronicler, and so on, the *Chronicle* itself being the only concern. The chapter from which Jamesy's one reference to *Ulysses* comes is a chronicle-within-a-chronicle. It is a chapter in which one writer after another is evoked and then absorbed not so much by his successor as by Jamesy, by the chronicle itself. To recognize the writers to whom the chapter points is to recognize that they were also persons. To recognize Jamesy in the chronicle of *Ulysses*, on the other hand, is to recognize a reality from which everything personal has been removed.

LIQUIDATION?

Removal of persons. I might be talking about genocide. And with what cause? *Ulysses* certainly does not read as if it is devoted to implementing the Final Solution. How can Jamesy even covertly be accused of having removed what only Death can? Nobody has been "offed" so that Jamesy might exist. More than thirty of *Ulysses'* characters bear the names of persons who "walked round Dublin" in 1904: AE, Alf Bergan, Richard Best, William Braden, Davy Byrne, and so on through the alphabet to Dudley White. [10] Each name is itself a discernible connection between replacing character and person replaced. But since the persons have been replaced only in a manner of speaking, most went about their days unthreatened by the chronicle that replaces them. Nor has any threatening removal been worked on those persons for whom Jamesy's knowledge of Leopold Bloom substitutes. There are at least three alleged prototypes for Bloom: Ettore Schmitz, Alfred Hunter, and Charles Chance. [11] Like the little watch, Bloom was almost but not seen in any one of these people, and was only almost seen again in Milo O'Shea, the person who portrayed him in Joseph Strick's film *Ulysses*. Like the little watch, Bloom was almost but never seen. Bloom therefore replaces no one person who was implicated in the phenomena of the "real" Dublin or the "real" Anywhere Else. No one has been removed so that Jamesy's knowledge of Bloom might be. The costs that attend Bloom's dominating presence in *Ulysses* would therefore seem to be nil.

IMPOSSIBLE COSTS

But while Jamesy's knowledge of his principal and lesser characters has not cost any person his or her life, *Ulysses* is not without its costs. It is because I feel I must assess these costs that I have been writing about *Ulysses* as if persons are capable of submitting to Jamesy's superior intelligence—submitting to it, that is, as *Jamesy's* and not just as that superiority implicit in any omniscient narrative. It costs me little enough to submit to conventional omniscience: the narrating intelligence asks no more of me than that I accede to its authority on the matters it presents. The costs of submitting to Jamesy's omniscience, by contrast, are exorbitant. I meet these costs only if I submit (1) to the proposition that *Ulysses'* parts of speech are "more acceptable" than those "less acceptable phenomena" to which I am subject when I am not reading *Ulysses* and (2) to the removal of all "less acceptable phenomena," of all phenomena that supply me with less access to omniscience than I am privileged to have when I am reading *Ulysses*.

If I am to submit to Jamesy's omniscience, I must find that characters in *Ulysses* are more acceptable to me than persons. Such submission might understandably cost me one or more of my friends, but I would also have to pay by denying myself any impulse to discriminate between *Ulysses'* characters. It would not be only Bloom, Molly, or Stephen that I would have to find more acceptable than any person, including myself. Bantam Lyons, Haines, Old Gummy Granny, even Lenehan—*any* character in *Ulysses* becomes more acceptable than a person in that the "least" among them is inseparable from Jamesy's all-knowing being. Insofar as every character is the disclosure of something Jamesy knows, all are the One Thing and there can be nothing to choose between them. As a substitute for a person, a substitute that is more acceptable than a person, each character is as acceptable as the next. Since each is the same within Jamesy's omniscience, I must make each the same to me or fail in my submission to all he knows.

And I can of course only fail. However willing I might be to submit, I cannot do so without magically dismantling my sensibility. For as it subjects me to phenomena that are precisely not the same but different from one to the next, my sensibility subjects me as well to the operation of distinguishing between them. Though they are the same for Jamesy, though my submitting to Jamesy's omniscience requires that they be the same for me, Lenehan and Bloom are not the same for me. Because I remain subject to my sensibility, I cannot submit.

COSTS OF DISCLOSING WHAT NO PERSON CAN KNOW

Jamesy, who knows everything, knows that I cannot submit. He knows that the inferior intelligence of mere persons stops them from knowing reality as in itself it really is. He knows about persons that they can begin to form some notion of reality only in personal terms. That is why he indulges them with comparatives. Because he knows that I am subject to making distinctions, he not only resorts to the terms "superior" and "inferior," "more" and "less" but also offers quantitatively less of some characters than of others. Because he knows that persons could not hear the unwavering and timeless, single pitch of his selfsameness, *Ulysses* is multiform and startling, plural, long. Though his disclosures are all-knowing and therefore real as substance is real, though his only traffic with the phenomenal is his pure and certain knowledge of its impure uncertainties, Jamesy condescends to inferior intelligence by allowing *Ulysses* to be as evocative of "less acceptable phenomena" as any written thing.

But in condescending, Jamesy's intelligence remains exclusively for itself. Because it involves stooping to one who is known to be inferior, condescension precludes the indebtedness mere persons incur when they do things in a world with other persons. For all his knowledge about persons, for all the condescending adjustments he may be making in the light of that knowledge, Jamesy's disclosures are not what they are so they might be for persons but are quite simply what they are. He sees to it that *Ulysses* is intelligible to persons. But just as his reality would be uncompromised if there were no discernible connections between *Ulysses* and the phenomenal world, so too is it incidental to his being that persons are able to follow *Ulysses* through its many turns. Jamesy *is* because his followable disclosures are unstained by even the slightest concern for persons. What he discloses in *Ulysses* is not for persons but rather and solely for itself.

It can be for its omniscient self only if it meets two requirements. The first is the more obvious and the more easily met. *Ulysses* discloses what I have so far simply been assuming that it does: that Jamesy thinks everything and therefore cannot possibly be wrong in anything he thinks. As he knows everything else about the Dublin of *Ulysses*, Jamesy knows what each of his characters thinks in different places at the same time, knows what Gerty, Bloom, and Stephen never so much as manage to think about their buried psyches. He knows each form and property of water that Bloom has marvelled at throughout his thirty-eight years, and knows that Bloom had always been in the dark about where Moses was when the candle went out. He knows that Molly thinks Bloom does not know she knows he carries a rubber with him. "As God is looking down on me this night," it is Jamesy alone who knows whether the scullerymaid Mary Driscoll "ever . . . laid a hand to them oylsters" (15: 880–81).

While it costs Jamesy nothing to meet the first requirement, his expenses in meeting the second are considerable. *Ulysses* can be for its omniscient self only if it discloses that Jamesy knows everything in the one way that is all-knowing. Jamesy can know it in that one way only if other omniscient narrators know less than he knows. Only if there are real and not just phenomenal distinctions to be made between Jamesy and other so-called omniscient narrators can *Ulysses* be for its omniscient self. The convention of the omniscient narrator is phenomenal only and not real: it is the convening of various materials that allow mere persons to read the narrative as the disclosures of an all-knowing intelligence. But how *Ulysses* is read is of no concern to Jamesy, whose unconcern is essential to his being. An omniscient narrator either is or is not according to whether or not he knows everything in the one way that is all-knowing, and that one way cannot be conventional. Jamesy *is* insofar as his omniscience is distinguishable from conventional omniscience.

The less conventional Jamesy's omniscience, the more distinguishable he is from other "omniscient" narrators who, by contrast with him if he is exceptional, are less than all-knowing. The conventionally omniscient narrator is impersonal. In order to avoid being conventionally omniscient—and this is the cost—Jamesy must seem to be personal.

To recognize Jamesy as seeming to be personal is not the same as to mistake him for being personal. Though his condescension in allowing his disclosures to be intelligible may be mistaken as personal, Jamesy *is* insofar as his disclosures are not for persons but only for himself. Disclosing his omniscience is costly to Jamesy not because it may be mistaken as personal but rather because the more distinguishable he is from conventionally omniscient narrators, the more that distinction really carries with it the semblance of the personal.

DISTURBING INTRUSIONS

If the most conventionally omniscient narrative is the most conventionally impersonal, Jamesy's chronicle disturbs that convention from its first page. By letting his characters play at thinking a sizeable portion of it on their own, Jamesy offers the illusion that what he knows about them is more personal than it needs to be. Had it been enough for him to disclose that he knows everything his characters think and do not think, he could have availed himself of such conventional (if less insipid) formulas as "It would never have occurred to Mr Bloom that . . . ," and "As he noticed the gold points on Mulligan's teeth, Stephen was reminded of. . . ."

Jamesy's use of interior monologue, though, is only the first disturbance in what might be a far more placidly impersonal narrative. *Ulysses* is less conventionally omniscient than a narrative that includes interior monologue but also protects the narrator's knowledge from the base perceptions of his characters. But whether less conventional or more, it is still conventions that supplant conventions that supplant conventions. Though hardly a rapprochement with his people-replacing characters, Jamesy's making room for their perceptions within the dominant mode of his complete, past-tense sentences is in its turn a convention that remains intact through chapter 6 and is not dismissed completely for several chapters more.

Its dismissal is imminent, though, as the first words of the seventh chapter warn: "IN THE HEART OF THE HIBERNIAN METROPOLIS." The chapter's sixty-three headlines are the first of Jamesy's extraordinary intrusions into what chapters 1 through 6 had established as the narrator's ordinary business at hand. Conventions that had presented Jamesy as a relatively impersonal overseer explode in centered, capital

letters that keep intruding into the narrative as if to proclaim NOTICE
ME, or at the very least REMEMBER WHO IS CALLING THE SHOTS. Because
they continue to disclose a narrator who knows everything as persons
do not, these intrusions are in reality impersonal. But they offer a semblance of the personal as well. As substitutes for persons, Stephen and
Bloom repeatedly intrude into the past-tense narrative of the first six
chapters with their separate, unheard reflections. Jamesy can be read as
taking his seemingly personal turn with interior monologue in chapter
7's headlines, for they too intrude silently into the narrative, intrude
into it so silently, in fact, that the "(E)" in "HOUSE OF KEY(E)S" (7: 141)
would be lost altogether if Jamesy's were a spoken and not a written
business.[12]

INTRUSIONS BOUND BY RULES

Chapter 7 is the beginning of an extended series of chapters that
Jamesy disturbs by way of small and large intrusions. Insofar as it disturbs what would otherwise have been a more conventionally impersonal omniscience, each intrusion seems to be personal, and it seems
to be more personal the more it disturbs the convention. In the presence of the most disturbing intrusions, therefore, Jamesy's omniscience
must either give way altogether, taking Jamesy's being with it, or it
must hold its own by containing the disturbance. However unconventional because however seemingly personal, Jamesy's intrusions are
bound by a number of rules that secure his omniscient being. Here is a
summary of the rules.

(1) Each chapter into which Jamesy intrudes would be no less intelligible if it lacked his intrusions. Each intrusion is in this way
perfectly gratuitous. But each also retains an explicable relationship
with the rest of the intrusions within its chapter. HOUSE OF KEY(E)S
is like the rest of the phrases in boldface within its chapter insofar
as each can be imagined as having a place above a column of news-
print. The rest of the intrusions into the twelfth chapter are like
"Ga Ga Gara. Klook Klook Klook. Black Liz is our hen. She lays
eggs for us. When she lays her egg she is so glad. Gara. Klook
Klook Klook. Then comes good uncle Leo. He puts his hand under
black Liz and takes her fresh egg. Ga ga ga ga Gara. Klook Klook
Klook" (12: 846–49), in that each assumes a different point of view
than the barfly-narrator's and then proceeds to elaborate ridicu-
lously on something in his narrative.

(2) While each intrusion is gratuitous, it also maintains an explicable relationship with the narrative into which it intrudes. Like

the rest of the phrases in capital letters within its chapter, HOUSE OF KEY(E)s introduces other phrases within the particular section of narrative that immediately follows it. "Alexander Keyes, tea, wine and spirit merchant" (7: 143). "—The idea, Mr Bloom said, is the house of keys. You know, councillor, the Manx parliament. Innuendo of home rule" (7: 149–50). Like the rest of Jamesy's intrusions into the barfly's narrative, "Ga Ga Gara" is introduced by a phrase that immediately precedes it. "Gob," the barfly had just said of Bloom, "he'd have a soft hand under a hen" (12: 845).

(3) Each of Jamesy's intrusions is distinct from and parasitic on his perfectly impersonal omniscience. What Bloom said to the councillor, what the anonymous barfly said about his hour in Barney Kiernan's to his equally anonymous audience—these are things that Jamesy knows with certainty, as he knows all things. By contrast, HOUSE OF KEY(E)s and "Ga Ga Gara" have the flightiness of mere observation. Seemingly personal, they relate to Jamesy's knowledge very much the way his characters' perceptions do. Because they are excrescences on what he knows and because they can be read as having puckish good fun at its expense, each intrusion in *Ulysses* seems to impugn the authority of what Jamesy knows about that Dublin at one remove that its first chapters were just beginning to present. But just as it is this Dublin that Jamesy knows, so too does his knowledge of it remain undiminished in its reality despite all the disturbances within what might otherwise have been a more conventionally impersonal omniscient narrative.

(4) Throughout *Ulysses*, therefore, it is not what Jamesy knows that the intrusions parody: instead, they parody people who have thoughts. Though many of the intrusions seem to be personal at least to the degree that they seem the work of a madcap profligate who wants nothing more than to make people laugh, they are parodies of what anyone might have but no one has observed about Jamesy's perfectly impersonal knowledge. Identifying Jamesy in any one of his intrusions is easy enough, just as it is easy enough to identify each of his characters by what each thinks or says. Simon Dedalus can be heard in any of his one-liners, Mulligan in his burlesques, Lenehan in his barely tolerable puns. It is not only Bloom who hears Alf Bergan in the postcard "U. p: up." (12: 269): Joe Hynes thinks it is Bergan's style too. "—Was it you did it, Alf? says Joe. The truth, the whole truth and nothing but the truth, so help you Jimmy Johnson. / —Me? says Alf. Don't cast your nasturtiums on my character" (12: 1038–40).[13] Unlike Dedalus, Mulligan, Lenehan, or Bergan, on the other hand, Jamesy does not have a consistent style but varies wildly in his intrusions from chapter to chap-

ter.[14] As HOUSE OF KEY(E)s diverges stylistically from "Ga Ga Gara" (and "Ga Ga Gara" from other intrusions even within its own chapter), so does each diverge from Jamesy's attack on Bloom for having masturbated. "Has he not nearer home a seedfield that lies fallow for the want of the ploughshare?" (14: 929–30) the interloper asks rhetorically about Bloom. "A habit reprehensible at puberty is second nature and an opprobrium in middle life" (14: 930–31). Were the attacker substituting for a consistent and identifiable person, the attack itself might be more formidable. Because it is merely another in a series of skirmishes that are consistent only in that they would not be fought by any one person, the attack is turned away by everything Jamesy discloses about the damage done to Bloom's and Molly's sexual compatibility by Rudy's death. Because Bloom is what Jamesy knows about him, Bloom is not reduced to an object of parody. What the attack parodies is not Bloom but rather the personal impulse to reprove—an impulse, in this case, that the real and therefore impulse-free Jamesy only seems to have.

TO IMPERSONATE

It takes a person to intrude into what would otherwise be an omniscience uncorrupted by personal perception or thought. Because he must only seem to be personal if he is to be omniscient in the one way that is all-knowing, Jamesy's intrusions must not be and are not recognizable as those of a narrator who is substituting for a person. The person for whom Jamesy might have substituted has been removed before he or she could be disclosed.[15] What is disclosed in his or her place is Jamesy the Impersonator.

To substitute for a person is to substitute for whatever a person is subject to. To impersonate, on the other hand, as Jamesy does, is to feign such subjection while preserving intact the impersonator's immunity to it. Jamesy is not subject to personal concerns. Because I am a person and can therefore conceive of Jamesy in no other way, I have implied that he has concerns. To imply that Jamesy cares what happens is to distort what he is. By reading *Ulysses* as his completion of a "task," the task of substituting other more acceptable phenomena (*Ulysses*, or Dublin at one remove) in place of the less acceptable phenomena to be removed (whatever mere persons take any place to be at any time), I have distorted what is at once least personal and most real about Jamesy. *Ulysses* is Jamesy's completion of a task only insofar as he impersonates that already removed "someone" who would be concerned enough to begin the task and then complete it. There is in reality no time for Jamesy to do either. Since with the removal of the person time is removed too, there is no time for Jamesy to be concerned that he will be mistaken for just any old omniscient narrator, no time for him to disturb conventional omniscience so that he might be omniscient in the one unshared way that is all-knowing.

And yet what Jamesy is is inseparable from his impersonation, from his seeming to be a person with time, a person subject to concerns. What seems to concern him most, basically enough, is that he cannot be personal but must only seem to be. One rule that Jamesy can think of not observing, can seem not to observe but must observe, is the rule according to which he cannot be both personal and omniscient being. Jamesy impersonates "someone" who is unhappy with this rule. Merely a person, I can only speculate on the unhappiness. One of my guesses is that the rule keeps him just that hairbreadth away from omnipotence, from the power to be whatever he pleases even if what he pleases to be is nothing more than a person. Another guess is that he is unhappy with the rule for reasons that resemble God's reasons for creating the universe: to ask why Jamesy wants to be personal may be to ask why God dispersed his unity into stars, his eternity into time, why he let there be people.

Such speculation is idle, of course, since Jamesy is not really unhappy but only seems to be. And yet for all I do to remember that he is impersonal, I read the impersonating Jamesy as an intelligence that does its superior best to be personal but knows its best is not good enough. Before I begin to review in some detail the deep middle of the book—that portion of *Ulysses* in which Jamesy's impersonating is its sharpest and most unignorable—I want to look more generally at the shape of his impersonating as a whole, I want to look at what must come of it since Jamesy, who knows everything, knows that it must keep him at one absolute remove from being personal.[16]

BUTTINGS-OUT

Jamesy's impersonating does not keep him there without his seeming to use one other ploy. Knowing that his intrusions into the narrative cancel whatever personal quality they might have had if they were less hyperbolic, Jamesy seems to change tactics. Butting in having kept him impersonal, he butts out. Though he does so somewhat tentatively at first and never with the abandon that would characterize an inferior intelligence, he abdicates in favor of three characters who do his narrating for him.[17] Because of these abdications, I included the term CHARACTER on the ladder to the impersonal *Chronicle*. Since each of these three narrating characters is unlike Jamesy in that each is substituting for a person, the chronicle as a whole is the more personal for their narratives.

"I was just passing the time of day with Old Troy of the D. M. P.," the twelfth chapter begins. Though Jamesy himself will issue a first-person "vow" two chapters later, the first-person narrator of chapter 12 is not Jamesy but an unnamed barfly. This first abdication seems to come hard for Jamesy. If he were any easier about having yielded the narrative to a mere character, he might not have riddled the chapter with intrusions that, rather than disrupting the impersonal narrator's hold on the narrative, return it to him again and again.

Perhaps because in having given way to the barfly he had become accustomed to such stepping-aside, Jamesy is far less peremptory in Gerty's portion of the next chapter. Because Gerty's is a third- and not a first-person narrative, Jamesy retains at least the pronominal lineaments of his impersonal omniscience and can therefore be easier about his own withdrawal. In the story she tells herself about herself, Gerty does not know what Jamesy knows about her: that she is sublimating her sexual appetite while at the same time refusing to acknowledge the handicap that makes it all the less likely that her sublime fantasies will be fulfilled. And as his superior intelligence enables him to stay more than just one up on her throughout her narrative, the rest of the chapter is securely Jamesy's insofar as it returns—though for the last time— to that mixture of omniscience and interior monologue with which *Ulysses* began.

The guest narrator of the sixteenth chapter is Leopold Bloom. In chapter 4, after he had read *Matcham's Masterstroke* by Mr. Philip Beaufoy, Bloom had thought that he himself should have a go at writing. At the cabman's shelter, the thought comes back. "To improve the shining hour he wondered whether he might meet with anything approaching the same luck as Mr Philip Beaufoy if taken down in writing suppose he were to pen something out of the common groove (as he fully intended doing) at the rate of one guinea per column, *My Experiences*, let us say, *in a Cabman's Shelter*" (16: 1227–31). Like Gerty's, Bloom's narrative is third-person and allows Jamesy to show up the very character for whom he has decamped. "*My Experiences*, let us say, *in a Cabman's Shelter*" is laden with a syntax and phrases heavy enough to sink it. Unlike Gerty's, which avoids sinking mostly because it documents the interesting if pitiful life she plays at living, Bloom's stays afloat not because it is interesting to see how pitifully he would write but because it is both funny and poignant to be no less close to his sensibility even when he is putting on the airs of a writer.[18] Unlike Gerty's, Bloom's narrative extends throughout its chapter and is therefore the one chapter-long narrative that Jamesy neither mediates as a conventionally impersonal intelligence nor disrupts with his impersonations.

SLOW, POSSIBLY EVEN INCOMPLETE RESIGNATION

As impervious to conscience or reprisal as to the impossible news that a character has perceived, said, thought, or felt something he himself did not already know, Jamesy has been removed from all communities of people by order of the rules that let him *be*. His costs in having been removed would be trifling if he had remained indifferently "within or behind or beyond or above his handiwork" (*P*, 215). But whether out of sheer superiority, disdain, or a loneliness that seeks retribution, he flails away at what it is to be a person in his buttings-in. It is a rule of Jamesy's being that he must be timeless: and while this too is a rule by which he abides, he comes across in his buttings-out like an intelligence-in-process, an intelligence that only very slowly resigns itself to the personal costs of having been effaced.

If he completes that resignation by ceding all of the sixteenth chapter to Bloom, he cannot backslide thereafter but must instead confirm that he has passed beyond his doomed flirtation with the personal. Chapters 17 and 18 try his resolve again and again, for what they continue to tell about Stephen, Bloom, and Molly makes them the most personal chapters in the book. Except in that sense in which he himself is every phrase of *Ulysses*, Jamesy stays out of chapter 18 altogether. Because the chapter is interior monologue and not third-person narrative in the past tense, it is even more completely Molly's than chapter 16 is Bloom's. For once and at last, in Molly's chapter, Jamesy's removal is not accompanied by his resistance to the inevitable.

His compliance in chapter 17, by contrast, is obtrusive if only slightly less thorough. In its "catechetical interrogation" (17: 2249), Jamesy is the questions and answers to one thing after another, each of them materializing as if by itself and in the absence of any sensibility that might sort out the treasures from the junk. The fatuous "versicle" on a card "from Mr + Mrs M. Comerford" (17: 1782) weighs no differently with Jamesy than the words that Bloom remembers from his father's suicide note. Bloom's and Stephen's handshake is "the lines of their valedictory arms, meeting at any point and forming any angle less than the sum of two right angles" (17: 1222–23), the reflection of Bloom's face in the mirror a "composite asymmetrical image" (17:

1348). Technical and antiseptic, Jamesy's phrases empower him to present the personal with perfect dispassion.

But even as late as chapter 17, his detachment from his characters is hard-won if it is won at all. If there were nothing personal for Jamesy in what he knows about Bloom, if it were easy to put Bloom to sleep forever, "the childman weary, the manchild in the womb" (17: 2317–18), would not have made its way onto the chapter's last page. The phrases do not go uncontested. "Womb? Weary?" (17: 2319), the diction-monitoring, flawlessly impersonal part of Jamesy asks. Called to account for having momentarily forgotten itself and gone mushy, it is another, more personal part of Jamesy that answers amply and with poise "He rests. He has travelled" (17: 2320).

There is a similar quality in what is for me the least conventional passage in *Ulysses*. It is a passage that occurs roughly halfway through the book and is therefore prior to the last stages of Jamesy's submission as an impersonal intelligence. The passage seems to parody Gerty's sentimentality in that it takes its tone and direction, as her narrative does, from "that book *The Lamplighter* by Miss Cummins, author of *Mabel Vaughan* and other tales" (13: 632–34). But instead of being sentimental itself and thereby parodying any person's feelings at twilight, it offers Jamesy's most nearly personal view of Dublin and of Bloom. The parody is there, surely, but it is unignorable only in the words "lonely" and "everwelcome." Only in those two words has Jamesy been removed from perceptions and feelings only he could have who knows all that Jamesy knows.

A last lonely candle wandered up the sky from Mirus bazaar in search of funds for Mercer's hospital and broke, drooping, and shed a cluster of violet but one white stars. They floated, fell: they faded. The shepherd's hour: the hour of folding: hour of tryst. From house to house, giving his everwelcome double knock, went the nine o'clock postman, the glowworm's lamp at his belt gleaming here and there through the laurel hedges. And among the five young trees a hoisted lintstock lit the lamp at Leahy's terrace. By screens of lighted windows, by equal gardens a shrill voice went crying, wailing: *Evening Telegraph, stop press edition! Result of the Gold Cup races!* and from the door of Dignam's house a boy ran out and called. Twittering the bat flew here, flew there. Far out over the sands and coming surf crept, grey. Howth settled for slumber, tired of long days, of yumyum rhododendrons (he was old) and felt gladly the night breeze lift, ruffle his fell of ferns. He lay but opened a red eye unsleeping, deep and slowly breathing, slumberous but awake.

And far on Kish bank the anchored lightship twinkled, winked at Mr Bloom. (13: 1166–81)

The Impersonator

The first three chapters of *Ulysses* point me toward the person for whom Stephen Dedalus substitutes, chapters 4 through 6 toward the person Bloom would be if he, like Stephen and every other character, were a person and not a substitute, not a person at one remove. Without requiring that I particularly like Stephen, without requiring that I condone Bloom's ways, the first six chapters of *Ulysses* cohere because these characters cohere. The parts of speech that constitute Stephen and Bloom have a self-consistency that persons have. Persons are of course not perfectly self-consistent. If they were, whatever they did or said would be tiresomely transparent not only to other persons but also to themselves. But a person's inconsistencies have a more or less self-consistent range. Just as someone is an acquaintance or a friend only because he is enough the same from time to time for me to remember what I have come to be familiar with in him, Stephen's sensibility and acts are recognizable to me as Stephen's, Bloom's as Bloom's. If *Ulysses* were no longer than its first six chapters, it would impress me because of the rigor with which it points toward persons.

That the rigor of that pointing continues throughout *Ulysses* is a subtle but considerable surprise once I have read chapter 7. That chapter makes it clear that I am at the mercy of an intelligence that does just what it pleases. Since one of the things it pleases to do in Chapter 7 is to upstage its characters by pretending to be a character in its own right, I begin to feel well advised not to expect much more in the way of coherent disclosure about Stephen and about Bloom. Maybe I have heard the last of them, now that the narrator seems bent on my noticing him. Or maybe I have heard the last by which they would be recognizable to me. As I read on, though, I am surprised to find that there is as much knowledgeable and self-consistent pointing toward persons after chapter 6 as there is before. While subsequent chapters remind me again and again that I am relying for my news about Stephen and Bloom on Jamesy's characterlike whimsy as the teller of that news, there are two things that Jamesy is not whimsical about in the least: he keeps the news about his characters coming, and he keeps it coming in a way that does not disrupt the consistency of any one of them.[19] For all its changes in other respects, the narrative from chapter 7 on keeps pointing me toward persons. And far from diminishing it, as I had at first expected they would, the changes Jamesy introduces augment the pointing, they move me to take *Ulysses* all the more personally after chapter 6. My concern here is to say why.

The simpler part of the explanation is that Jamesy's shenanigans serve as a foil. Against the backdrop of his gestures toward upstaging them, the persons for whom his characters substitute appear to be especially sturdy creatures. Over the course of *Ulysses* as a whole, Jamesy's characters manage to withstand everything he throws at them—his bombastic disruption of the measured and respectful tone in which he had begun to tell their story, his feigned derision of them, his unfeigned and vast indifference to what they care about most. It is only because Jamesy seems dedicated to wresting the center away from them that persons remain as central to *Ulysses* as they do.

The part that is harder to explain obliges me to survey what Jamesy's changed ways tell me not about his characters but rather about himself. Through the first six chapters, I participate in a convention according to which omniscient narrators are perfectly sufficient as long as they know everything about persons. Within this convention, an omniscient narrator cannot be personal since persons know less than everything. Through chapter 6 of *Ulysses*, the convention is intact for me because the narrator is both a conduit of complete knowledge about persons *and* impersonal: for all I know, for all the convention allows me to think about it, the narrator is complete *because* impersonal. Intact for me, which is to say intact because I participate in it unhesitantly, the convention precludes my thinking there might be still more to the narrator if he were everything he is but also personal. In terms of substance, in real terms, there could be no more to Jamesy than there already is: because he is what he knows and because he knows all, Jamesy's being is at once all there and all there really is. For as long as the convention is intact, real terms are the only terms that apply.

Jamesy is as real as ever throughout *Ulysses*. There is no less of him after the convention loosens, as it begins to in chapter 7. What changes in chapter 7 is that Jamesy pretends there is something missing in the narrator of the first six and that he himself had better make up for lost time. He begins to impersonate. As he does so, he implies that the first narrator is missing whatever is not missing in a person who, because he or she is born, is subject to a peculiar body, sensibility, and compound of conditions. Once Jamesy's semblance of the personal begins to register with me, my participation in the narrative changes markedly. Instead of taking the narrator's sufficiency for granted, as I do when only real terms apply, I apply personal terms not only to the narrative but to the narrator as well.

In real terms, Jamesy is one and the same with the first narrator. In personal as in real terms, Jamesy and the first narrator are one and the same in that neither has been born and neither substitutes for a person who has been born. Jamesy differs from the first narrator, on the other hand, in that his impersonating pretends (1) to acknowledge a difference between real and personal terms, and (2) to favor the personal. Jamesy's acknowledgment and preference are pretense only, and so real terms continue to apply. But the pretense itself prompts me to apply personal terms to the narrator as if such terms were not only separable from real terms but the very terms Jamesy wants me to apply. As I follow his intermittent but increasingly flagrant impersonating from chapter 7 through chapter 14, I find that Jamesy is personal and not real to the degree that he wants to be a person.

To know everything is to be real and therefore impersonal. To be subject to the merely "living realities" of a body, sensibility, and conditions is to know less than everything, as persons who are born to die know less than everything. In personal but not in real terms, Jamesy wants what he cannot have: to be subject, as you and I are, to the world as each person merely takes it to be. The world as I take it to be is a world with other persons whose waking time, like mine, is a sequence of perceptions and judgments. For most of us, that sequence ends too soon. Before falling asleep, I am sometimes startled awake by the thought that I have lived more than half my life, possibly much more than half. Just as I often want to know what I cannot know, I often want never to die. If I were Jamesy (who is what Stephen wants to be), I would have what I often want.

At his one "more acceptable" remove from the "real" Dublin and every other so-called real place, Jamesy is the first, last, and only Word of *Ulysses*, the substance of his Word filling every imaginable gap and filling it forever. "Beware of what you wish for in youth," Stephen says during his lecture on *Hamlet*, "because you will get it in middle life" (9: 451–52). In Jamesy, I identify James Joyce's restlessness with the rule that to write something is sooner or later to have written it for all time. Few written things exhibit the deific thoroughness of *Ulysses*. To have written *Ulysses* is no longer to appear as a person whose debtorship for things done obliges him to respond again and again, but rather as an impersonal, godlike intelligence above obligation and outside time. In Jamesy's impersonating, Joyce dramatizes his own unease with rules without which he could not have written *Ulysses* and thereby risked being mistaken for the most superior of intelligences—which is to say for something other than a person. Jamesy the Impersonator of chapters 10 through 14 is personal insofar as he feels deprived of mortality and incomplete knowledge.[20] Though he merely feigns that deprivation, he discloses that he knows all there is to know about persons and debts. In Jamesy's impersonating, Joyce's restlessness with written closure shows.

When that restlessness appears for me, I am given a chance I would not otherwise have to judge as almost adequate my deprivations as a person.

PERCEIVING AND JUDGING

I am perceiving when I apply one or more of my faculties to whatever is present for them. I will call this "perceiving" to distinguish it from "judging"—a wobbly distinction, I admit, because to perceive is also to judge. Because I know less than everything and may therefore be wrong, I am obviously judging one thing or another to be the case whenever I perceive this thing or that. The distinction between perceiving and judging is useful to me, though, because I am varyingly answerable for my perceptions and "judgment" is a term that helps me keep track of such variation. If I mistake mirage for water or water for mirage, I am varyingly answerable depending on my own or someone else's need for water, upon whether I am on foot or in a dependable conveyance. I will have little to answer for if, simply wanting to know what I am seeing, I determine that it is one or the other and am wrong. I would describe this or a roughly comparable circumstance as perceiving. Though the difference between the two is not at all simple, I will reserve the term *judging* for determinations in which a person or a character has more rather than less to answer for when he or she perceives.

In substituting for a person, a character substitutes for what a person is subject to. The character named Jimmy Henry substitutes for a person. Subject to his sensibility, Jimmy Henry cannot know everything: the best he can do is to perceive that one thing or another seems to be the case. While he had perceived that John Howard Parnell had not been where he should have been some minutes before, he could come no closer than that to knowing with certainty where John Howard Parnell was. "Where was the marshal, he wanted to know, to keep order in the council chamber" (10: 1007–8). Jimmy Henry wanted to know not simply to know, of course, but so he could make something of it, so he could have that knowledge as an exhibit in support of his judgment that John Howard Parnell is a shirker. If to perceive and to judge is to be unable to know that one's perceptions and judgments are the whole truth, to judge has more rather than less to do with opinion, appraisal, feeling. Not mistaken in his perception that the city marshal was not at the council chamber where it was his elected duty to have been, Jimmy Henry's self-righteous delight in that fact implies his judgment of John Howard Parnell's fitness to serve: not knowing where the marshal was, Jimmy Henry is answerable for that judgment since it may turn out that John Howard Parnell was occupied all the while with more pressing civic business.

As the most panoramic of Jamesy's cityscapes, chapter 10 discloses that he knows with certainty what every character in Dublin is doing, saying and thinking between the hours of three and four in the afternoon. Since Jamesy is his omniscience, he cannot *not* know John Howard Parnell's whereabouts. "—Is that he? Haines asked, twisting round in his seat" (10: 1098) in the Dublin Bakery Company tearoom on the page following Jimmy Henry's question. "—Yes, Mulligan said. That's John Howard, his brother, our city marshal" (10: 1049). Ineradicably different from Jimmy Henry as from each of his characters, Jamesy is immune not only to perception but to judgment as well. Because Jamesy knows what Jimmy Henry wants to know but does not—that the marshal is diddling away the hour over a chessboard—Jamesy does not judge and therefore has nothing to answer for on the matter of John Howard Parnell.

NO TWO WAYS

Within chapter 10, as within *Ulysses* as a whole, a character's perceptions and judgments are intimately, almost even compulsively related. There are exceptions. Tom Kernan thinks, "The windscreen of that motorcar in the sun there" (10: 1759): the purely designative temper of the words "that" and "there" leaves him answerable for very little. But chapter 10 includes the interior monologues of no fewer than nine characters, and the first perception of each involves a judgment of one sort of another, however slight. Kernan himself is no exception. Satisfied that he had coaxed an order out of Mr. Crimmins with carefully chosen small talk, Kernan judges that he had "Got round him all right" (10: 720). "Five to three," Father Conmee observes. "Just nice time to walk to Artane" (10: 2–3). Boylan assesses the shopgirl's cleavage and concludes that she is a "young pullet" (10: 327). "Palefaces" (10: 341), Stephen thinks of tourists on a tram. Miss Dunne, displeased with the novel she is reading, decides that there's "too much mystery business in it" (10: 371). Anticipating that a "fellow might damn easy get a nasty fall there coming along tight in the dark" (10: 513–14), M'Coy transfers a banana peel from path to gutter. Bloom notices the "crooked botched print" (10: 586) of the book he is glancing at. Dilly Dedalus laments the loss of "those lovely curtains" (10: 646) her family's penury has forced her to auction off for five shillings. And Master Patrick Aloysius Dignam remembers that it was "too blooming dull sitting in the parlour" (10: 1124–25) with his father's mourners.

None of the examples I have just cited is as blatantly judgmental as Jimmy Henry's indictment of John Howard Parnell. And yet however moderate it is, each of the nine is only one of the many ways in which value might be assigned to the matter addressed. Jamesy's omniscience obviously precludes the assigning of values: because he knows everything in the one way that is certainty, because there are no two ways about the matters he knows, Jamesy is not answerable. Not so for his characters, who are answerable to one another for the differing values each assigns to matters they have in common. Five minutes to three is a matter Father Conmee has in common with every other Dubliner in *Ulysses*. Since his world is one in which he is not reduced to begging on crutches, what any time of day is worth to Conmee differs starkly from what it is worth to the onelegged sailor who jerks himself from street to street behind the growl "—For England. . . . *home and beauty*" (10: 232–33).

It is of course only for readers of *Ulysses* that the differing values of Conmee and the sailor intersect. Substituting for persons who do not know what readers of *Ulysses* know, the characters in chapter 10 pass obliquely on the street, some of them attending to the physical presences of these others, some talking with them, but none being privy to what those others think but do not say. Though Crimmins might suspect as much, he does not know with Jamesy's certainty that Kernan has judged him to be no more than someone to get round. It should be safe to assume that Crimmins does not judge himself that way. Had he known what Kernan was thinking about him, as readers do, the differing judgments of customer and salesman might have collided head-on, the latter being left with much to answer for. That collision avoided and the order booked, what may yet collide with Kernan's judgment of Crimmins are different readers' judgments of Kernan. Any reader who has wondered if he or she was being had in a commercial transaction will not be disposed to applaud Kernan's self-congratulatory relief over having made Crimmins his dupe.

How *Ulysses* is read depends on the uncountable judgments its characters' judgments elicit from its readers. Clive Hart has judged that the judgment M'Coy exercises in his one short bit of interior monologue is enough to distinguish him favorably from his less sympathetic companion, Lenehan. The effect is quite the reverse, Hart writes, with Boylan's "a young pullet."[21] Neither of these judgments is the last word on its matter. My agreeing with Hart on both matters is obviously not a last word either since you may not agree with him about them, and since someone else again may arrive at different, interesting readings of the same phrases. Judgments never really settle a matter but summon more judgments still.

"FATHER CONMEE WAS WONDERFULLY WELL INDEED"

Since Jamesy's real-because-certain knowledge is free of the indeterminacy with which judgments are burdened, he himself is free to have the last word on any matter in *Ulysses*. He would have that last word in chapter 10 if it were not for his impersonation of someone bent on maligning Father Conmee.

> Father Conmee crossed to Mountjoy square. He thought, but not for long, of soldiers and sailors, whose legs had been shot off by cannonballs, ending their days in some pauper ward, and of cardinal Wolsey's words: *If I had served my God as I have served my king He would not have abandoned me in my old days.* He walked by the treeshade of sunnywinking leaves: and towards him came the wife of Mr David Sheehy M. P.
> —Very well, indeed, father. And you, father?
> Father Conmee was wonderfully well indeed. He would go to Buxton probably for the waters. And her boys, were they getting on well at Belvedere? Was that so? Father Conmee was very glad indeed to hear that. (10: 12–21)

The attack by Jamesy is surreptitious, to be sure, for it emanates from third-person, past-tense sentences that bring with them into the chapter the aura of omniscient indifference they help develop and sustain throughout much of the preceding nine.

But the sentences above are not those of the Great Imperson Jamesy. The *impersonal* touch would have been to omit the phrase "but not for long" and to present Conmee's hyper-polite exchange with Mrs. Sheehy in direct discourse. Whereas Jamesy might have gone along his well-established way by letting what he knows about Conmee accumulate to Conmee's undeniable disgrace, he goes out of his way both to point up Conmee's hypocrisy and to level sarcasm at his mannered use of the word "indeed." Since I read Conmee's use of the word as a fit emblem for his fussy, shallow dealings with the souls entrusted to his pastoral care, I cannot deny that it is at least mildly embarrassing. What I do deny, what the impersonating Jamesy pretends to want me to deny is that it is as reprehensible as he makes it out to be. If it were just that reprehensible, I would not sense—as I do—that Jamesy is picking on Conmee. By not granting him the direct discourse through which Conmee might play at speaking the word for himself, Jamesy goes out of his way to imply that Conmee's use of it is less excusable than Mrs. Sheehy's. The word is after all her contribution to their chat, not Conmee's. If Conmee could have resisted using it once it had been introduced, a nonimpersonating Jamesy would certainly have resisted lambasting him for having used it.

Jamesy does not resist. Instead, he impersonates someone who cannot let Conmee's use of the word pass unjudged. Rather than impressing me as an intelligence that *knows* that Conmee spoke the word "indeed," Jamesy seems to have *judged* that Conmee is a disgraceful character and must be judged as such. But while I might otherwise have been inclined to judge Conmee in that way, I have been distracted from Conmee's use of the word by Jamesy's feigned judgment of him for having used it. Though he has done so with relatively little ado, Jamesy has shifted attention away from what he knows about Conmee and onto himself.

JUDGING AND SAYING

With that shift I begin to attend to Jamesy not solely as a knower who discloses but also as a judge who says what his judgments are. Judging is inextricably allied with saying. Judgments are predicated on apprehensions, on a person's seizing from unsayableness the particular matter to be judged. As in Kernan's "the windscreen of that motorcar in the sun there," a person can say things to another person or to himself without at the same time implying a judgment. But judgments cannot be made without saying things if only to oneself. Jamesy impersonates whenever he pretends to forgo his very real omniscience in favor of what a mere person might say and thus be answerable for. If the impersonal-because-omniscient Jamesy discloses what he knows, Jamesy the Impersonator pretends to say what he judges to be the case.

His impersonating in chapter 10, as I have said, is limited primarily to the section on Conmee. And even within that section Jamesy remains mostly impersonal, is mostly content to disclose about Conmee what only a superior intelligence could know. When I read the paragraphs in which Conmee imagines "the book that might be written" (10: 162) about Mary Rochfort, for example, I am tempted to think I am dealing with a disclosure of Jamesy's certain knowledge. As Conmee goes on constructing her story for himself, he arrives at what I take to be his compelling interest in it: the enigma of whether or not she ever "committed adultery fully," with "ejaculation of semen within the natural female organ." I say *I* take this to be what moves Conmee to imagine writing the book because these are paragraphs in which Jamesy maintains his more or less conventionally impersonal omniscience. Because they include nothing that resembles an act of judgment on Jamesy's part, because they are in this respect unlike the passage in which Conmee greets Mrs. Sheehy, they tempt me to think that what I learn from them is certain.

But is it? The temptation is just the reverse when I go on a hundred words or so and read that "the lychgate of a field showed Father Conmee breadths of cabbages, curtseying to him with ample underleaves" (10: 180–81). If Jamesy had been content to know how Conmee saw the cabbages, he could have supplied that knowledge by granting Conmee the interior monologue within which his character could play at seeing them for himself. I would then be able to read what Jamesy knows as evidence on which I and other readers, but not also Jamesy, might base judgments about Conmee. But any evidence the sentence may present is nearly indistinguishable from Jamesy's judgment that Conmee is lascivious enough to be titillated by cabbage leaves, sublimating enough to conceal his lust from himself by assuming that cabbage ladies are only being courteous when they expose their "unmentionables." The sentence reads to me as if it is an outgrowth of this very judgment and not evidence at all. Since it is a judgment to which Jamesy seems to have beaten me and everyone else, might it not also have motivated the paragraphs on Mary Rochfort and possibly even Conmee's portrait as a whole? I think it can be said of Conmee that his hypocrisy owes as much to repressed prurience as to anything else. But who has said as much about Conmee, Jamesy, or myself? Given the coolness with which he impersonates in Chapter 10, I am unable to tell.

HEATING IT UP

That coolness gives way in chapter 11. Having only implied that his characters are what he says they are, Jamesy intensifies his impersonation of someone who judges: he goes on and makes it explicit. Chapter 11 is a chapter in which Jamesy conducts an ardent show of wanting *Ulysses* to be recognized as things that he himself has said.

"Leopold cut liverslices. As said before he ate with relish the inner organs" (11: 519–20), and "Bloom ate liv as said before" (11: 569). Though the phrase "as said before" is restricted literally to words Jamesy himself and no one of his characters has "said" at some earlier point in the book, it calls enough attention to the origin of what is said that it extends to words that may have appeared to issue from a character but did not. If I had read chapter 7 as asking me to think of "onehandled" (7: 1018) as a word Stephen and not Jamesy "said" in referring to Nelson's statue, chapter 11 asks me to think again. "Blazes Boylan's smart tan shoes creaked on the barfloor, said before. Jingle by monuments of sir John Gray, Horatio onehandled Nelson, reverend father Theobald

Mathew, jaunted, as said before just now" (11: 761–63). With their emphasis on what has been "said before," these sentences call my attention to the fact that *Ulysses* must all of it have been "said" by Jamesy "before" Stephen could play at saying "onehandled."

Chapter 11 has it that his characters "say" one word or another only "after" Jamesy has said the whole of *Ulysses*. "Before" the blind stripling could utter his version of the curse in chapter 10 (10: 1119), Jamesy must have said "God's curse on bitch's bastard" (11: 285) in chapter 11. "Before" Tom Kernan could be quoted in chapter 6 as having a weakness for the locution "retrospective arrangement" (6: 150), Jamesy must have said in chapter 11 that "Tom Kernan, harking back in a retrospective sort of arrangement talked to listening Father Cowley, who played a voluntary, who nodded as he played" (11: 797–99). By emphasizing that he himself is the sayer of *Ulysses*, Jamesy feigns descent from his atemporal omniscience. As his impersonation in chapter 11 pretends that he gives up his timelessness for a succession of afters and befores, it also pretends that *Ulysses* is not the disclosure of what is real and true but rather and merely what "someone" has judged worthy to be said.

DOUBLE WHAMMY

This "someone," though, is an impersonator. Jamesy is personal only at one absolute remove. As the tone of his impersonating in chapter 11 makes clear, Jamesy knows that he is irrecoverably impersonal. No person would pepper what he or she says with smug and daffy "said before"s, confessions in which Jamesy seems to remember being forgetful and pointedly refuses to do anything about it.[22] That refusal is perfectly in order: Jamesy does not think twice about his words because, impersonal, he is not answerable for them, there is no answering Jamesy because there are no two ways about whatever he says. In contrast with Jamesy, a person is answerable because there are at least two ways about what he or she says. What a person says is at best a *version*, "an account resting upon limited authority"[23] that turns from one thing to another and may be answered in its turn. Nothing turns for Jamesy, who is timeless. Whatever he says is the unturning, one word "Jamesy," or "I AM WHO AM." Chapter 11 is Jamesy's revelation that the order in which things "happen" in *Ulysses* is no index to their cause. Only if he is the cause of what follows it can Jamesy have said chapter 11's overture, a foretelling of the chapter's motifs in which the word "Done" immediately precedes the word "Begin!" There are "events" in *Ulysses* only if Jamesy causes them to be by saying them.

If I am to read chapter 11 for its impersonal elements, I must suspend my readiness to answer for *Ulysses'* characters: for it is in this chapter that I am asked to recognize them as nothing more than an arbitrarily related series of phrases. Chapter 11 reminds me that Bloom, like everything else in *Ulysses*, is whatever Jamesy says. Jamesy's ardor in chapter 11 issues largely from what he wants to be recognized as having said about his protagonist. While he only snipes at Conmee from behind the cover of an omniscient indifference, Jamesy urges me to catch him unloading his whole arsenal against Bloom. Jamesy's is an especially versatile and comprehensive weaponry. Because it consists of everything he himself has said in *Ulysses*, it lets him see to it that Bloom both gets what he deserves and deserves what he gets.

Jamesy has only to say it and Bloom is at once a victim of sexual jealousy and a most cooperative cuckold. As Jamesy says it, Bloom has orchestrated Boylan's affair with Molly. That might be crime enough in a character who is at the same time intensely jealous of his wife's lover. But there is more. Bloom spots Boylan's car outside the Ormond hotel at this the hour of Boylan's tryst with Molly: then he decides to "sit tight" in the dining room there so that he might "see, not be seen" (11: 357–58). What follows punishes Bloom as unrelentingly as he punishes himself by continuing to think about his plight. Having said Bloom noticed that his and Molly's bed jingles (4: 59), Jamesy now says Bloom hears Boylan's car "jing" as it pulls away. "Bloom heard a jing, a little sound. He's off" (11: 457). If Bloom happens to think the word "off" because it describes Boylan's going, Jamesy wants to be recognized as having said Bloom thinks it so that it might also describe Boylan's coming: for within the intricacies of the "jingle" motif, Jamesy has gone out of his way to elide the car's trek to 7 Eccles Street with Boylan's getting it off with Molly once he is there. "P. S. The rum tum tum," Bloom lilts to himself as he adds a postcript to Martha: "How will you pun? You punish me?" (11: 890–91). If he is at first oblivious to the pun on the word "off," the sense in which it establishes him as masochistic witness to his own cuckolding is there for him in Nighttown as he hallucinates watching Boylan have his way with Molly.

Jamesy has assigned Bloom the same first name as Leopold von Sacher Masoch, whose *Tales of the Ghetto* Bloom owns to having read. If punishment is what Bloom not only deserves but craves, Jamesy more than obliges. To remind him that *Cosi fan tutte*, all women are like that, Jamesy supplies provocative and flirtatious barmaids, one of whom holds a vaginalike shell to her ear and then caresses the "smooth jutting beerpull" (11: 1112), its "cool firm white enamel baton protruding through" the "sliding ring" of her hand (11: 1116–17). Just as "tenors get women by the score" (11: 686), music, in chapter 11, is sex, its harmonies a matter of "quitting all languor" (11: 736) and of getting the timing right, of waiting and coming, "don't spin it out too long" (11: 746) and "why did he go so quick when I?" (11: 463). And each song Bloom hears in the Ormond is rife with application to his woe. *M'appari* from Flowtow's *Martha* reminds him that he has had to turn squalidly to an invisible, pathetic-if-titillating pen pal, *All is lost now* that all is just now lost, *The Croppy Boy* that as a Bloom or Virag he too is the "last of his name and race" (11: 1064–65).

Nor does Jamesy settle for kill in his assault on Bloom. Overkill is what it takes to make it unmistakably clear that Bloom's awful luck is not happenstance but rather Jamesy's pleasure-filled doing. Again and again throughout chapter 11 he seems to revel in alluding to Bloom's predicament as a cuckold. To Simon Dedalus's announcement that "Mrs Marion Bloom has left off clothes of all descriptions" (11: 496–97), Jamesy first splices the news that "jingle jaunted down the quays" (11: 498), then returns the narrative briefly to the Ormond only to turn it back again to Boylan. "By Bachelor's walk jogjaunty jingled Blazes Boylan, bachelor, in sun, in heat, mare's glossy rump atrot, with flick of whip, on bounding tyres: sprawled, warmseated, Boylan impatience, ardentbold. Horn. Have you the? Horn. Have you the? Haw haw horn" (11: 524–27). Though he is about to, Bloom has not yet played at thinking the word "hawthorn" (11: 633). That may be what is ("haw haw") funniest to Jamesy. For just as he is free to delight in having "said" that Boylan fucks Molly "before" the sequence of chapters brings a reader to Molly's confirmation of that fact, so too can Jamesy delight in having extracted from a word Bloom has not yet "thought" both his own laughter at Bloom-the-cuckold and the cuckold's sign.

ONLY SEEMING TO

Bloom is used to being laughed at by Dubliners who talk as if they know that Molly is "doing the other business" (11: 487). Jamesy impersonates someone who could be one of their company. By alluding repeatedly to the business Molly and Boylan are about to do, Jamesy seems to be joining Dedalus and his chums at their "old game" (15: 975) of having bad dirty fun at Bloom's expense. Jamesy only seems to join them, of course, because Bloom's detractors cannot really be joined. Because they are only and forever what Jamesy has said, Jamesy presents only the semblance of joining them. Since he knows too much to play at being a person, he cannot join them even in play. For him to join them in the judgments they play at making, it would have to be possible for him to be wrong about how many and which natural male organs Molly's natural female organ has accommodated. Despite the implication of promiscuity when she thinks "I never in all my life felt anyone had one the size" (18: 149–50) of Boylan's penis, Molly's monologue establishes that she has had sexual intercourse only with Boylan and with Bloom: since it is Jamesy himself who has said as much, he cannot be wrong about it and can therefore only seem to join.

In the same way, he can only seem to judge Bloom. Each of Jamesy's characters is perfectly manipulable for Jamesy, who has said whatever must be said to imply at least some minimal fit between their assorted punishments and crimes. In chapter 11, it is his very obtrusive use of this double whammy that underscores the fact that Jamesy is not judging Bloom at all but only seeming to, only impersonating someone who judges. As a person at one remove, Bloom is no more the author of his own "crimes" than of the punishing "coincidences" that befall him. Because his own words are Jamesy's words first, because there is no person named Bloom who, because he was born, may offer even the slightest resistance to the intelligence that has said him, Bloom can only seem to be judged by Jamesy. Jamesy can join the company of persons only if he, like they, are intelligences to whom birth and death and other things are not just said to happen, but happen. For until it is subjected to the conditions that follow biological birth, not even the most knowing of intelligences can judge and be answerable for its judgments.

Unable to join or to judge while seeming to do both, the impersonating Jamesy gives way in chapters 12 and 13 to two characters who unknowingly assume his purely authorial position as chronicler. As characters, the barfly and Gerty MacDowell are halfway up the ladder to the impersonal *Chronicle*. As chroniclers and not just narrators or characters, they have some claim even to the rungs above them. But that is a claim they do not and cannot make since, unlike Jamesy, they know nothing of the chronicle's very real existence. Innocent of their elevation, Gerty and the barfly substitute for intelligences on the lowest rung. The barfly's apprehensions and judgments are said loud and clear, Gerty's unsaid but very nearly sayable-to-herself. Because their successive chronicles are convincing substitutes for the less-than-all-knowing saying that persons do, they are essential to Jamesy's impersonation.

And they are essential to it in another way. Jamesy is able to impersonate only because he knows what persons are subject to when they talk to themselves or to one another. Thinking is talking to oneself. Jamesy's thinking differs from mine in that there are no persons for Jamesy to talk to, and none to talk to him: unanswerable, Jamesy thinks everything in the one way that is all-knowing. By contrast, as Jamesy knows, I am subject to a world with other persons who think and speak: because I cannot know how you might answer what I think, I think less than everything. Because there are other persons for any person, what a person thinks or says is merely a version and therefore suspect. While Gerty and the barfly do not so much as play at knowing what is suspect about their respective chronicles, Jamesy both knows and says it through his parody of each. What the barfly says depends at least in part on what other characters say. He reports their words more or less faithfully and then seems to respond to the proceedings with judgments of his own. The back-and-forth that is conversation is largely implicit in Gerty's chapter, but explicit in the barfly's. Because his chapter takes its direction from what a number of characters say, and because each character's words are scrutinized not only by the barfly but by Jamesy himself, chapter 12 is a good bit more complicated than chapter 13—which I will take up first.

GERTY'S DREAMS

Gerty's portion of the thirteenth chapter is an account of her dreams as those dreams appropriate and make a place for select "events" at twilight on Sandymount strand. Whereas the barfly's account is in the first person because he is saying it to someone, Gerty's is in the third because she cannot quite say it even to herself. Since "Gerty had her dreams that no-one knew of" (13: 634), not even her confessor, they are dreams that Gerty herself must not know.

Among all the people in the world including herself, it is to her confessor alone that Gerty may say in the first person what her dreams are and what they lead her to do. If she so much as thinks about her life by saying something to herself about herself, she must keep that thinking in line with what her confessor would have her believe it is all right to say to him. To do less than that would be to deny the Church's jurisdiction.

> He told her that time when she told him about that in confession, crimsoning up to the roots of her hair for fear he could see, not to be troubled because that was only the voice of nature and we were all subject to nature's laws, he said, in this life and that that was no sin because that came from the nature of woman instituted by God, he said, and that Our Blessed Lady herself said to the archangel Gabriel be it done unto me according to Thy Word. (13: 453–59)

Whereas the Church demands that Gerty come close enough to saying profane things so that she may be understood and judged accordingly, it also insists that there are more and less sacred ways to say them. Relieved to hear her understander say that what she had confessed to

was not a sin, she had also been instructed in how to think and talk
about it. Through his repeated appeal to the word "that," the priest
had reminded her that certain antecedents may be discreetly relegated
to pronouns and thereby brought into closer harmony with the Word
of God.

Gerty puts the same lesson to a related use. It is not only her body's
yearnings and deeds that she must almost but not quite say: there is also
the almost unutterable subject of her body's dysfunction. Just as she
repeatedly approaches but avoids saying to herself that she has sexual
desires, so too does she approach but avoid saying that the body promoting those desires, her body, is a crippled body.

With its reliance on phrases and formulas she has culled from the
romances she reads, Gerty's account keeps bringing her to the verge of
acknowledging her handicap only to turn away. Imagining herself "as
fair a specimen of winsome Irish girlhood as one could wish to see" (13:
80–81), she does not neglect her feet in the detailed catalog of her
charms. "Edy Boardman prided herself that she was very *petite* but she
never had a foot like Gerty MacDowell, a five, and never would" (13:
165–67). "There was an innate refinement, a languid queenly *hauteur*
about Gerty which was unmistakably evidenced in her delicate hands
and higharched instep. Had kind fate but willed her to be" . . . (13:
96–99). The reference to her instep bringing her too close to an acknowledgment of her ill-fated accident, Gerty shifts the terms. Instead
of "had kind fate but willed her to be steady on her feet," her chronicle
reads "but willed her to be born a gentlewoman of high degree," and
the subject has once again been avoided. For Gerty to say to herself
that "she had a lucky hand" (13: 226) for lighting a fire is to have been
drawn toward the subject of her unlucky foot but to have avoided saying it.

Only once does she not avoid saying it. But for "that one shortcom-
ing she knew she need fear no competition and that was an accident
coming down Dalkey hill and she always tried to conceal it. But it must
end, she felt. If she saw that magic lure in his eyes there would be no
holding back for her" (13: 650–53). Having said what it is almost impossible for her to say—that her dreams of domestic bliss are less likely
to be realized because she limps—she goes on to say at least two things
at the same time, each of the two pivoting on the word "it" in the
sentence "but it must end, she felt." (1) With the pronoun taking an
*ante*cedent, Gerty is quickly suppressing her hard-won acknowledgment that the injury to her foot is an irreversible handicap in the
competition: she is saying that her limp must end, that she has already
had more than enough heartache because her limp turns men away. (2)
With the pronoun taking a reference that *follows* it, the acknowledg-

ment stands and she is saying that what must end is her frustration that no man has looked at her with "that magic lure in his eyes": "it must end, she felt" because that man is there in front of her right now and she feels he cannot take his eyes off her just yet.

Jamesy knows why Gerty has to say at least two things at the same time. He knows that for her to say only one of the things her body urges her to acknowledge would be for her to give up the one game her body and her culture let her care about playing. She can believe she has a chance in the game, Jamesy knows, only if the stories she tells herself about herself are at the same time miraculously hopeful and free of any desperate-because-too-miraculous cures. He knows that her equivocal, third-person, past-tense dreaming is a pep talk to herself, a pep talk without which she would be forced to give up not only the game itself but thinking and talking as well. He knows that Gerty would no longer be substituting for a person if she were to give all that up, for he knows that to be a person is to have the time to go on saying things if only to oneself.

Jamesy knows too that Gerty becomes more and more inclined to let her body do a univocal kind of talking, he knows that Gerty's body responds to what she sees Bloom saying with his. "If ever there was undisguised admiration in a man's passionate gaze it was there plain to be seen on that man's face. It is for you, Gertrude MacDowell, and you know it" (13: 564). "Admiration" is less what she sees than raw arousal, of course. And in keeping with that kind of repression she will continue to find words that only almost say what she cannot admit to herself in the first person that her body is saying. But then her body would not say it at all if it were not for small differences in what she says to herself. Because she lets herself know about her dreams that Bloom's passionate gaze is for her, past tense yields briefly to present, and third- yields to a second-person pronoun that is at least gesturing in the direction of first. "It is for you, Gertrude MacDowell, and you know it." However tawdry and pathetic the terms, Gerty has her say with Bloom. While she goes on deluding herself about her own forwardness and thereby avoids having to answer for it either to her confessor or to herself, she has said more than enough to be answerable to Bloom, to his judgment of what her body has said for him.

"HOW TO END THE CONVERSATION"

By the time she and Bloom have gotten it said with some measure of mutual consent and understanding, they have exchanged no words. "Still it was a kind of language between us" (13: 944), Bloom remembers. And he is right. Prior to his "fireworks," Gerty says to herself that "her every effort would be to share his thoughts" (13: 654). Exchanging words is the usual but obviously not the only way to share another person's thoughts. Seeing that Bloom's "hands and face were working" (13: 695), sharing with him the thought that he would very much like to see the insides of her upper thighs, Gerty does her best to expose them to his view. "She wasn't ashamed and he wasn't either to look in that immodest way like that because he couldn't resist. . . . And then a rocket sprang and bang shot blind blank and O!" (13: 730–37), and Bloom thinks later why: "Dress up and look and suggest and let you see and see more and defy you if you're a man to see that and, like a sneeze coming, legs, look, look and if you have any guts in you. Tip. Have to let fly" (13: 993–96).

As Gerty is answerable to Bloom in their silent colloquy, so is Bloom to Gerty. He is sure she knew that he was masturbating. But if she might therefore have judged him a fool, Bloom judges that he had at least avoided making an even "worse fool" (13: 942–43) of himself. "Suppose I spoke to her. What about? Bad plan however if you don't know how to end the conversation" (13: 862–63). People want to know how to end a conversation, Jamesy knows, because not to know is to have too little control over the various turns it might take. Not to be in control of a situation is of course to risk being a fool. Since he could have settled on the most innocuous, least foolish thing to say and then have gone ahead and said it, Bloom could presumably have controlled his opening words to Gerty. But without knowing how to end the conversation, he could not have controlled either the subsequent words between them or what Gerty herself might make of those words.

From his side of it, though—and with Gerty's univocal help—he had maintained control. Because the two of them had let their bodies say that they were there to act as exhibitionist and masturbating voyeur, Bloom and Gerty had "conversed." Drawn to talk to her by his hormones as well as by her obvious interest in what he had to say, he had come into her hearing for a short time and then gone off before he could be implicated in anything other than the agreed-upon business at hand. Which is to say that he did know how to end the conversation with her. Instead of being left with enough to answer for so that he was sorry he had begun the conversation in the first place, Bloom remained answerable to Gerty only for his shamelessness in allowing her to watch him bring himself to orgasm.

He had been more foolish, he recalls, in his exchanges with prostitutes. Since to talk with them at all was to abandon the control that resides in not talking, the first words were the riskiest. "Worst is beginning. How they change the venue when it's not what they like. Ask you do you like mushrooms because she once knew a gentlemen who.

Or ask you what someone was going to say when he changed his mind and stopped" (13: 879–82). More circumspect than Bloom, this "someone" had stopped himself from saying something he did not want to answer for. What, he might have thought just after starting to propose it, if she rejected or was offended by what he had in mind for their sexual interlude? Or worse, what if her willingness to enact his fantasy were to leave him emotionally in her debt? By interrupting what might otherwise have been a conversation with her about the matter, the man had stayed in control, had avoided a possible entanglement he could not have answered for simply with cash.

ENTANGLEMENTS

Instead, it was Bloom who had become entangled. Having begun to converse with her "about nothing," unable to know what the woman was going to say until she said it, he had been called upon to answer not only for himself but also for one of her former clients, a client who had kept his professional distance as Bloom had not. It is a mark of Bloom's having not kept it that the woman emerges from the plural "they"—"all prostitutes"—to the singular "she"—"this one prostitute" who, because his conversation with her had taken its uncontrollable turns, said something that still distinguishes her in his mind from others in her class.

Distinguishes her, that is to say, as a person. While he was with her, Bloom could remain unentangled and in control only so long as his apprehension of her as a prostitute was uncontested by his apprehension of her as a person. As she became however slightly more distinguishable as a person through what she said for him, she sent slight but uncontrollable tremors through what he was saying and would later say to himself about her. Because he remembers that she had called upon him to answer words of her own, he had not cancelled his obligation to her simply by paying her for her services, he was still if only minimally in her debt, entangled, not altogether in control.

Though part of that entanglement and debt can be traced to his having not been able to answer for "someone" else, there is also, for Bloom, a more general indebtedness, one that issues from the economy within which people talk to one another. People talk because they learn fairly early in their lives that talking sometimes gets results. If said for an adult's hearing and heard by that adult, the child's saying "Terry hit me" or "I'm hungry" may remedy her lack of control over her bruiser of a sibling or the refrigerator door. But neither remedy will come without her also having learned, if somewhat more slowly, that she is placing herself in the debt of at least one other person with that quiet but audible power play. Having learned that talking gets results only if it entangles another person, she has had to learn as well that she too becomes entangled in whatever responses she has occasioned—the noticeably less than enthusiastic good offices of the adult, say, or Terry's enthusiastic if delayed retaliation. Bloom is seeking a remedy of his own whenever he begins a conversation with a prostitute. Sometimes it is a breeze. "Wonderful of course if you say: good evening, and you see she's on for it: good evening"(13: 865–66). But even then he is aware that he is becoming entangled and obliged. Simply by talking with a prostitute who answers, Bloom understands, he in turn becomes answerable to one more person in a world of people who talk.

BELONGING

If Jamesy knew less than everything about persons, his verve as an impersonator would be proportionately less. Chapters 13 and 12 are complementary displays of what he knows about people who talk. He knows that people want to control what happens to them in their lives. Since words at least seem to them to be more controllable than circumstance, Jamesy knows, people find that saying things compensates them for their lack of control if it rarely remedies it outright. But persons also learn that they incur unpredictable debts when they so much as pass the time of day with one another: Jamesy knows that they are therefore reluctant to talk unless their talk includes escape clauses, ways out of having to answer for what they say.

The barfly's monologue in chapter 12 is replete with such ways out. Though his account of an hour in Barney Kiernan's pub requires that he himself have listened to what was said there, he is not answerable for what he says about it since his incessant surface of talk does not let his listener or listeners get a word in edgewise. Nor is he going on at such length without "anything in the way of liquid refreshment" (12: 758–59). And so while his unanswerably holding forth offers one kind of immunity for his talk, the "porter" (12: 1362) he is treated to as he holds forth offers still another.

Drinking and talking clearly go together for the barfly, but only on the condition that no one in the company of drinkers stirs up a fuss with his talk. A fuss is anything that entangles people with one another by prompting diverging responses for which they then become answerable. Since a fuss is anything about which there may be more than the barfly's one way, judgments are notorious disturbers of the unanimity for which he strives. Breen might well have a case in court over the postcard "U. p: up," says J. J. O'Molloy. "Who wants your opinion" (12: 1074), the barfly thinks but waits to say until O'Molloy cannot hear him and therefore cannot respond. "Let us drink our pints in peace. Gob, we won't be let even do that much itself" (12: 1074–75).

The barfly has this "peace" when he is with same-minded souls who want to drink their pints with one another without someone "kicking up a bloody murder about bloody nothing. Gob, it'd turn the porter sour in your guts, so it would" (12: 1794–95), to have to witness the wars brought about by talk. The barfly's is not the peace of drunken stupor, though. Neither is it the peace of silence.[24] He listens and talks because he is continually having to remind himself that he belongs. What belonging means is that there is safety in numbers. It means his best chance for peace is that he is numbered among a group of people who hold a mandate and will not be gainsaid.

Little matter if the group's membership is a bit vague—the vaguer, perhaps, the farther-reaching. Many of those who drink will be given the benefit of the doubt, and all the more so if they happen to be treating. Still, there must be some who do not belong if there is to be such a thing as belonging. The barfly identifies at least three recalcitrants: Bob Doran, the citizen, and Bloom. Compared to the citizen's and to Bloom's, the fuss Doran stirs up is easily quelled. In the name of Barney Kiernan's "respectable licensed premises" (12: 394) and all who belong there, Doran is told "to keep quiet, that they didn't want that kind of talk" (12: 393–94).[25]

A comparable injunction might be directed at the citizen, who the barfly knows is forever "only waiting for the wink of the word" (12: 479) to go off into another of his peace-disturbing tirades. But while he can always be expected to shatter what the barfly regards as the last refuge of those who belong, the citizen also happens to be the most forceful spokesman for the group itself and is therefore harder to exclude. "—*Sinn Fein!* says the citizen" (12: 523) so Bloom cannot fail to get the point. "*Sinn fein amhain!* The friends we love are by our side and the foes we hate before us" (12: 523–24). The barfly can be surer he belongs because the citizen is there to say that there are those who do not. He has it both ways with the citizen, who, because he does the dirty work of telling the outcasts they are outcasts, can in turn be cast out as a course loudmouth, "all wind and piss like a tanyard cat" (12: 1311–12).

The hour would have been much less vexing for the barfly, obviously, if Bloom had not showed up. With Bloom as a target, the citizen's advocacy of the group becomes a very heated advocacy of the group-as-*nation*. Having heard the citizen say "We want no more strangers in our house" (12: 1150–51), "Bloom was talking and talking with John Wyse" (12: 1414).

—Persecution, says he, all the history of the world is full of it. Perpetuating national hatred among nations.
—But do you know what a nation means? says John Wyse.
—Yes, says Bloom.
—What is it? says John Wyse.
—A nation? says Bloom. A nation is the same people living in the same place. (12: 1417–23)

The barfly would like to think that the group he belongs to could be defined as encompassingly as "the same people living in the same place." Sameness appeals to the barfly. As long as everyone in his company thinks the same way he does—and if his listeners think otherwise they never say so—then he need not answer for his words. And yet if the group is a "nation" and not an assortment of good fellows, all of whom want nothing more than to drink their pints in peace, a discomforting proposition follows. The people of a nation are the "same people" only if the nation makes room for their differences. And making that room requires not just one monologue but many conversations.[26]

Moved to speak for himself-as-stranger, Bloom's exchanges with the patrons become a conversation to the degree that the talk between them takes turn after unpredictable turn. When he refers to estranging "hatred," he cannot know that he will be called upon for his sense of "what a nation means." Nor can he know what his answer will bring in the way of derision.

—A nation? says Bloom. A nation is the same people living in the same place.
—By God, then, says Ned, laughing, if that's so I'm a nation for I'm living in the same place for the past five years.
So of course everyone had the laugh at Bloom and says he, trying to muck out of it:
—Or also living in different places.
—That covers my case, says Joe. (12: 1422–29)

Ned's comeback strikes "everyone" funny. Joe's might have too if the citizen had not been ready with more solemn business. Laughter at Bloom's expense is selfsame from person to person, Bloom excluded. Because that selfsameness temporarily interrupts the series of turns that are conversation, it temporarily restores the barfly's peace.

RULES AND CASES

But the retorts that prompt the laughter take an interesting turn of their own. Ned Lambert's seemingly ridiculous "I'm a nation" is a surprisingly accurate reading of Bloom's words. Bloom had been speaking not only for himself but also for each person whom "hatred" has estranged, those within the group as well as those without. A nation, for Bloom, is not a collectivity that answers for its members by substituting national hatred for individual responsibilities: it is instead each of its persons as each remains answerable to other persons "living in the same place." By referring to himself as a "case," Joe Hynes too is unintentionally advancing what Bloom has in mind. As a nation is each of its persons, each person is again and again a case to be judged by other persons.

While the ridicule aimed at Bloom may temporarily stall the conversation in laughter, it also begins to say what Bloom himself might have said but did not. If it might have been more comfortable for the patrons merely to laugh Bloom off as an outcast who does not know what he is talking about, the citizen has other ideas.

—What is your nation if I may ask? says the citizen.
—Ireland, says Bloom. I was born here. Ireland.
    The citizen said nothing only cleared the spit out of his gullet and, gob, he spat a Red bank oyster out of him right in the corner.
—After you with the push, Joe, says he, taking out his handkerchief to swab himself dry. (12: 1430–35)

The citizen is sure that the group-as-nation has a more than adequate rule for dealing with Bloom's case. This rule says that Ireland need not suffer Jews, that Ireland should give Jews the push just as they have been given it by every nation worthy of the name. "Ahasuerus I call him" (12: 1667), the citizen says of him after Bloom steps out to the courthouse. For the citizen as for most Dubliners, Bloom is one more "Wandering Jew" whom God has cursed.

Having become practiced at being hated because of his race, Bloom had remembered that his definition of a nation should not be limited to "the same people living in the same place." As different Jews are the "same people" insofar as they are Jews, Jews constitute a nation in 1904 only if they are living not in the same but rather in "different places."

—And I belong to a race too, says Bloom, that is hated and persecuted. Also now. This very moment. This very instant.
    Gob, he near burnt his fingers with the butt of his old cigar.
—Robbed, says he. Plundered. Insulted. Persecuted. Taking what belongs to us by right. At this very moment, says he, putting up his fist, sold by auction in Morocco like slaves or cattle.
—Are you talking about the new Jerusalem? says the citizen.
—I'm talking about injustice, says Bloom.

—Right, says John Wyse. Stand up to it then with force like men. (12: 1467–75)

Bloom would have been talking about the new Jerusalem if belonging were all he had to answer for. He is talking about his nation and his race, surely: but he is talking about them from the perspective to which he is most subject—the perspective that is his as a person. By tacitly acknowledging that he himself is being insulted and persecuted "this very moment. This very instant," he is saying that the targets of nationally or racially inspired hatreds are not nations or races but rather persons.

RULES ARE OLD "SAID BEFORE"S

By "talking about injustice," Bloom is asking to be recognized as having a case. Bloom substitutes for a person who calls to other persons out of his need. He will have a case only with those persons who respond justly to his call. To respond justly is to give your tacit promise that you want to make sense of what another person's sometimes only tacit call to you comes to, it is to promise that you will judge that sense and be answerable for your judgment of it. Jamesy knows that persons can respond to only so many cases. Because each judgment is fraught with responsibility, because each judgment weighs upon its judge, individual judges are loath to bear alone the weight of all the cases it might be possible for them to hear. Though it imperils justice to do so, Jamesy knows, people necessarily look for and find ways to spread that weight around.

Just as belonging to the group spreads it around, so too is it spread around by invoking the rules that are any group's collective past, a past that is summoned simply by talking since all talk is informed by grammatical and institutional rules.[27] Jamesy knows that rules may be appealed to in the judgment of a case because they are there to be appealed to, because in any talking there have to be and are innumerable and subtle "said before"s. Before any two people contract with one another, there are more and less appropriate contracts that do not have to be said anew: into the most appropriate of these, with some adjustments, their transaction may then be placed, the persons themselves being substituted for by phrases that were ready and waiting. As "said purchaser" and "said vendor" (12: 42), Michael E. Geraghty, Esquire, and Moses Herzog are answerable to one another because the law makes at least a show of having spread around and absorbed the weight of their financial responsibilities to one another.

Under the law, it was ruled that a "said amount shall have been duly paid" (12: 47–48) by Geraghty for "said nonperishable goods" (12: 44) supplied to him by Herzog. Said amount was not duly paid. But were Herzog to bring his case to a court of law, it might well be that other rules than those spelled out in the contract would be invoked. For within that court, as within the court of Dublin public opinion, Herzog is likely to be substituted for not by the phrase "said vendor" but rather by stated and unstated phrases which rule that he is an interloping, usurious stranger to whom nothing belongs "by right." By invoking this rule, Dubliners can avoid hearing Herzog's case because they can avoid acknowledging that persons judge, as they are judged, subjectively.

A PERSON IS A CASE TOO NEW FOR RULES

Because it is persons who judge, all judgments are subjective. No appeal to so-called objective rules will absolve me from having to answer for the personal peculiarities that, because I am subject to them, are necessarily at work in every judgment I make. A person does not have a case with me, I do not hear his or her case until it entangles me as a responsible person, a person whose appeal to escape clauses is bound to fail because I cannot be acquitted but must answer for the way I hear the case.

A case is not heard until it somehow makes its way into the entangling turns that are conversation. Conversation, as I have said, is the turns persons take as they say their differing versions of things for one another, the turns themselves being possible only if the respondents tacitly promise to judge what they hear and to be answerable for their separate and differing judgments of it. Jamesy knows that it is only in conversation that each person responds as a person to what he or she has just heard. In a conversation, each response is a beginning, however laden with old "said before"s. In a conversation, each response is heard and judged as a first-time saying. Because each respondent in a conversation acknowledges that he or she is dealing with a case too new for rules, each asks to be heard and judged in turn as a new case.

INTERRUPTED CONVERSATION

"Didn't I tell you?," the barfly stops to remind his listeners about Bloom's contrariness and unremitting talk. "As true as I'm drinking this porter if he was at his last gasp he'd try to downface you that dying was living" (12: 1362–63). "I declare to my antimacassar if you took up a straw from the bloody floor and if you said to Bloom: *Look at, Bloom. Do you see that straw? That's a straw.* Declare to my aunt he'd talk about it for an hour so he would and talk steady" (12: 893–96). The barfly's interruptions sound as if he has heard and judged Bloom's case, but he has done neither because he has managed not to respond. The barfly assumes that among his listeners there is none who will gainsay his assessment of Bloom. Rather than conversing, rather than acknowledging that his judgment of Bloom might in turn be judged as it would be in conversation, the barfly repeatedly interrupts his account of conversational wars in order to restore the myopic peace that his treating cronies may prize as much as he does.

His monologue would be that very peace if Jamesy were not busy interrupting him. Again and again, Jamesy breaks into the monologue with his impersonations. Having pretended in chapter 11 to be one more Dubliner who delights in Bloom's cuckoldry, Jamesy pretends in chapter 12 to be a composite of at least three characters. One of the three is the citizen: Jamesy's catalogues of Irish wonders bear a more than accidental resemblance to the citizen's encomium to "our flax and our damask from the looms of Antrim and our Limerick lace, our tanneries and our white flint glass down there by Ballybough . . . nothing like it in the whole wide world" (12: 1243–48). The writer of the "skit in the *United Irishman* today about that Zulu chief" (12: 1509–10) is a second character whom Jamesy pretends to be, for the skit conforms in both style and tone with Jamesy's takeoffs on seances, talking dogs, a boxing match, Bloom's leavetaking, nuptial trees, and so on.

A third character Jamesy pretends to be is of course the barfly himself. Jamesy is like the barfly insofar as each interrupts what one character or another says, and the resemblance does not stop there. As the barfly's do, Jamesy's interruptions make it sound as if he is judging cases though he is not. Even the condemned, after all, are afforded a time to speak: a judgment that may not be responded to within the judge's hearing is not a judgment at all but rather a harangue. Just as the barfly stops all conversation between himself and his listeners, the written *Ulysses* is interrupted conversation insofar as it takes place outside a time in which there are persons who talk back and forth.

And yet Jamesy knows that persons who read *Ulysses* converse with it unstoppably in their different ways. My conversation with *Ulysses* is all the more compellingly ongoing because Jamesy impersonates the judge that only I can be in my reading of the book. When I read *Ulysses* I cannot resist judging the matters it presents, matters the impersonating Jamesy only seems to judge and therefore resists judging. Secure in the knowledge that I cannot resist it as he both can and does, Jamesy impersonates me by challenging me to try. If I could resist, his challenge runs, then I would be absorbed into Jamesy himself, into the wholly impersonal writtenness of *Ulysses*. Jamesy's impersonation of me consists of his knowledge that I will not let my conversation with *Ulys-*

ses stay interrupted. He knows that all he has to do to get me to inter-rogate the barfly's words is to seem to judge them himself. By only seem-ing to judge them, Jamesy keeps that peace which I disturb by holding the barfly answerable for what he says. Because *Ulysses* is written and done with, the barfly has of course said all he is going to say and there-fore cannot answer. But challenged by Jamesy's impersonation of me as someone who questions and wants answers, I respond to the written as if it might be personal, as if there might be behind it a person with whom I could converse.

"SIR, TO YOU MY HAND"

Jamesy's references to himself in chapter 14 toy with the possibility of his being that very person. This is the only chapter in which he condescends to use the first-person pronoun. "Thou art, I vow," he writes of Theodore Purefoy, "the remarkablest progenitor barring none in this chaffering allincluding most farraginous chronicle" (14: 1411–12). To chaffer is to haggle over trade. It implies an exchange between persons. Because chapter 14 is replete with Jamesy's "I hear"s, "I tell thee"s, "I know not what"s and "No, say I"s, it presents him as some-one readers might call upon to answer for *Ulysses*' haggling ways. When he offers Purefoy his "hand" (14: 1343), Jamesy even goes so far as to pretend that he, like most persons, has at least that one bodily property if not also all the rest.

But impersonating pretense it is. Jamesy knows that to have the body of a person waits upon that person's being born to his or her body. And Jamesy—who is written, unborn, and all-knowing—knows that he does not have a body. He knows as well that this fact will not be lost on readers, knows they will also understand that Purefoy himself does not have a hand with which to accept congratulations. Like Mina and their whole brood, Theodore Purefoy too is written and not born. While each character substitutes for a person, each has been written into being which, as being, is inseparable from Jamesy's own. As birth is separation, as being born is to be placed outside the mother, apart from her and as a visible part of the world, the newest Purefoy is merely a substitute for a person who was born. Though Jamesy impersonates, though he feigns the separateness that is every person's, he alone among all those named in *Ulysses* does not substitute for a person. Jamesy is neither a part of the world nor a substitute for such a part. He is instead the whole of *Ulysses*.

As the whole of *Ulysses*, Jamesy is all of its characters as well as what may be said to happen to them. In Jamesy's being there are no differ-ences. Because each character is inseparable from Jamesy, because each merely substitutes for a person who is separate, there is no real difference between Jamesy and any one of his characters.

But there is between them a difference for me. Though Jamesy and any one of his characters are the same insofar as he and all of them are at one absolute remove from being persons, each of his characters has a crucial-if-merely-substituted-for resemblance to me: as each is subject to Jamesy's knowledge of persons, I am subject to the very things he knows about them. Knowing that persons are subject to visible bodies and that most persons' bodies have hands, Jamesy declares that Theodore Purefoy "is to be seen any fair sabbath with a pair of his boys off Bullock harbour dapping on the sound with a heavybraked reel" (14: 518–20). With Mina, Jamesy's declarative mood shifts to the imperative. "Reverently look at her as she reclines there with the motherlight in her eyes, that longing hunger for baby fingers (a pretty sight it is to see)" (14: 315–17). As it would be for the persons for whom Theodore, Mina, and the newborn Mortimer Edward substitute, it would be absurd for me to pretend to have the hands I may be seen to have.[28] It is not at all absurd for Jamesy to pretend as much since he does not so much as substitute for a person who may be seen to have them. There is derision in his pretense, as if nothing could be funnier than to feign having a mortal body without having to have one. Unable to forget what I myself am subject to or that characters are substitutes for persons, I find unsurprisingly that I resemble any one of Jamesy's characters more than I resemble Jamesy.

THE GOD BRINGFORTH

Despite all he knows and can relate about persons, Jamesy acknowledges in chapter 14 that he himself does not resemble persons as closely as his characters do. His way of acknowledging it is to suspend his operation as an impersonator and submit to being god. Predictably, though, he does not submit without an impersonating twist: in chapter 14, the god Jamesy submits to being is like a person to the degree that persons are sometimes angry and say why.

What he pretends to be angry about is itself the very basis of any resemblance between characters and persons, the very basis, that is, of his own unlikeness from both. He pretends to be angry that the company gathered at Horne's Lying-in Hospital is intolerably disrespectful of the miraculous, great boon of human birth. His characters' irreverent talk about childbearing having taken one too many disobedient turns, "a black crack of noise in the street here, alack, bawled back" (14: 408). When Dixon, Lynch, Madden, Lenehan, Crotthers, Costello, Dedalus, and Bloom hear it "long rumblingly over all the heavens" but

(14: 422) do not at once repudiate the sterilities that attend lust, Jamesy intervenes with the truth about what the thunder meant: "that," he proclaims, "was the voice of the god that was in a very grievous rage that he would presently lift his arm up and spill their souls for their abuses and their spillings done by them contrariwise to his word which forth to bring brenningly biddeth" (14: 470–73).

For Jamesy as "the god Bringforth" (14: 435–36), these "right witty scholars" (14: 202) constitute a "wretched company" (14: 470). Each is punishable because he uses his gift of sex to the end of pleasure alone: seeking only to be brought off, he profanes the sacred bringing forth that is procreation. "Maledicity!" (14: 771), the blaspheming Bannon exclaims about having been unequipped for sexual intercourse with Milly Bloom. "Would to God that foresight had but remembered me to take my cloak along!" (14: 772–73). Bloom himself is one of the wretched, "stained," as he is, "by the mire of an indelible dishonour" (14: 1218–19), his recent masturbation on the strand in view of Gerty's drawers.

Because it seems to respond to their onanistic and contraceptive impossibilizing of "Godpossibled souls" (14: 225), of persons, Jamesy's seeming anger seems to be personal. There is a personal cast as well to his more temperate but unequivocal insistence that all persons must be strong advocates for childbirth, as if how one talks about a subject makes a difference in what oneself and others do about it. Early in the chapter he sets it forth that "it behoves every most just citizen to become the exhortator and admonisher of his semblables and to tremble lest what had in the past by the nation excellently commenced might be in the future not with similar excellence accomplished" (14: 21–25). As if persons were his "semblables" and not pathetic underlings, as if he himself were "with any as any with any" (17: 68) and not the remote and exalted deity, Jamesy exhorts and admonishes, keeps calling throughout the chapter for the births of more and more persons.

WHAT TO CHERISH

But who is Jamesy to be making such a call—or more really and with less seeming, what does he know himself to be in making it? He knows, of course, that he is his characters' all-in-all. "Merciful providence had been pleased to put a period to the sufferings of the lady who was *enceinte*" (14: 820–21). Jamesy knows that it is only because it pleases him to put a period to the sentence in which he relates it that baby Purefoy is "given birth." "God, I thank thee, as the Author of my days!" (14: 762–63), Bannon rejoices over the good fortune of his having met Milly, Jamesy having authored both that fortune and these thanks. And yet while he knows that his characters depend absolutely on what he relates about them, he knows too that he is the progenitor not of persons but of substitutes for persons. If he can pretend that he himself, as a person who has been brought forth, can have an active part in bringing forth more persons, he knows all along that he is not so much as substituting for such a person.

Rather than bringing persons forth as a natural progenitor does, Jamesy both calls forth characters—Bloom, Stephen, Milly, Bannon, the Purefoys—and calls for persons to be brought forth. Knowing the difference between characters and persons, knowing the difference between calling for persons to be brought forth and bringing them forth, Jamesy pretends not to know it. For it to be seen, Jamesy knows, a child's body must be brought forth into the light. He also knows, by contrast, that it takes only parts of speech to relate either that a child has been brought forth or that the bringing forth of children is a good thing. But with all he knows about the difference between visible persons and words about persons, Jamesy announces that the bringing forth of children is to be "cherished" "not merely in being seen but also even in being related worthy of being praised" (14: 56–57). Insofar as it relates that they are worthy of being praised, his dictum goes, what he himself relates about persons is at least the equivalent of persons.

HIS OWN APOLOGIST

The dictum is pretense. Knowing that praise for persons is not the equivalent of one born person, Jamesy impersonates his own apologist by pretending that his praise for them in *Ulysses* is better than mere persons. It is the premise of the apology that much can go wrong in childbearing, a premise dramatized throughout *Ulysses* by Rudy's death. "In fact when one comes to look into it," Jamesy pretends to reflect, "the wonder is that so many pregnancies and deliveries go off so well as they do, all things considered and in spite of our human shortcomings which often baulk nature in her intentions" (14: 1264–67). Whereas childbearing is imperfect, nothing is more perfect than Jamesy's disclosure that he knows everything about persons. Whereas persons live imperfectly, perfecting their lives only in their own deaths, each character in *Ulysses* is given timeless being in Jamesy's perfect knowledge. As "innocent" of *Ulysses* "as the babe unborn" (14: 1190), the lot of them subsist along with Jamesy in what he relates about them, character and all-knowing intelligence perfected together in "an arrest of embryonic development at some stage antecedent to the human" (14: 990–91).

I would not take Jamesy's characters as personally as I do if they were not in themselves strong praise for persons who are born. Whatever their respective blindnesses, incapacities, and griefs, the Dubliners of *Ulysses* do far more to recommend being born than do the Dubliners of *Dubliners*. If praising persons were the equivalent of persons, *Ulysses'* characters would be the equivalent of persons. It is not and they are not, as Jamesy knows. Impersonating his own apologist, Jamesy impersonates as well each character within the "wretched company" he pretends to condemn. Just as those characters cherish not the births that might follow upon their sexual pleasure but the pleasure itself, Jamesy pretends to cherish what he relates about persons and not persons. Whereas the birth of a person requires "that earthly mother which was but a dam to bear beastly" (14: 149–50) and to "bring forth in pain" (14: 209), there is nothing like pain for the unembodied Jamesy who pleases himself by relating this and that about his characters. "To tell the truth" (14: 535) he can "always bring himself off with his tongue" (14: 542–43). Because he is not subject to having a body as a person is, because it pleases him to disclose his perfectly indifferent knowledge of persons, Jamesy is supple enough to perform autofellatio just by having his say.

THERE IS NO SUBSTITUTE FOR BIRTH

As he does throughout *Ulysses*, Jamesy allows himself to be caught in his pretense. At the same time that he impersonates "someone" who holds that *Ulysses'* parts of speech are a more than adequate substitute for persons who are born, he acknowledges just the reverse. In the library, he has Mulligan say "—The most beautiful book that has come out of our country in my time. One thinks of Homer" (9: 1164–65). One can of course think only of *Ulysses*. The phrase comes back toward the end of chapter 14 and when it does the emphasis is decidedly away from talk and toward an altogether different kind of ejaculation. "Most beautiful book come out of Ireland my time. *Silentium!* Get a spurt on" (14: 1456–57).

When I catch Jamesy at his impersonating I address the simple wisdom that a person's birth cannot be substituted for, not even when the substitute is perfect knowledge that points toward persons as worthy of praise. No matter how laudatory, the pointing requires remove—a distance between the persons-pointed-toward and the-substitute-that-points. This is the very distance Jamesy maintains throughout his Dublin at one remove. Only one kind of knowledge closes this distance, and it is not Jamesy's kind. The distance between substitute and person is closed only in the carnal knowledge that engenders a new person. Contiguous in time and fecund, one person's egg and another's sperm disrupt the perfection of the-never-to-be-conceived.[29] Born, the new person is subject to his or her traffic with other persons and with the imperfect knowledge about them that we substitute for persons. This traffic is personal, I am convinced, only if there is always at least tacit reference to what cannot be substituted for, namely to persons who are born.

Notice that what is to be "cherished" according to Jamesy's dictum is not the births of individual persons but rather the birth of all of them, indiscriminately, in the aggregate. As if to give itself away as sham, Jamesy's call for more persons becomes grotesquely impersonal. When he declaims that infant mortality is "in the long run beneficial to the race in general in securing thereby the survival of the fittest" (14: 1284–85), he is playing dumb. He cannot have forgotten Rudy's death—because he is timeless, Jamesy can at most pretend to forget—and is therefore once again, as in the eleventh chapter, making Bloom the butt of a very bad joke. While Bloom does not know the joke exists, I do. Jamesy's indiscriminate call for more persons having come to what is a very bad joke for me, I find myself judging the value of procreation in general as that judgment intersects with my judgment of what particular lives are worth. Understanding that I have much to answer for in making even so self-evident a determination, I judge that the Purefoys should not have had a tenth child, that the Blooms should have a third.

I would be abler to suspend this and comparable judgments when I read *Ulysses* if Jamesy were impersonal but not also impersonating. Such judgments suspended, freed by that much from my subjection to the personal impulse to judge, I would be that much likelier to subsist along with him in his station high above "the small round floor that makes us passionate."[30] Elevated to that height, I could know everything *Ulysses* discloses not only about its characters but about its readers as well, I would be free to rest with that knowledge because I would be above persons, above any responses from me that they might otherwise summon and for which I would have to answer.

But Jamesy is the impersonating as well as the indifference, he is two things at once and I am therefore anything but free. Jamesy the Impersonator reminds me that I am sentimentalizing if I allow myself to enjoy liberties comparable to his, however appealing those liberties might be. Completed and therefore already outside the time in which persons respond to one another and are answerable for their responses, Jamesy is free to work as if backward in time from judgment to crime since a character's crime is whatever it pleases Jamesy to say it is. Because there is no Leopold Bloom outside those of Jamesy's phrases that substitute for the person Bloom would be if he had been born, Jamesy is free to impersonate someone who judges. Above justice, Jamesy is of course

only seemingly unjust. Through the whimsical cruelty of his impersonating, he directs me with such force toward the person Bloom substitutes for that it carries me on past Bloom toward the persons for whom
I am continuingly substituting characters in what I call my life. Different from Bloom in that they were born and not written into being, the
persons in my life are the same as Bloom in that they no less than he
are characters for me when I respond to them. Far from giving me some
respite from my immense debtorship, *Ulysses* steadily coerces me to incur it.

2.

S T E P H E N

In his famous dictum in *A Portrait*, Stephen Dedalus tells Lynch that "the artist, like the God of the creation, remains within or behind or beyond or above his handiwork, invisible, refined out of existence, indifferent, paring his fingernails. / —Trying to refine them also out of existence, said Lynch" (*P*, 215). In the fingernails of the hand that Jamesy offers Doady Purefoy, that refinement is achieved. To the degree that Jamesy pretends to substitute for a person who can be seen, Jamesy is peculiarly refined. Only feigning such substitution, Jamesy only feigns a restlessness with the invisibility essential to knowing all things in the one way that is all-knowing. It is through his akasic knowledge of it that Jamesy is of one substance with "all that ever anywhere wherever was." He could not at once both know and be *every* thing if his substitution for a visible *something* were other than the pretense it unmistakably is.

By the time Stephen remembers the lines "*I am the boy / That can enjoy / Invisibility*" (1: 260–62), Stephen seems bent on taking the advice implicit in their song's title: "Invisibility is just the thing for me." By that time he has already developed a program that points toward his writing and thereby becoming the peculiarly invisible Jamesy. In saying that Stephen's program "points toward" his becoming Jamesy, I mean that Stephen substitutes for a person who in 1904 can at most anticipate what an omniscience as impersonal as Jamesy's would disclose in the completed *Ulysses* more than seventeen years later. Stephen anticipates writing so authorial a book that it will empower him to transcend the visible body his mother gave birth to when she bore him. Karen Lawrence writes that Stephen's "idea of paternity frees him from biology." "In woman's womb word is made flesh," Stephen announces in the lying-in hospital, "but in the spirit of the maker all flesh that passes becomes the word that shall not pass away. This is the postcreation" (14: 292–94). The authority Stephen wants for his writing is paternal not in the procreative but in the postcreative sense: for him it is only after the maternal impulse to procreate has been supplanted that there can be such a thing as an abiologically "fathering source"—a source, that is, whose authority is absolute precisely because it alone among intelligences is no longer subject to the conditions that persons born to mothers are.

If it is to be a "source," there must be issue. Arguing that the word "author" comes from the Latin *augere*, to increase, Vicki Mahaffey writes "Authority is the principle of increase writ large; that status of the author is literally increased through the number of disciples he can remake in his own image."[2] The author that Stephen's program points toward his becoming is one that conforms exactly with Mahaffey's definition of the author as "a disembodied, omniscient voice . . . that can literally imprint readers with its own type."[3] To the degree that any reader is won over and away from the biological by Jamesy's proclamation that whatever he relates about persons improves upon them and renders them passé, that reader is made over in Jamesy's abiological image. It is that image that Stephen's program credits Shakespeare with having imprinted on his spiritual sons, Stephen tacitly numbering himself among them but aspiring all the while to be the author-father. For Stephen to be father and no longer son, his program implies, he will have to write the Shakespeare-replacing Jamesy. Within his program as *Ulysses* discloses it, Stephen is simultaneously Jamesy's son in 1904 and, outside of time, Jamesy himself as the invisible, biology-supplanting father of all his race.

And yet if Stephen were nothing other than Jamesy waiting to happen, his line would be much simpler to follow than it is. Along with its disclosures of Stephen's hopes for his writing, *Ulysses* discloses itself as the very writing on which Stephen's now-realized hopes forever rest. While Jamesy as the all-authoring father remains centerstage within *Ulysses*, "offstage," as Karen Lawrence writes, "the maternal silently undermines the patriarchal power."[4] There is already some undermining of this power in the word "father" itself: an *author* need not, but a *father* implies at least slightly both a male inseminator and persons who are born to mothers. Unlike Jamesy, Stephen substitutes for a person who had male and female progenitors, was born, and then underwent any number of changes in the course of his mortal life. Insofar as his character connects discernibly with the person named James Joyce, Stephen substitutes for a biologically generated person whose aspirations and interests as a writer might well have changed between 1904 and 1921, the year *Ulysses* was completed. Whereas the Jamesy whom Stephen sets his sights on becoming is an absolutely authorial, timeless, abiological "father," James Joyce is at most one person among others. What I propose to do is to follow Stephen's line not only as it points toward an imaginable junction with Jamesy's but also as it veers subtly away from Jamesy's toward that of James Joyce.

Mothers and Fathers

IN THE NAME OF LOVE

"And no more turn aside and brood / Upon love's bitter mystery" (1: 239–40). Having sung these lines for her, Stephen had gone to the bedside of his dying mother and asked her why she was crying. "For those words, Stephen: love's bitter mystery" (1: 252–53).

However she may have understood those words, love is bitterly mysterious to Stephen because it is procreative. It was in the name of love, he thinks, that he and everyone else was conceived in order to be born and to die. His mother has now died. Love is bitter to him at least in part because the sequence "Bridebed, childbed" yields inexorably to "bed of death, ghostcandled" (3: 396). But love is bitter too because life is. Again and again in the name of love his mother and father had "clasped and sundered," done "the coupler's will" (3: 47) by engendering child after child in what became a disastrously large family. What is it in the Irish, Stephen wonders, that keeps them bringing forth more and more Irish into the nightmarishly enslaved world that is Ireland? Despite the hopeless and unrelieved tedium of their lives, his people continue to propagate, thereby compounding their own collective woe. The bitterer the consequences for the people themselves, the deeper the mystery that they keep having children.

Why they keep having them, he feels, is his race's most guarded secret. Looking at one of his students, he thinks "like him was I, these sloping shoulders, this gracelessness" (2: 168), and, most of all, the secrecy behind the eyes. "Secrets, silent, stony sit in the dark palaces of both our hearts: secrets weary of their tyranny: tyrants, willing to be dethroned" (2: 170–72). Though he understands this tyranny as nature's and therefore general to all persons, its secretiveness has a particularly Irish cast for Stephen. However willing his people may be to dethrone their tyrannical impulse to procreate, they share a dark secret within which procreative bonding keeps taking place.

Stephen is now twenty-two. From at least his early teens he had been subject to the tyranny himself. Behind his burgeoning sexual drive "he felt some dark presence moving irresistibly upon him from the darkness, a presence subtle and murmurous as a flood filling him wholly with itself. Its murmur besieged his ears like the murmur of some multitude in sleep" (*P*, 99), a multitude of merely possible persons who, one by one, may be called to wakefulness with their respective births. Before joining his brothers and sisters in song one evening, "he heard the choir of voices in the kitchen echoed and multiplied through an endless reverberation of the choirs of endless generations of children: and heard in all the echoes an echo also of the recurring note of weariness and pain." Convinced that "all seemed weary of life even before entering upon it" (P, 164), Stephen sets out to save his people from themselves.

TOWARD A RADICAL EUGENICS

The agency of their rescue will be writing that Stephen has not yet done but wants terribly to do. He does not know what to write and that confounds him. But he is at least clear that what he writes must put an end to the recurring note of his people's weariness and pain. Vaguely at first, and in a way that often leaves off before it becomes explicit, he undertakes what becomes in *Ulysses* a remarkable program for the writing he hopes to do, a program that aims at nothing less than the eradication of human birth.

The program begins, appropriately enough, with himself. If he is to save others, he himself must first be a saint. His terms for his own salvation require that he withstand nature's tyranny, which presents its most serious threat to him in Emma, his "beloved" in A *Portrait*. For Stephen merely to look at her is for him to suppose that "the secret of her race lay behind those dark eyes" (P, 220) and that with those eyes she is summoning him to fall. Wary lest she lead him into a sexual union that might produce a child, he writes a villanelle in which he chastises her for her guile. Is she not tired of being the universal "temptress"? Has she not had enough of holding men's "longing gaze" with her "languorous look and lavish limb"? "*Are you not weary of ardent ways, / Lure of the fallen seraphim?*" (P, 223).

Stephen considers giving Emma the poem but decides not to. And so while he writes as if he is questioning her directly in the second person, Emma cannot know she is being questioned and therefore cannot respond. Had she been able to, she might fairly have asked Stephen for a tally on these fallen seraphim she has lured. Just how many of them are there? *All*, Stephen would be inclined to answer. Because he thinks of her as all women insofar as she perpetuates nature's tyranny, he is charging her with having seduced all men who have not said no to their natural desire to couple with a woman. Though addressed to her, the poem is not for Emma but for Stephen himself. With its implicit warning that he keep his distance from her, it becomes his alibi for not seeing her at all.

While Stephen's program begins there, it goes well beyond his private refusal to procreate. Alternately euphoric and despondent about his chances as a writer, he is steadily committed to a writing that is for the public weal. His people, he thinks, are "a race of clodhoppers" (P,

249), and he puzzles how his writing might engineer a more refined genetic strain. "How could he hit their conscience or how cast his shadow over the imaginations of their daughters, before their squires begat upon them, that they might breed a race less ignoble than their own?" (*P*, 238). The question is largely rhetorical. Stephen is not close to being able to imagine how he as a writer might speak to his people. And no wonder, since what he wants most to say to them is that they are too many, that even two of them would be too many if those two could keep the race alive. Stephen's mission is both paradoxical and perfect: he can save his people from themselves only by persuading them to let themselves die out. The more he fears that his mission will fail because his people are too crude to be won over by his writing, the stronger his impulse to be shut of them altogether.

It is an impulse that will not let him hear what they might have to say about their lives and needs. Stephen is sure he has already heard enough from them about that. By the end of *A Portrait*, it is not to persons that he listens but rather to a personification of his need to leave them behind.

> 16 *April*: Away! Away!
>
> The spell of arms and voices: the white arms of roads, their promise of close embraces and the black arms of tall ships that stand against the moon, their tale of distant nations. They are held out to say: We are alone. Come. And the voices say with them: We are your kinsmen. And the air is thick with their company as they call to me, their kinsman, making ready to go, shaking the wings of their exultant and terrible youth. (*P*, 252)

Stephen feels his people have come to be too much for him. If he is ever to save them, he must first save himself from them by going away. Feeling he must escape the miserable consequences of his nature in having been born Irish and a Dedalus, he leaves Dublin for Paris.

It is clear from the beginning of *Ulysses* that his self-imposed exile has not worked. Having been called back to his nature by the telegram with its misprint, "—Nother dying come home father" (3: 199), Stephen has been unable to save his mother's body or to pray for her soul. He knows that her surviving children are there to be saved, that it is his responsibility as eldest to save them, and that he cannot. Like his father and most other Dubliners, he will be out of a job "tomorrow or next day" (16: 157). He is virtually friendless and does not know where he will spend the night. He feels no closer to being a writer than when he first determined that writing was to be his vocation. And who would read him if he had already written what he hopes to write? His compatriots keep having children. Would they understand if he were to tell them to stop propagating, to stop supplying nature with the bodies it must have? And who is he to tell them? With each new "goad of the flesh" he is reminded that he himself is no nearer salvation than they.

NATURE, ACCIDENT, SIN

Stephen considers himself enslaved to his nature within a country whose outlook for self-determination is dim, within a family reduced to living from day to day on handouts. He believes this servile, deathlike fate has fallen to him—as it has to all his people—because of "original sin, committed by another in whose sin he too has sinned" (9: 1008–9). Through his reading of *Hamlet* he constructs the scenario for a radical deliverance from nature, accident, and sin. The fullest articulation of that reading is the ninth chapter of *Ulysses*.

"If you want to shake my belief that Shakespeare is Hamlet," John Eglinton warns him as Stephen is beginning his lecture on the subject, "you have a stern task before you" (9: 370–71). Because the eighteen chapters of *Ulysses* are not available to them, all but one of Stephen's auditors in the library hear in what he says a relatively disinterested exposition on Shakespeare. He tells them that King Hamlet's ghost is to Shakespeare as Hamlet is to Shakespeare's dead son Hamnet, that Gertrude is to the ghost as the cuckolding Ann Hathaway is to Shakespeare, that Claudius is to Gertrude as two of Shakespeare's brothers are to Ann.

Among those who hear them, Mulligan alone knows these analogies proceed from the one analogy that matters to Stephen: as Shakespeare is, so may I be. "Wait till you hear him on Hamlet, Haines" (1: 487), Mulligan had advertised in the first chapter. "He proves by algebra that Hamlet's grandson is Shakespeare's grandfather and that he himself is the ghost of his own father. / —What? Haines said, beginning to point at Stephen. He himself?" (1: 555–58). Mulligan knows that the reading of *Hamlet* is Stephen's credo. He knows too that fatherhood is its central article of belief. Whatever more he may know about it gives way to his own ribald caricatures of its onanism and asceticism. Stephen's reading proposes that writing as great as Shakespeare's is the only true paternity: instead of being conceived naturally, through sexual intercourse with a mother, a father's true progeny are written into being. To Mulligan, who offers "his dutiful yeoman services for the fecundation of any female of what grade of life soever who should there direct to him with the desire of fulfilling the functions of her natural" (14: 686–88), Stephen's is a needlessly joyless way to become a father.

Except for that variety of it that Mulligan calls "A Honeymoon in the Hand" (9: 1173), sexual activity obviously requires two. The products generated by such activity are the products of two. Stephen is no stranger to heterosexual desire and its satisfactions. But he is troubled that such desire is activated within him by another than himself.[5] For that other is invariably a woman, and he thinks that a woman's sexual fidelity with a man is no more to be trusted than Ann's was with Shakespeare. In the philosophical terms familiar to Stephen through his scholastic education, the man who depends for kinship on the sexual bond with a mother has only an accidental, not a substantial, relationship with those kin. That man cannot know if he is father or, being not yet father, still son. The brute natural fact of fleshly birth brings only "incertitude" (9: 842) to that "mystical estate" and "apostolic succession" (9: 838) that is fatherhood.[6] According to Stephen's reading of *Hamlet*, a man who wants to know that he is truly father must first master his natural desire to be one of the two who join to make a natural child: then he must perform the miracle of speaking into being an entire race of spiritual sons who become his sons by understanding what he has said.

It was to the end of being our sole progenitor in just this way, Stephen says, that Shakespeare "studied *Hamlet* all the years of his life which were not vanity in order to play the part of the spectre" (9: 166–68). Only by speaking from the ghost's side of bodily death can Shakespeare proclaim himself masterfully, authoritatively to be father. From that side of death he is beyond Ann's reach—though from her side of it, still, she and her whole sex can both reach and corrupt his potential sons. What the ghostly father says to these sons is that nature is accident and full of sin. The letter of what he says will necessarily be lost on most, so strong is woman's and nature's hold. Because the father's word is heard "only in the heart of him who is the substance of his shadow, the son consubstantial with the father" (9: 480–81), the son is literally given his being by hearing that word in the one way it is meant. There is no substantial difference between the meaning of his word and those souls who either speak or hear it in this one way. Speaker-father and hearer-son are no longer two, as they are in nature.[7] For through the potency of the father's speech, both are conjoined as substance within the one meaning.

WRITING, SUBSTANCE, PERFECTION

What Shakespeare says is available, Stephen knows, only because it has been written.

When Rutlandbaconsouthamptonshakespeare or another poet of the same name in the comedy of errors wrote *Hamlet* he was not the father of his own son merely but, being no more a son, he was and felt himself the father of all his race, the father of his own grandfather, the father of his unborn grandson who, by the same token, never was born, for nature, as Mr Magee understands her, abhors perfection. (9: 865–71)

Mulligan had prefaced his summary of this part of the reading by saying "It's quite simple" (1: 555). While its leapfrogging of generations must be unravelled, it is simpler than it seems. Through his writing, Shakespeare speaks to "all his race"—many of whom died before he spoke, many of whom are still unborn. Because what he speaks is "heard only in the heart of him who is the substance of his shadow, the son consubstantial with the father," he undoes Mother Nature's accidental, imperfect succession in which embodied fathers and sons are related only through her untrustworthy exercise of language. He has wrested from woman the power she uses when she says "You are my son's father" to the man who may not yet be father but only son, he has replaced her insubstantial, meaningless act of naming with the substance that is his word.

It is some hours later that Stephen summarizes his own program by referring to what he calls "the postcreation" (14: 294). Mothers and their male inseminators make sinfully "all flesh that passes" (14: 293). But a male inseminator is not to be confused with a father. Born to his natural mother Ann Hathaway but not yet fathered, Hamnet Shakespeare died. Within Stephen's program, far better to be given substantial, fathered "birth" as Hamlet the Dane than to be born Hamnet Shakespeare. For Stephen, it is within substance alone that fathers are fathers, sons sons. By having written "the word that shall not pass away," Shakespeare spoke himself into the "postcreation" that is substance. Within that substance, grandfathers, fathers, and sons do not succeed one another lineally, as they do in perfection-abhorring nature. Because his word foretells an end to the tyrannical sequence of the generations, Shakespeare is at once his own grandfather, father, and son.

WHY THERE ARE FATHERS

The instrument through which nature sustains its tyranny is of course the woman. In Stephen's view, it is she who keeps fathers and sons estranged. Since she is in the business of breeding sons and fathers who depend on her for their relatedness, "who is the father of any son that any son should love him or he any son?" (9: 844–45). That a father with Shakespeare's great verbal power should be mistaken for the dis-

possessed young prince—this, for Stephen, is more than sufficient tes-
timony to the "unlikelihood" (9: 842) that sons of women ever hear
their father's call.

And how could they hear it? That call can come only through language, and language, for Stephen, is a system of relationships that begins with the mother's need to assign the name "father" as she sees fit.
As Stephen had thought earlier in the day while looking at his student,
nature enforces this need.

> Ugly and futile: lean neck and thick hair and a stain of ink, a snail's
> bed. Yet someone had loved him, borne him in her arms and in her
> heart. But for her the race of the world would have trampled him
> underfoot, a squashed boneless snail. She had loved his weak wa-
> tery blood drained from her own. Was that then real? The only true
> thing in life? . . . *Amor matris*: subjective and objective genitive.
> With her weak blood and wheysour milk she had fed him and hid
> from sight of others his swaddlingbands. (2: 139–43, 165–67)

"*Amor matris*, subjective and objective genitive," Stephen says in the
library, "may be the only true thing in life. Paternity may be a legal
fiction" (9: 842–44), "a necessary evil" (9: 828). "Fatherhood, in the
sense of conscious begetting, is unknown to man" (9: 837–38). For
Stephen, the natural bond between mother and child consigns all natural fathers to the role of the Blessed Virgin Mary's bewildered husband, Joseph the Joiner.

Stephen seems to understand that it is nothing other than nature
that obliges the human species to devise the language without which
there could be no such things as fathers, the fathers without whom
there could be neither language nor a species that speaks and writes.
How nature does this is something he does not work out for himself in
any detail. At the risk of intruding into what he has worked out about
it, I am going to borrow from a recent theory about mothers, fathers,
and language—a theory, I should emphasize, that points to woman as
the source of language, not to man.[8] This theory accords so closely with
Stephen's thoughts about the subject, I feel, that Stephen himself
would appeal to it in support of his reading of *Hamlet*.[9]

Language is possible only for animals with large brains, brains too
large to pass through the birth-canal. An infant Homo sapiens is born
and then has to live a full twenty months in the world before even its
gestation is complete. Its infancy lasts another four years after that. The
condition that makes language possible for the child, a large brain, is
therefore the very condition that renders the child peculiarly vulnerable among its competing species. Without its mother or a satisfactory
surrogate, neither the child nor the species of which it is an individual

can survive. For the duration of its natural dependence on her, which is long, the child is less related to its mother than proper to her: no mother to care for it, no child. Its relatedness to its "father" proceeds wholly from the mother's sense that her child will be likelier to survive if she has help in its nurturing. Urged both by her natural inclination to preserve her child and by the circumstances that threaten it, she is moved to speak. She tells a man—often but not always its male progenitor—that he is related to her child. If he accepts what she says, he understands that along with his enlarged responsibilities he now has enlarged sexual privileges with her.

From generation to generation, the species as a whole has done either better or worse because mothers at some point began to name men fathers. The theory argues that the mother's two natural bonds with an adult male and then her child were not enough. Had they been, had fathers been as unnecessary for Homo sapiens as for all other species, then the possibility of language itself would have been a mutation that simply was not selected for, any person's capacity for conceptualizing just one more trait that came and went its way. It is because "paternity" has worked that we have the multitude of legal fictions that make up what we say and hear said, what we read and write. More so than has that of any one of our other verbal inventions, the legacy of the word "father" has urged us to keep relating different things—this child with that man, those separate objects with one another, the blow I took on the head and this uncomfortable lump.

HAVING READERS

It is much more than Stephen's fear of cuckoldry that moves him to imagine a less problematical paternity than the one requiring a fertile, receptive, and word-wielding female, an inseminating male, and then, as issue of their "ruttime" (9: 540), the newborn child. Insofar as all acts of naming derive from the advantages that accrue to the species because men can be said to be fathers, the child is woman's occasion to be proprietress of language as well as of the races of people who use it. Because the child is hers, all people are related through her, these people in turn finding certain "family resemblances" between things that would otherwise remain unrelated. [10] What torments Stephen about being stuck on nature's side of the written and perfect "postcreation" is that the natural father is merely like someone to whom the child—and therefore language—is proper. Shakespeare did not settle for being accidentally like the writer-father, Stephen believes, and so neither will he. What he must do instead is to write something that ensures that he will have with the reader-son those substantial properties that are the meaning of his word.

Readers who are merely related to a writer, Stephen thinks, are readers who give his word a less-than-substantial reading. For Stephen, mere relationships are unsubstantial. They require the substance-denying separateness of the things related. Compared with the natural truth that is love of mother/mother's love, a truth that ensures nature's and the body's sway over the spirit of all who are born to die, mere relationship is a gap in being. Until he exercises such control over the bodies of his readers that their properties and his are indistinguishable, until he has them in that way, Stephen fears that he himself will remain confined to the role of the son, his word unheard, unheeded. If he is to be truly and not just analogically father, he thinks, his writing must do what Shakespeare's does: it must dissolve within it the accidental and grossly physical bodies that separate each person from the plenary meaning that is the one true substance. Only then will Stephen himself have fathered "the postcreation," an entity that because immortal will be even more his own than the natural death-bound child is properly the mother's.

LAST THINGS FIRST

Before having so much as begun to be a writer in his understanding of the term, Stephen has become obsessed with what he thinks the end of his writing must be. The obsession to know exactly where he is headed comes from the Church, which has disposed him to take last things first.

If he is not quite sure that he has a vocation, the director had warned him in A *Portrait*, it would be terrible to find later that he does not. "Once a priest always a priest," for the sacrament of Holy Orders "imprints on the soul an indelible spiritual mark which can never be effaced" (P, 160). When Stephen subsequently rejected all that God was willing to offer him for ever and ever, he had been left with only his enthusiasm, his "doubt and selfmistrust" (P, 177), and his untested promise as a writer. Brilliant, young, impatient, poor, bearing the indelible mental imprints of scholastic philosophy, he continues to want the impossible assurance that the course his life is taking is not "folly" (P, 225). Though it is clear to him that he should not have become a priest, maybe he should not have become a writer either. Is he doing the right thing?

Only if he is a seer can he know. Toward the end of A *Portrait*, having recently written the villanelle, he had stood on the steps of the National Library watching birds in flight. Though he had not been aware of the analogy at first, he'd seen the birds fly "in straight and curving lines" (*P*, 224), like writing, and like writing in his and other Western languages, they had seemed to him to be moving always "from left to right." It had come to him slowly that he was watching the birds for "an augury," for what they might tell him about the outcome of his life as a writer. In *Ulysses*, on the strand, he scribbles down a four-line stanza. It is when he notices his "augur's rod of ash" that he asks himself "Who ever anywhere will read these written words?" (3: 414–15). The "folly" of his wanting to write, he thinks, is that he cannot know in advance that anyone will ever bother to read him.

Cannot know and yet must. It is Stephen's implacable need to control how his writing is read that has prompted him to author his writing's future rather than the writing itself. He remembers books he was going to write "with letters for titles. Have you read his F? O yes, but I prefer Q. Yes, but W is wonderful. O yes, W" (3: 139–40). As if from a point in time beyond his death, he remembers, he had indulged his proclivity for last things by beginning a testimonial to his unwritten great oeuvre. "When one reads these strange pages of one long gone one feels that one is at one with one who once . . ." (3: 144–46), an ellipsis being the only suitable conclusion to the rhapsody, since going on to say what the writer had done could only weaken the unity that none of the differences between Stephen Dedalus and his various readers had managed to divide or interrupt.

When "one is at one with one who once . . . ," writer and reader are no longer two. Even as he derides himself with it, such arithmetic appeals powerfully to Stephen. He knows that no other person can care as much about his writing as he does himself. "Who ever anywhere will read these written words?" is a writer's grudging concession that he will never be what he wants most to be if he cannot be God: his own reader. Stephen dramatizes any writer's uneasy dependence on people who read. Because they may either take his writing or leave it, they are never reciprocally dependent on him.

TO SIRE "THE POSTCREATION"

Until it is read, writing is a first thing only. Once he has completed any one piece of writing, Stephen knows, once each of its words has assumed its place within the selfsame order constituted by all its words, there are only two things that he as its writer can do with it. Having lost the war to make it better, he can either destroy it, or—if only by preserving it in a drawer—surrender it to possible readers. Its fate as captive depends on those, if any, into whose hands it falls. They are its last things. If they happen to be people whose interest it generates, it will survive.

Not so surely as it would, though, if it could generate the people themselves. Between himself and readers, as between life and death, too many things can and do go wrong for Stephen or any writer to be sanguine about the odds that his or her word will be remembered. But any writing potent enough to supply the complete genetic makeup of its readers would dispense with this "between," this gap, this "inter-" within which a reader's interest either will or will not take hold as a fragile dependent of chance. More than anything else that it may also be, Stephen's reading of *Hamlet* implies his own will to be at once the beginning and the end of what he himself goes on to write—its beginning insofar as he is its writer, its end insofar as its readers are completely under his control.

Because Stephen wants what he writes to be exempt from the hazards of any two-sided exchange, he determines that "father," "son," "writer," and "reader" merely seem to differ from one another, seem to because natural sons and daughters mistakenly suppose that these words are predicated of people already born, and therefore different from one another as from Stephen himself. The only birth Stephen lets himself care about is that rebirth in meaning wherein "all flesh that passes becomes the word that shall not pass away" (14: 293–94). He condemns to illegitimacy and corruption those naturally engendered readers unfortunate enough to miss the meaning of his still-unwritten but forthcoming word. The saved, on the other hand, will be so filled with his meaning that their natural genesis, genus, and genders will be dislodged and replaced by Stephen's spiritualizing genius, a "queer thing" (9: 303) that empowers him to father himself by fathering a race of sons so perfect that they are the same as himself. In this perfecting transfer, Stephen's substance-giving meaning will supplant those merely accidental differences that currently linger on and plague the unregenerate, himself included.

If it were not for persons there could be fathers and sons! The more literal Stephen's emphasis on becoming father, the more misanthropic his program. To the degree that each person reminds him that the words he writes may not be interesting, each becomes insufferable to him. Since naturally born readers may not turn out to be interested enough in his writing to ensure its and his own substance-as-father, then to hell with them, he and substance would have been better off if they had never been born.

Stephen's program for precluding readers born to nature will be analogical and not true only to those who persist in crediting their separate births and lives as matters of some importance. The program itself is as follows. As the father is "Himself His Own Son" in the meaningful substance of His Word, so is the writer Himself His Own Reader. Writing is to meaning as father is to son: unless daughters are prepared to undergo a sex change, they need not apply to Stephen's word. If the program stopped there, it would negate natural generation by eliminating mothers. But it is more extravagant still. As father and son are to the number one, so also are writing and meaning: no reader of either sex need apply unless prepared to concede that "the postcreation" Stephen writes into being is meaningful without readers ever finding it to be so. Their natural progenitors will have done Stephen and the race no favor by having sinfully conceived, given birth to, and nurtured mortal readers whom he later redeems as his spiritual progeny. For while readers live and die in need of its redemptive power, the meaning of Stephen's word does not need them. Since "in the economy of heaven, foretold by Hamlet, there are no more marriages, glorified man, an androgynous angel, being a wife unto himself" (9: 1051–52), the more people there are who both need and atone with Stephen's meaning, the fewer people there will be. If Stephen has his way, they will eventually get it right.

Meaning

TO BELIEVE THAT MEANING IS SUBSTANCE

His reading of *Hamlet* supplies Stephen with a theoretical formula for becoming the father of his race, his one meaning ultimately replacing the diversity of people. Applied, Stephen's program would abolish any disquieting difference between Stephen and other persons because, applied, it would abolish persons. At one with Stephen, all persons who might otherwise have reproduced their kind will just say no. In place of their differing and mortal natures, they will have the selfsame perfection of Stephen's word, a word within whose meaning they will be immortally of one substance with Stephen himself.

Or so Stephen would have it be. Fantastical, his program taxes even his belief that it could ever be applied. If it is to do its almost impossible work of freeing persons from nature's tyranny, it must have the requisite power. Stephen keeps his belief in his program alive by tenaciously arranging all his thoughts under this one paradigm: meaning fills, it totalizes, its written demarcations are the limits of what *is*. Believing in his program demands from Stephen the belief that meaning is substance.

Whenever Stephen tests his belief in anything, his standard is the power with which he had once felt he would literally go to hell if he did not amend his life. The lineaments of that power, for him, are dialectical terms whose meanings issue from their relationships, good and bad, to the terms "salvation" and "damnation." Simple. Even over-simple. But, with Stephen, all the more powerful for that. Though he has rejected the Church, he has not managed to discard the Church-inspired notion that the meanings of the two terms in any binary pair complete one another, that insofar as they include all the possibilities they exclude nothing, exclude it, that is, in an active way, the word "nothing" functioning in this sentence as "no thing," as "every merely accidental *thing which is not*." By virtue of its structure, therefore, meaning, for Stephen as for the Church, is substance. Because Stephen knows that mothers' sons will fail to complete the circuit WRITEREADER whenever they miss his meaning or ignore it altogether, he wants to believe that meaning is itself this perfect circuit, its structure including always as one of its two terms whatever threatens to remain other for it.

In the third chapter of A *Portrait*, Stephen feels that he himself is intransigent and of no substance. He and his other "dear little brothers in Christ" (*P*, 108) are then implored by Father Arnall to remember only their last things. Urged to think so far ahead as to remember what has not happened yet, what must happen last of all, Stephen finds his life so stunningly foreshortened by the sermon that "the next day brought death and judgment" (*P*, 111)—not at all merely the concepts "death" and "judgment" but rather, and far more terrifyingly, death and judgment themselves. The words Stephen hears touch him so immediately that there is no gap for him between their meaning and their substance, they translate him out of the world of accident, they perfect him, bring him to term. "—*Remember only thy last things and thou shalt not sin for ever*—" (*P*, 108). This equation offers Stephen a simple and powerful certitude: "Do Z and it will forever yield A, your expectations satisfied to the full without your having to wait." He proves to himself soon afterward that the equation works. Provided that he think only of death, judgment, heaven, and hell, he discovers, "every instance of consciousness could be made to revibrate in heaven" with "immediate repercussion" (*P*, 148). By submitting to this arrangement, he installs within his mind and heart an economy that protects him against both waste and delay.

Its greatest comfort, though, is that it allows him to feel he is in control of the results. His soul presses the keys of a "great cash register" (*P*, 148), and what he has paid for with his devotion shows forth instantly in heaven. When the initial terror and euphoria wear off, he is once again unprotected from the imperfect world of accident and its temptations. Prior to his conversion he had allowed his sexual desire to master him. If he is to avoid returning to the world as its slave, then he must learn to resist its sirenlike call by committing himself constantly to the mortification of his senses, he must remind himself constantly of his last things by taking each of his senses as if to its death. It is in this way alone that he feels within him "a warm movement like that of some newly born life or virtue of the soul itself" (P, 150), a movement that is his access to substance. The only possible beginnings for his soul are therefore those that follow upon his having effectively ended his receptivity to the world. And he must end it from moment to moment if the world is not to have its way with him again. He need not let it. That he might relinquish his power and "undo all that he had done" (P, 152) is a titillating prospect, one that makes him feel all the more powerful when he acknowledges, probably in the very next instant, that he has neither "yielded nor undone all." Because they let him feel that he is active and productive, that what he is doing truly comes to something, his spiritual exercises and the vigilant appraisal of his soul's health are everything to him. They are "all." Anything else that he might do is therefore nothing.

POWER

His single-mindedness on this point is his power, a power that depends for its life on what it overpowers and excludes, on an otherness against which its selfsameness can be defined with perfect, meaningful clarity and continue to hold sway. So much is this so that despite the fact that his becoming a priest would follow logically from the power that accrues to him in his devoutness, despite the fact that it might even strengthen that power, the director's asking him if he has a vocation exposes him to a possibility that, though he had foreseen it, he had not managed perfectly to foreclose. Because the question lies in its otherness outside the venue of his power, it renders him impotent. He feels, after reflecting on it, that he must answer "no." And then "fall." "The snares of the world were its ways of sin. He would fall. He had not yet fallen but he would fall silently, in an instant. Not to fall was too hard, too hard: and he felt the silent lapse of his soul, as it would be at some instant to come, falling, falling but not yet fallen, still unfallen but about to fall" (P, 162). Though it has not happened yet, the conclusion is foregone. Just as he would be saved by remembering only his last things, so too will he be damned by forgetting them. The original equation is no less powerful for his inverted relationship to its terms. The terms themselves are "all." Rather than give up the power he had once been able to feel was his, he consigns his soul to hell. That

way he knows what his life means. Far better to be clear on his desti-
nation than to have to be in doubt from moment to moment about
whether he is headed anywhere at all. And, since he is now going to
be turning away from God's will and into the world, far better to remain
clear on what the world is. If the world's time is time in which to fall,
the world's space is "snares." As his first one was, his next fall will be a
fall from chastity. He will be ensnared by a woman of "eyepleasing
exterior" (14: 449) and he will fall.

DIALECTIC

Stephen has learned all too well that sin has its meaningful wages.
Throughout the rest of A *Portrait* and then in *Ulysses* too, he explains
his and his race's misery as the consequence of sexual transgression.
Since every person he sees was "wombed in sin darkness" (3: 45) as he
was, why should their lives be any better than they are? To explain why
he and everyone else is a slave is at least to master that meaning. Such
elevating transformation from one to the other is as instantaneous and
self-contained as the workings of meaning itself. Each term of his explanation means nothing unless always and silently accompanied by its
opposing term—"sin" by "perfection," "slave" by "master," "fall" by
"rise," and so on, each pair of terms a variation on the original couple
"bad" and "good." Stephen had earlier managed to force what would
otherwise have been purposeless and empty to yield at once those two
clearly meaningful terms "damned" and "saved." So too now. The
more certain he is that his misery means he is fallen, the more certainly
he rises by that understanding, his explanation of his and Ireland's
plight more substantial than the accidents it explains.

Or so he hopes. The dialectical operations of meaning inspire his
trust insofar as they are everything at once. Requiring nothing external
to themselves, they seem to subsist in much the same way God does.
But are they actually subsistent or only potentially so? Two is an exor-
bitantly large number for Stephen, and so he remains suspicious of anything that comes from it. He knows that even the most comprehensive
and unified understanding is unlike unchanging and selfsame substance
in that it must unfold in time as the sum of separate meanings, each of
which is as much the product of two opposing terms as a child is the
product of two individuals from the opposing sexes. "Dialectic," Stephen says, is the one "useful discovery" man learns from woman, Soc-
rates having learned "from his mother how to bring thoughts into the
world" (9: 235–36). For any written term to mean, it must bring along
with it, as its invisible but necessary complement, its most appropriately opposing term. Any one term may of course have as many oppos-

ing terms as its context suggests for it. Since the meaning of each term within a given context depends as well upon its store of possible opposing terms, the possibilities for any one term multiply geometrically until the limits of the language are reached. However multiple the possibilities for any term within a context, though, each possibility can be screened by submitting it to the question "Is this it, is this this term's most appropriately opposing term?" If all possible oppositions are screened, each can be answered with a simple "yes" or "no."

It is in this way that all meaning is dialectical. Since the meaning of any written word invariably comes from two terms, only one of which appears, the other having to be settled on by a reader who does the screening in no doggedly computerlike way, Stephen knows that the words he writes may be nothing more than accidental signs, that his meaning may wait and wait to be but never be. He believes that he must somehow exercise so proprietary an influence over both terms that his meaning will rise in the heart of the reader-son who, through its rising, will be of one substance with the writer-father, with Stephen himself.

PAIRS

To the end of determining once and for all what his words mean, he has aligned most of his thinking according to a set of dialectical terms whose fixed meanings offer him the illusion of a changeless, selfsame substance that stands under his changing understanding of what it means to be alive. Here is a crude approximation of his dialectic.

> slave/master
> accident/substance
> diversity/unity
> sensation/thought
> body/mind
> thing/signature
> corpse/soul
> mother, the unholy ghost/God, the father
> copulator/celibate

In each pair, the term on the right is shorthand for what he either emulates or feels compelled to emulate, the term on the left for what he fears will hold him back. Right relates to good only arbitrarily, of course, as left does to bad. But Stephen cannot allow himself to think there is anything arbitrary about the relationships he is maintaining between the terms, and these relationships are very simply those of good and bad. It is good to be master, bad to be slave.[11] Just as the slave will find the signatures of things unreadable and will therefore move as if by accident from sensation to sensation on his soulless way to death, the master will retain his pure and godlike unity though persistently besieged by temptations from diverse bodies in the world. Good is what truly is, and substance must wait until a father's meaning generates what is because it is good. Fearing an otherness so radical that it renders good and bad indistinguishable, an otherness far more threatening than his last things, Stephen wants to believe his dialectic enforces a meaning that is itself the very being of the father and the son.

He knows it can do so only under his diligent custody, for the terms within the set are variously wayward. I have arranged the list according to the relative ease or strain with which he excludes other possible opposing terms for any one term, the pairs toward the bottom of the list exacting much more from him than those at the top. It is clear to him, for example, that he was born to the bad luck of having to be the servant of "two masters" (1: 638)—"the imperial British state . . . and the holy Roman catholic and apostolic church" (1: 643–44)—as well as of a third, Ireland, who wants him for "odd jobs" (1: 641). It is also clear to him that if he is ever to be master through his written words his vow must continue to be what it was in his last conversation in *A Portrait*: "I will not serve" (*P*, 239). Master and slave therefore depend on one another for their respective meanings, they complete one another, neither can slide off into any less definitive meaning when Stephen temporarily forgets them as terms and attends to something else. The relationship between them is steady enough that he does not have to exert much force to keep their meanings fixed. Celibacy, on the other hand, does not always mean virtuous abstinence to Stephen—a considerable surprise in light of his program for "glorified man" (9: 1052). Since the two characters in his *Parable of the Plums* are virgins and not copulators, and since he is obviously satirizing them, at least one thing that his parable means is that Ireland is sterile. To maintain a meaningful connection between the terms in the pair at the bottom of the list, he must therefore borrow the Church's injunction against sexual intercourse. And when he does so—as he does in claiming that Shakespeare's seduction by Ann Hathaway "darkened his understanding, weakened his will and left in him a strong inclination to evil" (9: 1006–7)—he places his entire dialectic in jeopardy by indenturing his thoughts to the most powerful of his masters, the Church.

THE ONE GOOD

Because the good is and is one, Stephen thinks, meaning will be less than substantial only if it fails to resolve which of its two terms is good.

To move horizontally on the list from "slave" to "master" or from "body" to "mind" involves a dialectical relationship without which none of these words can mean. But when his thoughts move vertically among the terms in either the left- or right-hand columns of the list, Stephen assumes that much more than a gap-requiring relationship is at work. "Slave" and "body" do not relate to one another as separate terms: instead, they are not. Nor do "master" and "mind" have a relationship: they are what is and is good-because-one. Stephen's dialectic exerts a regulatory power over his thoughts only because he works very hard at believing that the meaning it produces is not the product of two, as children are, but rather of the one good. This power will last for as long as the vertical alignment of its terms remains strong. For when his dialectic weakens—as it does when he tells his parable—it no longer contains all the meaning, its meaning is no longer full, complete, subsistent, one and the same. Rather than reconciling within it a variety of binary terms, each of which is other for the term with which it is paired, it degenerates to just an other among them, to the imperfect status of a term that is merely related to, and not one with, the perfect term that it is not.

Stephen thinks that one of two terms will perfect his now-imperfect life: he will either write "the word that shall not pass away," or he will die. If he is truly to live, if he is to write the word before he himself passes away, it will not be enough for the words he thinks to be like the plenitude of meaning: instead, his thoughts and meaning-filled substance must be the same. A tall, tall order, as Stephen knows all too well. He knows that his thoughts are not one but multiple. And because they are contaminated by the sensations with which they are paired in his dialectic, he knows too that his thoughts cannot always and everywhere accord with the one substantial and selfsame good. Walking by himself on the strand and wanting to test the grip that space has on his thoughts, he closes his eyes only to hear his boots, one after the other, "crush crackling wrack and shells" (3: 10–11)—audible time enforcing his awareness that, whether he sees it or not, he is traversing visible space. He keeps his eyes closed long enough to imagine that everything may have vanished into perfection since he last looked. It has not. "See now. There all the time without you: and ever shall be, world without end" (3: 27–28).

Because his own and other separate bodies take up space in time, for Stephen to see them is for him constantly to be reminded of his current estrangement from substance, from the good that is one. What he wants to believe is that that very reminder, determinable as meaning, is *in* those bodies, in them, that is, to the diaphanous limit at which their material intrusion into mind leaves off. However discouraging the thought that what he sees is less substantial than thought itself, there can be in his seeing it at least that very thought. "At least that if no more, thought through my eyes" (3: 1–2). Because thought enables him to know that what he sees is inevitably material, he attributes to the visible an "ineluctable modality" and is therefore confident that what he sees has at least that much meaning if no more. "That lies in space which I in time must come to, ineluctably" (9: 1200–1201). "Signatures of all things I am here to read" (3: 2). If that is why he is here, if that is what Stephen was meant to do, if he was meant to read "things" for the signatures that are their substance, then he can allow himself to believe that to predicate is to substantiate, to render substantial and good those otherwise merely accidental "things" with which he is compelled to deal.

OTHER AND SAME

Of course not just any reading of these things will do. He must be sure that the meaning of his words is drawn to its one inevitable and good end by the terms of his dialectic, for then he can indulge the comforting feeling that he is moving not simply between one term and another, but rather within substance itself. If movement is always and already complete within a system of meanings that accommodates as it depends upon all possible opposing terms, what need is there to feel threatened by the manifold indeterminacies he meets as he moves between birth and death, indeterminacies that would usurp his confidence if he were to let them remind him that he may not yet have learned what they mean. It is safer to suppose that substance has been granted to the conjunction between "movement" and "stasis," "unlike" and "like." If substance has given its imprimatur to the likenesses he reads, then even "other" and "same" dissolve as they must if he is to be father. For if this most inclusive of all binary pairs is not truly one within the meaning his dialectic is forever ready to supply, if "other" and "same" is a relationship only, then Stephen is cast back into the "between" that separates as it connects the pair's two terms.

Whenever Stephen's thoughts remain truant and other for his dialectic, their indeterminacy reminds him too much of his own indeterminate future. Just as the possibility of his death is other for his projected writing, so too is the writing itself other insofar as he has not yet done it. Whereas the threat of the other is the threat of indeterminacy—what will he write to beget a race of people who will then and forever after be the same as himself?—it is the all-including and selfsame that assures and reassures. He knows that the selfsame words of his writing will appear in the same order from copy to copy. Since he makes some sense of his life only because the concepts he thinks are roughly the same each time he thinks them, he knows that his written words will take him from one relatively selfsame concept to another. And he wants each of these words simultaneously to generate and complete what is other for it according to a dialectic that is the same as itself. If he can therefore believe that "other" and "same" are enclosed within the one selfsame, meaning-filled substance in "the word that shall not pass away," he will have found a way around the unacceptably unanswerable question "Who ever anywhere will read these written words?" Writing itself will be the only meaningful generation, and so its meaning will be independent of what is most implacably other for it: already generated readers. "We walk through ourselves," Stephen insists, "meeting robbers, ghosts, giants, old men, young men, wives, widows, brothers-in-love, but always meeting ourselves" (9: 1044–46). Other persons are a threat to Stephen because he knows they will be there between his writing and its being found to mean. If he can be sure that to walk from here to there meeting them is in truth to be walking through and meeting only himself, then substance is intact, there are none of those interruptions in its oneness through which the meaning of his word might prove to be anything less than full.

Interest

BETWEEN

But however clearly Stephen's line points toward his becoming Jamesy, who is always at rest because he meets only himself, Stephen substitutes nonetheless for a person who is subject to a restlessness that Jamesy only feigns. Since Jamesy is of one substance with all visible things, there is no thing separate from Jamesy that might disrupt his restful indifference. Not so for Stephen. Between the visible person for whom Stephen substitutes and "all that ever anywhere wherever was" are visible and often interesting things. Some of these things are persons who both see and are seen. That he knows less than everything about these persons makes Stephen restless. While his thoughts about any one person resemble Jamesy's substance in that they are selfsame, that person's otherness resists those thoughts. There is the other person: there are the selfsame thoughts Stephen thinks that person prompts him to think. Between that person and Stephen's thoughts there is an indeterminable ratio of similarities and differences. Unlike Jamesy, who both knows and is the same as everything, Stephen is either more or less right about the person and cannot know which or how much.

Such uncertainty need not cancel his interest in the thoughts, for interest is itself what lies between.[12] Unlike underlying, selfsame, filled-with-meaning substance, interest is not the uniting of Stephen's thoughts and the person about whom he thinks: instead, it is their very separation. Whether or not Stephen's writing will be found to mean in the way his program requires, whether or not what it is found to mean will conform with his hopes for it, the otherness of these conditions is as separate from the selfsame words he wants to write as each person he meets is separate from any thoughts Stephen has about that person. He invokes his program largely as a defense against that "between" his writing will enter and remain lodged within for as long as there are just such other persons to read it.

I have been describing Stephen as someone for whom the closure of the "between" is a consummation devoutly to be wished. Stephen is tormented by "betweens." Between his biological birth and death, he finds himself among and between persons whom he wants to rescue from the inadequate world between them all. But that very rescue is stalled between (1) his having already articulated it as a program for his writing, and (2) his beginning to implement the program by beginning to write. Lodged in this unacceptable "between," Stephen keeps trying to imagine some continuity between here and there, this and that, now and then, same and other—a "continuity" that invariably remains on the side of "here," "this," "now," and "same," and is therefore discontinuous with the second term in each of these pairs. From the selfsameness of "this here now" with its frustrations for someone who has not yet written what he feels he must write so that he might *be*, Stephen wants to believe that his theory of father, meaning, and substance will carry him uninterruptedly into the writing that has so far refused to yield its otherness. But between "this" same and "that" other there is only an imaginable continuity and the better and worse uses to which it might be put. Stephen does not think of the theory itself as the very thing that he must write. Its use to him, therefore, is no more than preliminary. The theory need not hold him back indefinitely from starting to write. What it cannot do is take him through to having started.

THE COLLECTED WORKS

He knows he is not off to much of a start. By June 16, 1904, he has written

(1) the villanelle *"Are you not weary of ardent ways,"*
(2) an unfavorable and unpopular review of Lady Gregory's *Poets and Dreamers*, and

(3) a "capful of light odes" (14: 1119) which AE thinks so little of that he excludes every one of them from his anthology "of our younger poets' verses" (9: 291), which Stephen himself thinks so little of that a reader of *Ulysses* learns about them only through Lynch.

If Stephen is to write something new and better than the above, it will have to come from words that make their way into his brain and then register with him as worthy of being written down. During his hour alone on the strand he thinks the words "He comes, pale vampire, through storm his eyes, his bat sails bloodying the sea, mouth to her mouth's kiss" (3: 397–98), and promptly decides to write

> *On swift sail flaming*
> *From storm and south*
> *He comes, pale vampire,*
> *Mouth to my mouth.*   (7: 522–25)

It will of course be only gradually if at all that Stephen begins to make good on his hopes for himself as a writer. But these lines are much more a replay than a beginning, for they are anchored in a poem by Douglas Hyde.

> And my love came behind me—
> He came from the south;
> His breast to my bosom,
> His mouth to my mouth.[13]

Stephen writes "*On swift sail flaming*" because, having forgotten that he has read Hyde's poem but having read it, he can for once be comforted that the words themselves will certainly not die unread. It is his need to have his words read, venerated, and preserved that moves him to let Hyde's words supplant more promising words that he might otherwise give place to, words that might be a start.[14] By being interested exclusively in how his words will be received, Stephen precludes other possible interests out of which his best words will begin to come.

FACE

Insofar as his last things supplant what comes before them, Stephen is largely uninterested: he knows what he wants and therefore classifies as a hindrance everything between himself and that goal. Insofar as something resists such classification, though, insofar as that thing agitates him enough so that he is moved to distinguish it and relate it to other agitatingly separate things, his interest is at work supplanting the certain knowledge of what he wants.

If he were any more adept at filling his thoughts with meanings that proceed solely from the dialectic that transports him instantly to last things, the faces of persons would not be so unsettling for him as they are. At night in the dormitory at Clongowes "he saw the dark." "There were pale strange faces there, great eyes like carriagelamps. They were the ghosts of murderers, the figures of marshals who had received their death-wound on battlefields far away over the sea. What did they wish to say that their faces were so strange?" (*P*, 19).

From his father's "hairy face" on the first page of A *Portrait* to his sister Dilly's "Stuart face of nonesuch Charles" (10: 858) on the last page of Stephen's last interior monologue in *Ulysses*, images of other peoples' faces implode within his thoughts about them. During the lecture in A *Portrait*, MacAlister has asked a question from the bench below.

> Moynihan murmured from behind in his natural voice:
> —Isn't MacAlister a devil for his pound of flesh?
> Stephen looked down coldly on the oblong skull beneath him overgrown with tangled twinecoloured hair. The voice, the accent, the mind of the questioner offended him and he allowed the offence to carry him towards wilful unkindness, bidding his mind think that the student's father would have done better had he sent his son to Belfast to study and have saved something on the train fare by so doing.
> The oblong skull beneath did not turn to meet this shaft of thought and yet the shaft came back to its bowstring: for he saw in a moment the student's wheypale face.
> —That thought is not mine, he said to himself quickly. It came from the comic Irishman in the bench behind. (*P*, 193)

Thrust of thought, counterthrust to thought from face. Stephen responds to this sequence as to thesis and antithesis. Their synthesis uplifts him because it sets him on a line of thinking that he identifies as his own, not Moynihan's. Instead of promoting Stephen's interest, the sight of MacAlister's face is at most a corrective. Stephen sees the face of the other person. By then proceeding to a thought that is for him more properly selfsame than the first had been, he has enveloped other within same.

However unsettling its otherness may be as it registers with him, the face of another person is something that can be appropriated to its place as antithesis within his dialectic. When it does not interest him, or when he thinks of it with too little confidence in the interest it evokes, the other's face opposes. "Harsh gargoyle face that warred against me over our mess of hash of lights in rue Saint-André-des-Arts" (9: 576–77), he remembers of J.M. Synge. Even as he receives noncombative Lyster's question, the polarizing is there for Stephen in the "alarm" (9: 332) with which any one person faces another. "Hast thou found me, O mine enemy?" (9: 483) he thinks as he hears Mulligan's voice from the doorway and then sees coming toward him "a ribald face, sullen as a dean's" (9: 485). As Stephen summarizes it for himself just as he and Mulligan are about to leave the library, the other's visage produces within his thinking a symmetry of opposed wills: "My will: his will that fronts me. Seas between" (9: 1202).

THE "AUTONTIMORUMENOS"

These are the seas in which he is sure Dilly is "drowning. Agenbite. Save her. Agenbite. All against us. She will drown me with her, eyes and hair. Lank coils of seaweed hair around me, my heart, my soul. Salt green death" (10: 875–77). If he acts to save her, he thinks, she will drown him too. His cognizance of her will's otherness, his will to save himself—these conflicting strains of his thinking pass one another as if in opposite directions. The direction of interest, on the other hand, is unilaterally toward other from same. It is his interest in Dilly that led him to tell her of "Paris" (10: 859), that leads him—so as to encourage her interests—to "show no surprise" (10: 871) that she has bought a French primer "to learn French" (10: 869). But rather than acknowledge this interest he takes in her, rather than allow it to move him to offer her some of the money Deasy has paid him, he characteristically thinks his way past first things to his encompassing remorse. "Agenbite of inwit. Inwit's agenbite. Misery! Misery!" (10: 879–80). Insofar as his thoughts are disclosed only through interior monologue, these are the last words Stephen thinks. His powerlessness to help either Dilly or himself in some final way becomes his justification for self-cancelling movements of thought that only reinforce his paralysis. Its symmetrical journey complete and perfect, the dialectic of "other" and "same" fastens Stephen within a reading of his and Dilly's and their race's condition from which he thinks an "Irish nights entertainment" (9: 1105) is his only escape.

When Stephen sets about making good on his earlier plan to "Swill till eleven" (9: 1105), thereby drinking himself away forever from the interior monologue that presents his thinking, he is wanting to be delivered from the "*Autontimorumenos*" (9: 939), the self-tormentor who rules his thoughts. Stephen's thoughts are relentlessly self-tormenting because each "what" and "when" that he attends to implicates him within a world he did not choose to be born into, a world he has in common with others who did not choose it and who are not much happier than he. For him to be alive, awake, and even marginally sober is for him to be conscious of his relationship to this world by meeting the next word he thinks, meeting the pause that follows and separates it from the next word, all of it accreting in a sequence that he feels he must stop by beginning to write his word.

Within this self-torment, it is seldom enough for Stephen that a thought interest him. For him to be confident that the thought is substantial and therefore worth writing, he must believe that its meaning appropriates an entire race of unborn spiritual sons. Substance, for Stephen, is a hedge against the difference between two questions: (1) What might he find to write that interests him? (2) Might that interest interest someone else? If the meaning of a thought is less than full, he fears, it admits an interval through which substance might be lost.

"MUCH TO LEARN"

But then where are his still-undiscovered words to be found if not also in just such a gap? Shakespeare "found in the world without as actual what was in his world within as possible" (9: 1041–42). Stephen knows that he himself has not done that yet and that he must. Despite the threat contingency poses to his tightly determining dialectic, he suspects that he should be more patient with the seemingly expendable things that might interest him from day to day. Such patience, he hopes, will broaden his attention and prove as indispensible to the writing he has not yet done as time is indispensible to his moving from here to there, from now to then. Deasy's insistence that history's last things are God provokes Stephen to counter that God is "a shout in the street" (2: 386). For all its pomposity, this definition is Stephen's challenge to himself to think more flexibly about meaning and substance. When he steps out of the offices of the *Freeman* into Abbey Street and the syllables "Racing special!" (7: 914) are shouted in his ear, he hears them as a godlike imperative to learn what is there around him. "Dublin," he thinks. "I have much, much to learn" (7: 915). LET US HOPE, say the capital letters heading this section. Let us hope that you learn it.

"What have I learned?" he asks himself after concluding his lecture on *Hamlet.* "Of them? Of me?" (9: 1113). Though his not trying to answer implies that he has not learned enough to have made it worth his while, the questions are not simply rhetorical either. Only by intending them as questions and not as proof that it had all been "folly" (9: 42) can he think of his reading as a template for his life. Because "all events brought grist to his mill (9: 748), Shakespeare would have learned something from the hour. What has Stephen learned? His presentation of the reading in their company has taught him little about AE, Eglinton, Mulligan, Best, or Lyster. Nor has he learned much from having articulated the reading itself. Though he has told it somewhat differently this time, he has not altered its meaning in any way that qualifies with him as learning. Because his reading of Shakespeare is one that he had learned already, and because it is the reading of a spiritual father by his spiritual son, he cannot think of it as the learning he must do if he is ever to reach a time when he begins writing something that will make him father.

STEPHEN'S ANN

The gap between that time and this has its very intimate analogue with "the natural female organ" (17: 2279), the gap Stephen calls "woman's invisible weapon" (9: 461). According to the scenario implicit in his theory, he will begin writing something that pleases him only after some older but still toothsome woman has pleased him sexually. Like Shakespeare's, his learning will not be restricted to the ways of love. But also like Shakespeare's, his interest in these ways is an essential preliminary to his trusting that there are things in the world that are worthy of his attention. Though the self-tormentor in him has been telling him he should not, he finds women's bodies most worthy of his attention. Though he has come up with both heretical and orthodox ways of deferring his interest in meeting his own Ann Hathaway, her prominence in his theory at least allows him to acknowledge his own heterosexuality. "By cock, she was to blame," he tells his listeners of Ann. "She put the comether on him, sweet and twentysix." Bending over Shakespeare "as prologue to the swelling act," Ann "tumbles in a cornfield a lover younger than herself." "And my turn?" Stephen thinks. "When? / Come!" (9: 257–62). As a twenty-two-year-old who had fallen with a woman by the time he was sixteen, who brought back as his "rich booty" from Paris "five tattered numbers of *Pantalon Blanc et Culotte Rouge*" (3: 196–97) and the memory of what a prostitute had offered him for one franc more, who cries "*naked women!*" (3: 134) to the rain and prays "to the devil in Serpentine avenue that the fubsy widow in front might lift her clothes still more from the wet street" (3: 130–31), he is ready to be "wooed" by some Edwardian analogue of Ann who may turn out to be his induction to a world of things he does not yet know but must learn.

If she is to woo him, this woman obviously cannot be the mother of Jesus. Neither can she be a professional, though her experience in country matters would be more appreciated than not. Insofar as he depends on it to help him recognize her as the right one when he meets her, his reading of Ann Hathaway may also help release him from the dialectical strictures of the virgin and the whore, strictures that have been determining the meanings he assigns both to women and to what they arouse in him. However much he may want to sully her for his own pleasure, the woman whom he thinks of as altogether pure means precisely that to him, thereby affording him as much protection as he needs from having to learn anything else about her. The money he pays the prostitute offers him a comparable kind of protection: and because her livelihood depends on her not conceiving a child, she protects him from that possible meaning as well. Only if a woman is somewhat less than pure but not wholly impure either is the meaning of her attractiveness and her attraction to him indeterminate enough so that he might learn from it something he does not yet know. Though he is sure that it is much the safer course for him either to try to be a saint or to keep channelling his sexual needs and energies toward the clergyman's daughter, Georgina Johnson, in whose bed he has spent both his semen and the better part of a pound AE lent him, he is anxious to risk consummating a relationship with some one woman who will mean more to him than any woman with whom he remains chaste, any he hires.

His metaphor for the upcoming romance is martial as well as venereal, and he himself is at least temporarily to be the spoil. As if the war were God's with naked Eve, Stephen's sexual adversary will woo and win him, he will be "overborne" (9: 456) by her, brought away from his wanting to remain divinely and safely celibate and into the cyclical metabolic process in which endless generations, "wombed in sin darkness," submit in successive instants of "blind rut" (9: 859) to the "recurring note of weariness and pain" (*P*, 164) that is the life of people in the world. His emphasis on corruption and fatigue and torment reduces some of love's mystery by fastening it within the bitterness he hears in Shakespeare's revenge-bent ghost. In the general dialectic of the sexes, the one acceptable synthesis for the male is to pay woman back for having lured him to be, for a time only, her "man in the gap" (14: 895) that no one man can fill. According to Stephen, Ann overcomes Shakespeare's adolescent wariness of woman's wiles. The two create two children through their union. Hamnet dies. Ann cuckolds Shakespeare. Only then does "a lord" become "his dearmylove" (9: 658) as part of his revenge. Only then does he begin the "postcreation" by writing those plays in which he brands her with infamy, plays in which he establishes his self-sufficiency as an "androgynous angel," "a wife unto himself." Because Stephen is feeling all the urgency of his sexual nature, he reads in Shakespeare's life a chronology that instructs him that he too must go the narrow way between his woman-lover's thighs.

LIKE AND SAME

The last thing Stephen does when he is by himself is to sneak a look at an occult self-help book on sex. "How to win a woman's love," he reads as he picks it up. "For me this" (10: 847). Before he hears Dilly say over his shoulder "—What are you doing here, Stephen" and thinks "Shut the book quick. Don't let see" (10: 854, 856), he has had time to read only one talisman, which translates roughly "*My little heaven of blessed femininity! Love only me! Holy! Amen.*" While he is hardly desperate enough to entrust himself to this or any other charm, the possessiveness of its "*Love only me!*" is basic to his frustrations not only with women but also with potential readers. "To have or not to have," he proclaims in Nighttown, "that is the question" (15: 3522). If he could make the charm work, he would have a woman—as to his great distress he does not now. And not only would he be able to know his woman in the biblical sense, but he would also know that she would be forever his. Her constancy would be as much a fact as would the fact that he was knowing her carnally while he was knowing her carnally. Unlike a promise, the words of which may turn out to have been either good or bad or something in between, her troth to him would have all the incontrovertibility of a life already lived in complete faithfulness to him and made perfect in her death. She would in all matters be good to her word. If she were to tell him that he was father, it would mean that he was. He would believe her in the "one sense of the word" (1: 614) and therefore would not feel compelled to father himself and all his race by winning back from woman and her natural progeny that language women use to beguile and deceive. If Stephen's woman would herself be as much his as any revenge that he might take on her in his writing, then he could permit himself some other and perhaps less misery-ridden impetus for his art.

Perfection-abhorring nature, though, refuses to meet these conditions. Because woman is so clearly nature's favorite in her struggle with man, Stephen is convinced, she institutes the legal fictions of fatherhood and marriage, fictions that imply that man and woman are more like one another if they are called father and mother, husband and wife. If she can disguise how radically unlike one another they are by making man think that the two of them have more in common than the erotic inclination to do the "coupler's will," he will be the more malleable, and for longer. Behind the semblance that it is somehow in both their interests for the child to prosper, she tries to conceal from him the fact that their relationship is at best a series of amatory truces on which she herself depends for the offspring through which she wins the war. It is to her advantage to make room for a wide range of feelings between the man and herself. This room is the difference between like and same. If she can make the man feel that he is like her, if he likes her, he will be the slower to know his attraction to her for what it is in its selfsameness, slow enough, in many cases, for him to be had. Fearing that he may be dispossessed forever of the meaning through which his sons will recognize him as their consubstantial father, Stephen has taught himself to be unrelentingly suspicious of any subtleties in his feelings for the sex that is opposed to his "from everlasting to everlasting" (3: 43–44).

EMMA

Persuaded that his interest in a woman is meaningfully his only if it remains strictly sexual, he has been confounded by his feelings for Emma, who is so exclusively the object of his romantic interest in the last chapter of A *Portrait* that every unspecified feminine pronoun refers to her, her name alone too provoking for him to allow himself to think it. The "temptress of his villanelle" (*P*, 223), Emma's sexual difference is so agitating to him that it polarizes Stephen: it reminds him whenever he thinks about it that there can be no place in his life for pleasant exchanges with his foe. As long as he is not facing her, as long as she is in his mind only, he can see to it that she is the opposing term in a binary pair that he completes. His thoughts about her are his: they therefore stave off what is other. By thinking of her in a way that remains selfsame, especially when this way is supported by conflicting feelings that his dialectic aligns, he can continue to preclude all other meanings that his relationship with her might otherwise lead him toward.

He meets her one day on the street. If he could have, he would have avoided her. She tries with some confusion to keep him from running off by asking him about himself and about his writing. He responds by accusing her with his opaque sarcasm of having lured him to write poems about her. When he sees that she is now even more confused, he feels "sorry and mean" (*P*, 252). For the rest of their few minutes together he senses he is just enough like her that he is able to tap a friendlier "valve." He obliges her by answering the questions she had put to him, talks "rapidly" of himself and of his plans. "In the midst of it unluckily," he records in his journal,

> I made a sudden gesture of a revolutionary nature. I must have
> looked like a fellow throwing a handful of peas into the air. People

began to look at us. She shook hands a moment after and, in going
away, said she hoped I would do what I said.

Now I call that friendly, don't you?

Yes, I liked her today. A little or much? Don't know. I liked her
and it seems a new feeling to me. (*P*, 252)

Because he grants her the generosity of her wishes for him, and because
he acknowledges as new in his feelings for a desirable woman another
meaning than "some goad of the flesh" (9: 462), Emma has unwittingly
disrupted Stephen's preconceptions just enough to have taught him
something he could not have foreseen but is not sorry to have learned.

There is little evidence in *Ulysses* that he is still thinking of women
as people whom it is possible to like. Were he to allow himself to think
of them in that way, he would be giving up the misogyny that shields
him from having to distinguish among them, having to find between
himself and individuals of the other sex the subtle likenesses and differences that it is far more conclusive to construe as woman's odious guile.
He is cautious not to forget what he is sure each woman wants him to
forget: that she is same for herself and is committed to undoing those
completed and selfsame meanings through which man can know that
she is categorically other for him. Stephen is same, his notion of what
a woman means is same. By having determined in advance of his meeting her that she must break both his spirit and his heart, he is effectively nullifying the otherness of his lover-to-be. He has already
thought his way beyond her to what she must mean within the canon
of his writing, writing that his spiritual sons will know in all the selfsameness of its substance. From the moment he meets her she must
therefore act in conformity with the ten-year plan for his career or she
simply will not do.

What most disqualifies Emma as Stephen's woman is his having once
discovered that he liked her. Through a subterfuge innate to her sex,
he thinks, she had managed to exceed what he had thought of her, had
temporarily made him feel that there might be something of substance
between them. He is now quite sure there is not. For Stephen, relationship and likeness must either be on his terms or they will be on hers.
He is sure that he must make them same for himself if they are not to
be truly other. Emma is a compellingly other person, his portrait of
Ann is the same as itself. Stephen ensures that there is minimal traffic
between other and same by rendering Emma virtually unrecognizable
in his version of Ann. He thinks of Emma just once in *Ulysees*, and
then only because she may be there in the library as he leaves. "Is that
. . . ? Blueribboned hat . . . ? Idly writing . . . ? What? . . . Looked
. . . ?" (9: 1123).

"THING DONE"

His curiosity suggests that she still means something to him, even if what she means most is that he does not have a woman. Because he does not want Mulligan to see him stop and talk with her, he is saved from having to decide if he should, he is saved from going ahead and doing it. To "do," to "act," to carry something through until it is a "thing done" (9: 651)—these remedies of his paralysis seem to him now to be so specifically sexual that he would be forced to think that choosing to speak with her was an overture to the act of love, an act that can have no place in his relationship with someone he likes. "Do and do. Thing done." "One life is all. One body. Do. But do. Afar, in a reek of lust and squalor, hands are laid on whiteness" (9: 651, 653–54). These hands—imaginable, "afar"—are not his. He knows they could be his and he envies them. But doing has this reek to it. And though he will not himself be absolved once he is caught up in the "squalor" of his "pairing time" (9: 539) with his woman, and though his interests tell him that it is time for that time, he waits in the hope that he himself will not have to move, will not have to do, but will rather be done to.

And yet as he unfolds his reading of Ann and Shakespeare with its implications that it is "she" who must do the wooing, it comes to Stephen that this still-undisclosed woman might be so put off by his diffidence that she will not want to seduce him. "Wait to be wooed and won. Ay, meacock," he thinks, the "meacock" (9: 938) being repugnantly unvirile and having as its twin representatives "Eglinton Johannes, of arts a bachelor" (9: 1061), and Richard Best, the "blond ephebe" and "tame essence of Wilde" (9: 531–32). Recognizing that these two of his listeners are "unwed, unfancied, ware of wiles," Stephen supposes that they "fingerponder nightly each his variorum edition of *The Taming of the Shrew*" (9: 1062–63), the fecundity of Shakespeare's world lost on them because of their own sexual inversion, of which neither seems aware. When Stephen asks himself "Who will woo you?" (9: 938), it is less that he is anticipating than that he fears he resembles Best and Eglinton just enough so that no one will.

"S. D.: *sua donna*" (9: 940), he worries. The initials are at once his own and those for the Italian of "his woman." "*Già: di lui*": sure, his— as if he had one! "*Gelindo risolve di non amare*": he who is cold resolves not to love. The phrase troubles him as the description someone might fairly offer of Stephen Dedalus. He knows that he had seemed so to Emma, that he had belied his ardor for her by his resolutely ascetic manner in her presence, his less and less frequent visits to her house. When she had danced toward him in the round at the carnival ball, "her hand had lain in his an instant, a soft merchandise," and she had said to him:

—You are a great stranger now.
—Yes. I was born to be a monk.
—I am afraid you are a heretic.
—Are you much afraid?

For answer she had danced away from him along the chain of hands, dancing lightly and discreetly, giving herself to none. (P, 219)

How afraid had she been? "A little or much?" Angered and self-pitying because he fears his magnitude for her could not possibly match hers for him, he had refused to pursue the question beyond his teasing coaxing and had received the answer he deserved. Just how much he had meant to her became another of love's mysteries, mysteries that are currently the bitterer as he goes on waiting for some woman to declare by her sexual forwardness that she wants him to be her man.

WHO IS SHE?

"She, she, she. What she?" (3: 426). Not Emma, apparently. And not "the virgin" he had passed three days ago in front of a bookstore window. "Keen glance you gave her" (3: 428), he remembers, chiding himself for his inability to give her anything more. If he's becoming a little more emboldened, he is still left having to plead that some anonymous woman might do for him what he is reduced to having either to pay for or to do for himself. "Touch me," he had implored no one in particular as he had sat by himself on the strand. "Soft eyes. Soft soft soft hand. I am lonely here. O, touch me soon, now" (3: 434–35).

This theoretical woman resembles the writing he wants to do in that neither will simply materialize from his need. And yet because she is already in the world as his words-to-come are not, his thinking about the use to which he will put her cannot alleviate indefinitely her too-conspicuous absence in his life. He has learned from Shakespeare that there can be no bypass to the luscious peril of her sex. But who is she? If there is more to learn, it must be that it is the woman herself whom he cannot pass by. Because she will differ from the seductress he has forecast just as any person differs from an idea, he will find her only by acceding to those differences. Though finding her will be in part a matter of chance, he can foreclose even the slimmest of chances by not letting down his guard. As long as both his prototype for her and the dialectic that supports it remain intact, he will not find her.

But suppose that within the next few months or years Stephen gets his chance and takes it. Suppose he meets and allows himself to become interested in a woman, lets her interest him enough that he begins to regard her as the happy answer to his question "What she?" As his interest in her increases he will be less and less dependent on his dialectic. Meanings that he is currently protected from having to acknowledge will then be possible. Interested in her more as a person than as a type, he may find that even his injunction against nature, mothers, and babies loosens and gives way to an act in which he and this woman willingly conceive a child.

DEATH AS PARADIGM

For now, though, any child means first and last to Stephen a person who was born to die. As he himself thinks of it, what his natural parents began when they "clasped and sundered, did the coupler's will" (3: 47) was Stephen's death. He knows that dying will be the one perfect thing he does. For now, death is Stephen's paradigm for meaning. Because he feels that his awareness of death will escort him ineluctably to his term as a living being, he feels that each of his thoughts must be escorted to its term as meaning by the binary counterpart ineluctably fixed for it in his dialectic. Any meaning less clear than death's strikes him as imperfect, suspect, a beginning only, and therefore his exposure to another discomforting "between."

When he is reminded of midwifery and the beginnings of life by two women on the strand, Stephen suspects uncomfortably that he has merely *begun* to read the women's "signatures" (3: 2) for what they mean and are.

> They came down the steps from Leahy's terrace prudently, *Frauen-
> zimmer*: and down the shelving shore flabbily, their splayed feet
> sinking in the silted sand. Like me, like Algy, coming down to our
> mighty mother. Number one swung lourdily her midwife's bag, the
> other's gamp poked in the beach. From the liberties, out for the
> day. Mrs Florence MacCabe, relict of the late Patk MacCabe,
> deeply lamented, of Bride Street. One of her sisterhood lugged me
> squealing into life. Creation from nothing. What has she in the
> bag? A misbirth with a trailing navelcord, hushed in ruddy wool.
> The cords of all link back, strandentwining cable of all flesh. (3:
> 29–37)

Wanting substance to abide in the succession of words that are his thoughts about the women, he pursues their meaning and being until he thinks he has it all. While his appropriation of it is not lengthy, it concludes only after he invokes death, the first and most certain of his four last things. He imagines one of the women as a widow, and of "Bride Street," the dialectic of birth/death dictating to him the words of an obituary that recalls the couple's wedding in the address of the house to which she now and forever returns without her husband. As Stephen compounds the terms later in the hour, the meaning of "bride-bed, childbed" is full and therefore qualifies as substance only when accompanied unrelentingly by "bed of death, ghostcandled." Whatever else he might ask himself as he looks at the women is displaced by the question "What has she in the bag?," the only acceptable answer to which is one that accounts for everything: "a misbirth" that trails the "strandentwining cable" through which all flesh "links back" within the "womb of sin" that takes death as its wages. "*Omnis caro ad te veniet*" (3: 396): all flesh will come to thee.

"THE ART OF SURFEIT"

He stops thinking about the women because he had isolated their likeness to him and to all his kind and because that likeness has a meaning as determinate as death's. It turns out, though, that his reading has not perfected them, for he will think of them later in another way altogether. He gives this other way a chance when he thinks "From the liberties, out for the day." Maybe they have come down to the sea not so much because it is the life-giving and life-taking mighty mother of us all as because they live in a part of Dublin from which the strand offers them welcome relief.

At the time he thinks it, the thought is unimportant to Stephen. Beyond assigning one of them a name, he does not permit himself to be interested in how either of the women may prompt him to learn something he does not already know. But he is not through thinking about "Florence MacCabe," for she is to be one of the two virgins of his *Parable of the Plums*. Though she will then be ascribed a sterile past in an impotent and moribund Ireland, the thought of her will have remained incomplete enough to have fertilized Stephen's interest in the details by which his parable proceeds. "On now. Dare it," he urges himself as he is about to begin speaking. "Let there be life" (7: 930). Just as there can be no life without death, neither can there be life without some relationship between the living and their precinct. What might there be between himself and two old ladies "out for the day"? Motives: different reasons for doing things, for going one place or another. Different props: moneyboxes, silver and copper money, clothes, umbrellas, panloaf and brawn, the rain. And Dublin: its different possible points of arrival—the north city dining rooms in Marlborough street, Nelson's pillar one block to Stephen's right. The view from the top of the pillar, plumstones through the railings, the concrete below.

Stephen has rehearsed, until he knows them by heart, all the reasons for knowing nothing about the world. Now, though only intermittently, he seems to be as impatient with such reasons as with how little he knows. The women's otherness has moved him first to summon heterogeneous, everyday details and then—as if his interest in them were enough—to resist any impulse to gloss them as he goes along. The results temporarily baffle at least one of his hearers. "—Finished? Myles Crawford said" (7: 1031) in response to Stephen's having given an anxious and self-conscious "sudden loud young laugh as a close" (7: 1028). A similar obliqueness characterizes the method of his lecture on *Hamlet*. Because he thinks that Shakespeare's art is "the art of surfeit" (9: 626), Stephen wants his own discourse to be filled to excess with lore and diction that evoke the life of Shakespeare's time. Only by exceeding what he has to say to make the theory cohere can he be working toward those more expansive if less certain meanings in which the incidental acquires its possibly interesting place. "Work in all you know" (9: 158), he instructs himself—and it is largely under the strain of their embellishing details that Stephen's speeches bulge into the ellipses that keep me wondering if I am not missing something, and how much.

But whereas behind the gaps in his parable he is urging an unignorably bleak meaning that closes those gaps and implies a seamless, inescapable, deathlike truth about the Dublin that is his world, the gaps in his reading of *Hamlet* are comparatively room-making. Eglinton wants to hear more about Ann. Does Stephen mean to say that she was not "a Penelope stay-at-home" (9: 620)? He does mean that, and he could bring that meaning to its close by saying so directly. What he does instead is to go off into a series of associations that includes Antisthenes, an epithet for Helen as "the wooden mare of Troy in whom a score of heroes slept," Shakespeare's salary during his exile in London, Walt Whitman, Sir Walter Raleigh, Queen Elizabeth, the Queen of Sheba, John Manningham's three-sided story about a burgher's wife, Burbage and Shakespeare in which Shakespeare wins, Mistress Fitton, Lady Penelope Rich, Sir William Davenant of Oxford's mother, Henry VIII, and Alfred, Lord Tennyson. When Stephen eventually asks "But all those twenty years what do you suppose poor Penelope in Stratford was doing behind the diamond panes?" (9: 648–50), I can go back through the intervening words and find that at each juncture he is making a followable kind of sense while at the same time widening the angle of meaning between question and answer. Within that angle, he is able to inform, suggest, and dazzle, his cockiness freeing him, for the time, from his far more constricting requirements for meaning and substance.

RICHIE GOULDING, KEVIN EGAN

While Stephen's "art of surfeit" is not exactly James Joyce's, its vitality points in that direction more so than does Stephen's readiness to think of people always and collectively as the living dead. Stephen's reading of *Hamlet* is vital mostly because he thinks it is pretty good, because he is proud enough of it to feel that it will do for now as his position paper to the Dublin literati. And yet if he benefits from that pride by taking some measure of confidence in the words he uses to express his reading, the reading itself remains too firmly captive to his dialectic to lead him as far as he will have to go if he is to write *A Portrait* and *Ulysses*.

If he is to go that far, he will have to enlarge his trust in what interests him. Without being able to identify either interest as a possible beginning for something someone else might want to hear or read, Stephen is interested in both his uncle Richie Goulding and the expatriate Kevin Egan.[15] "Spurned" by his country, his common-law wife, and his son by her, Egan longs undespairingly for a home he will never have. Goulding is by contrast snugly domestic, the master of a house in which there's nothing to eat but "backache pills" (3: 98). Like the virgins' and the widow's, like Dilly's and Stephen's own, Goulding's and Egan's "houses" are for Stephen two more Irish "houses of decay" (3: 105). And yet while his unspoken, unwritten thoughts about both Egan and Goulding are enveloped within this one selfsame meaning, neither portrait proceeds as determinatively as the parable he is proud enough of to tell twice in the same day. As each portrait carries a less determinate meaning than either his parable or his reading of *Hamlet*, each promises more for Stephen as a writer.

If his uncle is so transparent that Stephen can predict how a visit with him would go, he continues to think about him less because he wants to persuade himself that he should not make the visit than because Richie interests him, as does Egan. Unlike Stephen's more inventive, more elegant thoughts on the strand—thoughts about the widows, the "jerkined dwarfs" (3: 304–5), the drowned corpse—his thoughts about Goulding and Egan seek less to appropriate them as objects than to defer to what Stephen knows must remain other in them. He imagines Richie ordering his son Walter to bring them some malt, imagines himself saying

—No, uncle Richie . . . .
—Call me Richie. Damn your lithia water. It lowers. Whusky!
—Uncle Richie, really. . . .
—Sit down or by the law Harry I'll knock you down. (3: 89–92)

In his version of a hospitality he would find the more cloying because he knows that what is offered is not available, his protests against it are thwarted by a figure who emerges less as his antagonist than as the focus of the sketch, Stephen himself serving only as a foil. And though his remembrances of Egan are nearly elegiac and thus might draw Stephen toward and into the levelling and selfsame binary thinking he is prone to whenever death is implied, Egan's difference from him is instead so generative that it keeps Stephen thinking about him more sustainedly than does any one other topic during his hour alone.

Stephen's memory of him includes many of Egan's own words. Egan tells a waitress proudly that he and Stephen are "*Deux irlandais*" (3: 220), she misunderstands, thinks he is ordering "a cheese *hollandais*." Does Stephen know the word "postprandial"? "There was a fellow I knew once in Barcelona, queer fellow, used to call it his postprandial" (3: 222–24). "You're your father's son. I know the voice" (3: 229). "I was a strapping young gossoon at that time, I tell you. I'll show you my likeness one day. I was, faith" (3: 245–46). "*The boys of Kilkenny are stout roaring blades.* Know that old lay?" He'd taught it, he says, to his son Patrice. "Goes like this. O, O" (3: 257–60). As he had begun to sing for Stephen this ballad about the francophile Irish revolutionary James Napper Tandy, Egan had touched him, Stephen's memory of that physical contact prompting a sentence that is for me the most attractive and haunting that Stephen thinks or speaks: "He takes me, Napper Tandy, by the hand" (3: 260). The "green fairy" (3: 226) that Egan sips and his "green eyes" (3: 238) are at once his Irishness and a necessarily barren envy of his own past. "Weak wasting hand on mine," Stephen recalls. "They have forgotten Kevin Egan, not he them" (3: 263–64). But while the details of his memory of Egan might have seemed to Stephen as if they were "ineluctably preconditioned" (15: 2120–21) to ornament the meaning death-in-life, their resonance denies the union of Egan and that meaning, it separates and remains between Egan and how Stephen might have read him as meaning mostly death.

Though he does not credit them as departures for something he might write, Stephen's interests both in Egan and in Goulding are discontinuous with the habits of mind that intercept such departures by demanding that all beginnings must at the same time end. If Egan and Goulding are ultimately nothing other than the living dead, if for all their incidental liveliness they are no less assimilable to Stephen's dialectic than are the dead living, his readings of them nevertheless leave the assimilation incomplete. He reads these others as if there were between himself and each a relationship whose interest temporarily dispels his predilection for transforming like to same. If his reading is at best only like what he reads and not of one substance with it, if what he reads therefore remains other than his selfsame reading of it, other is temporarily dislodged from the place his dialectic has made for it. Temporarily asymmetrical with its opposite, other neither completes nor is completed by same. Instead, it bears a relationship to same that is Stephen's interest. The thoughts that compose his interest are no less selfsame than the thoughts that align more closely with his dialectic. Interest differs from its absence not as from its opposite but rather in its direction. Rather than turn toward the selfsameness of his thoughts about Egan as if toward and into an enveloping protector, Stephen faces Egan. As he thinks it, his memory of Egan's "raw facebones under his peep of day boy's hat" (3: 240–41) is the same as itself. Egan's face is inexhaustibly other for that thought. Other and same, for Stephen, are temporarily disjunct. Instead of feeling threatened by their separation, Stephen directs his attention in such a way that it is enough for him, temporarily, that his interest lie between.

With Bloom

TO A CABMAN'S SHELTER

More than six hours after he meets Dilly at the bookstall and plunges into "Misery!" (10: 880), Stephen is once again a figure in the narrative, this time in the company of Bloom, who, eager that she be delivered of a natural son or daughter, has come to the lying-in hospital because of Mina Purefoy's "interesting condition" (14: 724). Of the "right witty scholars" (14: 202) gathered there to carouse, Stephen is "the most drunken that demanded still of more mead" (14: 194–95). Because Bloom bears "fast friendship to sir Simon" (14: 198), he stays to keep a protective eye on Stephen, follows him to Burke's and to Nighttown, and intervenes for him with Bella Cohen and with the police. Then he leads Stephen off to a cabman's shelter "where they might hit upon some drinkables in the shape of a milk and soda or a mineral" (16: 9–11).

Fully intending "to pen something out of the common groove" (16: 1229–30), "*My Experiences*, let us say, *in a Cabman's Shelter*" (16: 1231), Bloom is the guest-narrator of chapter 16. He therefore supplies an account of his interests that is unmatched by any such account of Stephen's own. Until Bloom's project of sobering him up begins to take with Stephen, Stephen is understandably indifferent to Bloom. Thereafter, he may make the thirteen-block walk to 7 Eccles Street with Bloom only because he has nothing else to do and nowhere else to go. Since interior monologue is no longer and never again an avenue to

Stephen's thoughts, since unlike Bloom he narrates only what the narrative reports him to have said, it is difficult to gauge the degree to which Stephen's returning to his wits coincides with his taking an interest in Bloom. This difficulty is itself the one determinable coincidence. For at the same time that Stephen and a reader of *Ulysses* are expelled from the enclosure within which they had been at one in Stephen's selfsame thinking, at the same time that Stephen's thoughts must begin to be inferred from what he says and does and thus might be misread as being other than they are, Stephen begins to surprise, if not also, and relatedly, to be surprised.

Before he and Bloom reach the cabman's shelter, Stephen is as pompous and glib with Bloom as he had been with Haines and Deasy. "I don't mean to presume to dictate to you in the slightest degree," Bloom says to him, "but why did you leave your father's house?" "—To seek misfortune, was Stephen's answer" (16: 251–53). And yet while his answer to Bloom's next question is no less glib and more sarcastic, Stephen unexpectedly follows it with a question of his own. Where is Stephen's father living now? "—I believe he is in Dublin somewhere, . . . Why?" (16: 258–59). Bloom is not insensitive to Stephen's rudeness. And so if Stephen utters this "Why?" as if to say "how could it matter less?" and even "leave me alone," Bloom would not hear it as a reluctant, weary, but nonetheless explicit invitation to keep talking, which he does. Simon "takes great pride" in Stephen (16: 261–62). Stephen could perhaps still go home. He certainly "won't get in" at Martello Tower "after what occurred at Westland Row station" (16: 250–51) with Mulligan.[16] Mulligan, Bloom goes on, is not to be trusted: though his humor is entertaining, though it is to his credit that he will soon be making a good living as a doctor, and though his having saved a man from drowning was an "exceedingly plucky deed" (16: 294), Mulligan is jealous of Stephen and is trying to pick his brains.

BLOOM PERSEVERES

These words tell Stephen that between himself and Bloom there is a world in which Mulligan's character might be talked about. But while he therefore responds with "two or three lowspirited remarks" (16: 303–4) of his own on that same topic, what he says defies Bloom's attempt to understand it. Whether out of boredom, exhaustion, cautiousness, an initial distaste for Bloom, or simply out of habit, Stephen is slow to respect this "unlookedfor occasion" (16: 1217) in which words about things that interest him might well be understood by another person. Indeed, until much later in the hour, Stephen is intent

on confusing Bloom, who misses the irony when Stephen assures him
that the existence of God "has been proved conclusively" (16: 772),
who tries to but finds "nothing particularly Roman" (16: 818–19) about
the knife that Stephen asks him to take away because it reminds him
of "Roman history." Doing his best neither to insist that Stephen be
clear nor to patronize his aggressive obscurity by allowing him to settle
back altogether into his own thoughts, Bloom keeps trying to draw him
out. Was he not right, he asks Stephen, to have told the citizen that
Christ was a Jew? "—*Ex quibus*, Stephen mumbled in a noncommittal
accent, their two or four eyes conversing, *Christus* or Bloom his name
is or after all any other, *secundum carnem*" (16: 1091–93): according to
the flesh, all are of that race.

Whatever trouble Bloom has with the Latin does not stop him. He
is becoming accustomed enough to Stephen's "dark" (3: 420) words to
persevere as if Stephen himself were a part of the conversation. "It's a
patent absurdity on the face of it," Bloom says,

> to hate people because they live round the corner and speak an-
> other vernacular, in the next house so to speak.
> —Memorable bloody bridge battle and seven minutes' war, Ste-
> phen assented, between Skinner's alley and Ormond market.
>   Yes, Mr Bloom thoroughly agreed, entirely endorsing the remark,
> that was overwhelmingly right. And the whole world was full of
> that sort of thing.
> —You just took the words out of my mouth, he said. A hocuspocus
> of conflicting evidence that candidly you couldn't remotely. . . .
> (16: 1101–10)

Whether Bloom speaks these last words or only thinks them, he breaks
them off because they are so applicable to the hocuspocus he is hearing
from Stephen that to go on with the line of thought would foreclose
any further talk.

CHANGING THE COUNTRY

Bloom keeps trying until Stephen stumps him completely by saying
"Ireland must be important because it belongs to me."

> —What belongs, queried Mr Bloom bending, fancying he was per-
> haps under some misapprehension. Excuse me. Unfortunately, I
> didn't catch the latter portion. What was it you . . . ?
>   Stephen, patently crosstempered, repeated and shoved aside his

mug of coffee or whatever you like to call it none too politely, adding:

—We can't change the country. Let us change the subject. (16: 1164–71)

But Bloom won't talk just to talk, and, "to change the subject," looks down "in a quandry, as he couldn't tell exactly what construction to put on belongs to," which to Bloom "sounded rather a far cry" (16: 1172–74).

As far a cry as Stephen's obsession to become Ireland's one true generative force through the writing of his word. Such megalomania is unrecognizable to Bloom, who has scrutinized Stephen's words during the past few hours, has heard him talk about both his writing and his country but understandably cannot fathom what the two have to do with one another in Stephen's mind. "Look forth now, my people" (14: 375), he had heard Stephen say in the lying-in hospital, "unto a land flowing with milk and money. But thou hast suckled me with a bitter milk: my moon and sun thou hast quenched for ever. And thou hast left me alone for ever in the dark ways of my bitterness." After Stephen's rebuke of him, Bloom wants to attribute Stephen's "curious bitter way" (16: 1176) to the bitter milk of drink, as if Stephen sober might be Stephen sweet.

Stephen's terms for ridding himself and the country of "love's bitter mystery" are that the country become his, its mortal citizenry transformed into "the word that shall not pass away." What had become of their friends from school, Bloom had heard Stephen asked.

You have spoken of the past and its phantoms, Stephen said. Why think of them? If I call them into life across the waters of Lethe will not the poor ghosts troop to my call? Who supposes it? I, Bous Stephanoumenos, bullockbefriending bard, am lord and giver of their life. He encircled his gadding hair with a coronal of vineleaves, smiling at Vincent. That answer and those leaves, Vincent said to him, will adorn you more fitly when something more, and greatly more, than a capful of light odes can call your genius father. All who wish you well hope this for you. All desire to see you bring forth the work you meditate, to acclaim you Stephaneforos. I heartily wish you may not fail them. O no, Vincent, Lenehan said, laying a hand on the shoulder near him. Have no fear. He could not leave his mother an orphan. The young man's face grew dark. All could see how hard it was for him to be reminded of his promise and of his recent loss. (14: 1112–25)

Though Stephen has told himself he has "much, much to learn" (7: 915) about the world he lives in, his bitterest, most self-doubting and possessive impulses tell him that he must remake that world, must become lord and giver of life to those otherwise merely engendered sons who will remain no more than "poor ghosts" until his genius simultaneously fathers their substance with his own. It is not enough for him that his words go forth to take their chances with already engendered sons and daughters between whom there is now and then the agreement of interest that language is. When Ireland at last becomes important by belonging to him, Stephen thinks, he will be at one with all his sons, there being no longer anything between them.

For now, at a cabman's shelter near Butt Bridge, there is between Stephen and another of Ireland's natural sons their remarkable similarities and differences, Bloom's interest in Stephen's interests, and the world. Despite Bloom's loneliness within it, despite the cause its circumstances and people have given him to be bitter toward it, the world interests Bloom. If Stephen is to rid himself of his embittering paralysis by becoming the writer he promises to be, Bloom thinks, then it's "interest and duty even to wait on and profit by the unlookedfor occasion," which this very evening may itself be. For with its "coincidence of meeting, discussion, dance, row, old salt of the here today and gone tomorrow type, night loafers, the whole galaxy of events" like those that brought grist to Shakespeare's mill, "all went to make up a miniature cameo of the world we live in" (16: 1222–25). It is unthinkable to Bloom that Stephen might want to make the world over in his own image.

"—His own image to a man with that queer thing genius is the standard of all experience" (9: 432–33), Stephen had pronounced in the library. If "the images of other males of his blood" continue to "repel" Stephen, if he continues to "see in them grotesque attempts of nature to foretell or repeat himself" (9: 434–35), if "man delights him not nor woman neither" (9: 1030), then Stephen will have met in Bloom not another person but merely one more reason to reconstitute the world as he would have it be. If Stephen is predisposed to hate all those who, "*secundum carnem*," are of the one race with himself, then it will not take long for Bloom to put this hatred in motion. As far as Stephen's own purposes are concerned, he need not give Bloom the time of day—a fact that his behavior may be declaring.

TALKING THINGS OVER

Bloom is used to comparable treatment from other Dubliners. And though he broods a bit on Stephen's "rebuke" (16: 1174) by prolonging

the silence, it is predictably Bloom himself and not Stephen who is the
next to speak. When Stephen manages some words of his own, Bloom
is "overjoyed to set his mind at rest" (16: 1272) that talk between them
is still a possibility. He does not want to press his luck, though, and so
waits awhile before speaking again. Stephen is not through perplexing
Bloom. But to Bloom's "—There was every indication they would arrive at that," Stephen asks perhaps inadvertently, perhaps almost in-
terestedly, but in any case at least intelligibly "—Who?" (16: 1295–
96).

The subject the other occupants of the shelter have arrived at is Parnell. Their talk inevitably turns to his adultery with Kitty O'Shea, and
it occurs to Bloom that he might just show Stephen a photograph of
Molly. Leaving it on the table "so that the other could drink in the
beauty for himself" (16: 1458–59), Bloom then looks away "thoughtfully with the intention of not further increasing the other's possible
embarrassment while gauging her symmetry of heaving *embonpoint*"
(16: 1466–68).[17] Stephen tells him the picture is "handsome" (16:
1479). Until "Miss Right" (16: 1557) comes along for Stephen, Bloom
thinks, "ladies' society" is "a *conditio sine qua non*" (16: 1557–58).
Bloom has "the gravest possible doubts" that Stephen "would find
much satisfaction basking in the boy and girl courtship idea" (16:
1561–62). Everything points to its being in Stephen's interest to have
an affair with Molly. Without admitting to himself that he is pimping,
and with a variety of other "utopian plans" for Stephen "flashing
through his (B's) busy brain" (16: 1652), Bloom proposes, "after mature reflection while prudently pocketing her photo," that Stephen just
come with him to his "diggings" and "talk things over" (16: 164–5).

"—Yes, that's the best, he assured Stephen to whom for the matter
of that Brazen Head or him or anywhere else was all more or less" (16:
1650–51). But if it is all more or less the same to Stephen whether he
goes with Bloom or not, his condescending passivity has begun gradually to give way. If he should have been able to penetrate the mystery
of why chairs are placed upside down on tables at night, his asking for
Bloom's help in the matter is a small but important interruption of his
static, self-enclosing pride. He allows his interest in the question to
overcome any hesitancy about betraying that interest and the ignorance it implies. Perhaps the question comes to him at all only because
he is with Bloom, because he senses that with Bloom it is somehow a
less trivial question than it would have been with anyone else he has
talked with all day. He had puzzled the question before. It is the kind
of question he will have to ask himself again and again if his art is to be
"the art of surfeit." Maybe asking the question has a place in what it
means to "talk things over," maybe he should lend more of himself to

conversing with Bloom.[18] Having "confessed to still feeling poorly and fagged out" (16: 1706), Stephen hears Bloom tell him that "the only thing is to walk then you'll feel a different man. Come. It's not far. Lean on me" (16: 1719–20). "—Yes, Stephen said uncertainly" (16: 1723).

"PARALLEL COURSES"

"So they turned on to chatting about music" (16: 1733), Bloom betraying his ignorance by referring to *Don Giovanni* as "light opera," to Mendelssohn as "the severe classical school" (16: 1752, 1754). Because Bloom more than suspects that Stephen has "his father's voice to bank his hopes on" (16: 1659), he wants very much to hear Stephen sing since the principal "utopian plan" is duets in Italian, Molly and Stephen, "concert tours in English watering resorts packed with hydros and seaside theatres, turning money away" (16: 1654–55). Bloom's limited familiarity with the literature of music has not constricted the acuteness of his ear for the human voice. He tells Stephen that just yesterday he had heard his "respected father" (16: 1759) sing Flotow's *M'appari*. Does Stephen sing that aria himself? Stephen "said he didn't sing it but launched out into praises of Shakespeare's songs" (16: 1761–62), his enthusiasm for this and for related subjects prompting him to go on at length about "the highly interesting old" (16: 1799)—Bloom does not know what, he has lost the thread.

Stephen may have been unclear. His new gregariousness with Bloom may have taken him from one thing to another too elliptically and thus made it too easy for Bloom to become "somewhat distracted" (16: 1798) when he sees "suddenly in evidence in the dark quite near . . . a big foolish nervous noodly kind of a horse" (16: 1782–89), which he proceeds to think about while Stephen keeps on talking. But Stephen has been neither deliberately nor disdainfully unclear: in this regard he is, as Bloom had promised, "a different man" (16: 1719). He is certainly no longer "standoffish" (16: 1614). Neither has he been "rambling on to himself or some unknown listener somewhere" (16: 885–86), but has instead been talking to Bloom. Without knowing that he had temporarily lost Bloom's attention or that it has now been fully restored, Stephen continues his preamble. Then he sings for Bloom in his "phenomenally beautiful tenor voice" (16: 1820) the first lines of a song "which boggled Bloom a bit":

> *Von der Sirenen Listigkeit*
> *Tun die Poeten dichten.*   (16: 1813–16)

Wanting to illuminate for Bloom what he suspects might otherwise remain dark words, Stephen interrupts his singing to translate. "Bloom, nodding, said he perfectly understood and begged him to go on by all means which he did" (16: 1817–19).

His debilitating thoughts may have begun to exercise a less powerful hold over Stephen. If so, the best evidence is his changed and changing community with Bloom. Because the two of them walk into chapter 17 and on toward Bloom's house along "parallel courses" (17: 1), Stephen consents to there being between himself and this other Dubliner the distance, pace, and direction necessary if they are to keep talking. Their deliberations include Paris, friendship, woman, prostitution, the Roman Catholic church, the Irish nation, Jesuit education, careers, the past day, and Stephen's collapse. The unimpeachable but obtuse narrator does not record how actively Stephen engages in the discussion, but no one of these subjects is without its interest for Stephen, who has begun to open up with Bloom as if with someone for whom he is willing to articulate what matters to him. If he is still somewhat less than solicitous of Bloom's companionship and conversation, he nonetheless spends more than a sixth of his last half hour in literature waiting at the area railings while Bloom regulates a gaslamp, lights a candle, takes off his boots and hat, and does whatever else he does before reappearing at the front door to let Stephen in. Over a cup of cocoa, both reminisce about their two prior meetings. Bloom describes an ad for Stephen, who reciprocates by constructing for Bloom the scene of a drama at a "solitary hotel" (17: 612). Stephen then volunteers his ready-made *Parable of the Plums*, speaks a sentence in Irish, and complies "doubly" (17: 775) with Bloom's request by writing his name not only in Irish characters but in Roman as well. As Bloom sings for him what is now the national anthem of Israel, he sees in Bloom the concealed identity of Christ's divine and human nature. "With amicability, gratefully," he declines Bloom's offer of "asylum" (17: 955, 954), agrees to meet and talk with Bloom again, shakes his hand, and leaves.

His time with Bloom may have pointed Stephen toward words-to-come. When he and Bloom discover that they have Dante Riordan in common, Stephen is led to further reminiscences, two of which manifest themselves in the first pages of *A Portrait*. The fire Bloom kindles for him moves Stephen to think of others who had done the same, all of whom emerge either in *A Portrait* or *Dubliners*, three of them along with their fires (17: 134).[19] These and comparable examples are of course only the beginnings of what Bloom may have contributed to Stephen's writing. Stephen's expanding congeniality with a character who interests the writer of *Ulysses* suggests the possibility that Stephen himself may begin to write *Ulysses* in ten years.

Just prior to their leave-taking, both men are "silent, each contemplating the other in both mirrors of the reciprocal flesh of theirhisnothis fellowfaces" (17: 1183). From Stephen's side of this moment, Bloom's face is other not just to Stephen's own but also to whatever selfsame words make up his contemplation of it. Stephen's thoughts are only directed toward Bloom's face. They are no more at one with it than references are at one with the referents toward which they point. And indeed in this one instance, even the references dissolve. For in the compound "theirhisnothis," what might have been the distinguishable words "not" and "his" are so irrevocably elided that they could just as sensibly be "no" and "this." "No," it is not an image of my own face I am seeing in the other: and though it is more his than mine, it is not so much "his" as "this," this one face in front of me, a face that neither atones with my concepts nor opposes them but rather disrupts what would otherwise be the sovereignty of my thoughts. Though I am free to preserve the selfsameness of each reference directed toward the person facing me, these references are momentarily undone by the otherness of the referent who keeps surprising my ideas of him by saying what I did not expect, by thinking only he knows what. He is always other than the person my thoughts would have caught up with. I am left with only my interest in him, an interest that directs me to do the catching up he keeps reminding me I cannot.

MOLLY AS STEPHEN'S ANN

But if there were things about the other person that Stephen had to learn before he could begin to be the writer he wants to be, and if he begins to learn these things with Bloom, his thinking that he will go on to write what he has learned may simply continue and reinforce the very sovereignty he has had to question. For he remains free to use Bloom, free to think of Bloom's otherness as material he can appropriate. If Stephen's cordiality with Bloom surprises, it need not follow that Bloom's generosity has surprised Stephen's misanthropy and roused him from it. Stephen may become the more agreeable with Bloom only so that he might extract as much as possible toward his writing. The "postcreation" he means to write must include "all in all in all of us" (9: 1049–50). If in going on to write Bloom and others who are different from himself he realizes his "own image" as the artist father of us all, his plan for his career will have remained intact. The "patient silhouette," Leopold Bloom, who "waited, listening" (9: 597) outside the door of the room in which Stephen spoke this plan will have been only a poor ghost who later troops to Stephen's call. In having met Bloom, Stephen will have begun to be the James Joyce who in Simon and Stephen Dedalus fathers both his father and himself, who fathers a race of the unborn in J. J. O'Molloy, Ned Lambert, Lenehan, Myles Crawford, Paddy Dignam, Bloom, and all the other characters in *Ulysses*. It might even be that Stephen has begun to father precisely that race of inert partisans he thinks he wants as reader-sons. Secure within the economy of a book that keeps promising and deferring his meeting with Bloom, Stephen may have read all the clues correctly and may thus have stayed on course.

Especially so if it is a course that takes him to Molly as to the seductress from whom he is convinced he must win back the subjugation of his race's spirit. His dream from the night before had augured an answer to the pressing question "Who will woo you?" (9: 938). "That man led me, spoke. I was not afraid. The melon he had he held against my face. Smiled: creamfruit smell. That was the rule, said. In. Come. Red carpet spread. You will see who" (3: 367–69). Although he had heard his companion Mr O'Madden Burke refer to Molly as "Dublin's prime favourite" (7: 610), Stephen does not at first identify Bloom as the pander who will lead him to his Ann-like heartbreaker. But the dream returns, in the context of his search for clues to the course his life should take. Leaving the library,

> About to pass through the doorway, feeling one behind, he stood aside.
>
> Part. The moment is now. Where then? If Socrates leave his house today, if Judas go forth tonight. Why? That lies in space which I in time must come to, ineluctably.
>
> My will: his will that fronts me. Seas between. A man passed out between them, bowing, greeting.
>
> —Good day again, Buck Mulligan said. The portico.
>
> Here I watched the birds for augury. Aengus of the birds. They go, they come. Last night I flew. Easily flew. Men wondered. Street of harlots after. A creamfruit melon he held to me. In. You will see.
>
> —The wandering jew, Buck Mulligan whispered with clown's awe. (9: 1197–1209)

The Wandering Jew has had a dream of his own. "Dreamt last night? Wait. Something confused. She had red slippers on. Turkish" (13: 1240–41). Though Bloom summons from the dream only its oriental flavor, the color red, and that "she" is Molly, these memories are enough to supplement Stephen's dream and draw the narrative on toward Bloom's half-conscious proffering of his wife's "yellow smellow melons" (17: 2241) to his newfound friend. All the signs are that Molly is the woman to make Dedalus fly as his name predestines him to.

"My wife . . . would have the greatest of pleasure in making your acquaintance" (16: 1800–1802), Bloom tells Stephen on their walk to Eccles Street. As Stephen may intuit, Bloom is not wrong. After Bloom tells Molly that he has showed her photo to "Stephen Dedalus, professor and author" (17: 2270) and that Stephen has agreed to give her lessons in Italian pronunciation, she plans her "union" with the "young stranger" (18: 1315) that her cards had foretold that morning. To be her most compelling, she will have to "get a nice pair of red slippers like those Turks" (18: 1494–95). If she could "only get in with a handsome young poet" (18: 1359) at her age! She'll "read and study" all she can, even "learn a bit off by heart" so he will not think her stupid. And she will "teach him the other part" (18: 1361–63). "I'll make him feel all over him till he half faints under me then hell write about me lover and mistress publicly too with our 2 photographs in all the papers when he becomes famous" (18: 1363–66).

Molly is Stephen's "Galatea" (8: 924). Not long after he wills an Ann Hathaway of his own, he sees a representation of a woman who, when she comes to life for him as it promises she is soon to do, will fulfil all his predetermined requirements for her. "Sweet and twentysix" (9: 258) in the photo Bloom displays, "hot in the blood, once a wooer, twice a wooer" (9: 669), Molly is more than ready to be the "goddess who bends over the boy Adonis, stooping to conquer, as prologue to the swelling act" (9: 258–59).[20] Stephen could not have arranged his immediate future more perfectly if he had been the author of it himself—which he may have been. "Greater love than this, he said, no man hath that a man lay down his wife for a friend. Go thou and do likewise" (14: 360–62). Having heard Stephen say this, Bloom has gone and done likewise. Since Stephen has been thinking that his career will turn on his "turn" (9: 261) with a provocative woman, his will and his words seem to have appropriated this woman's otherness to his selfsame plan. As if he had spoken both their roles into being, he need now only act his out. "Speech, speech," he had thought toward the close of his lecture. "But act. Act speech." "Act. Be acted on" (9: 978–79). Now, in Bloom's kitchen, he sees hanging from a clothesline "one pair of ladies' grey hose" (17: 153): italicizing what one of his next acts could be, he notices at the "point of junction" between the two legs an "erect wooden" peg (17: 155–56).

THE BALLAD OF LITTLE HARRY HUGHES

Because Stephen's way to Molly is through her particularly cooperative husband, because she herself is as if of one substance with Stephen's purposes and terms, all that is left is for Stephen to consent. As he chats with Bloom in the kitchen, he may simply be waiting for

Bloom to propose a time for his first tryst with Molly. His wider patience with Bloom may be nothing more in itself than his capitulation
to his own good fortune. He may, as he waits, be thanking his stars that
he is at last on his way into the greatness he had until now been able
only to desire, prescribe, and envy.

But if so, he does a very curious thing. He sings for Bloom, whom he
knows to be a Jew, a ballad about a Jew's daughter who lures a gentile
away from his schoolfellows and then cuts off his head. So Bloom will
not miss the analogy, Stephen interprets it for him. "One of all, the
least of all, is the victim predestined. Once by inadvertence, twice by
design he challenges his destiny. It comes when he is abandoned and
challenges him reluctant and, as an apparition of hope and youth,
holds him unresisting. It leads him to a strange habitation, to a secret
infidel apartment, and there, implacable, immolates him, consenting"
(17: 833–37). What Stephen says suggests that he reads his meeting
with Bloom not as an initiation into the maturity he has longed for but
rather as a sacrifice he has been fated to endure. And yet if he is "unresisting," "consenting," why the resistance and dissent in his song and
commentary? Because the prospect of Molly's immolating sensuality
gives him cold feet? Because he has coveted the glamorous melancholy
of his paralysis all along and now blames Bloom for having made it this
easy to move?

I read it that he insults Bloom because he sees that Bloom is procur-
ing for him, because to pretend he does not see it would be to settle for
Bloom's meaning less to him than he does. Though Bloom is willing
and able to bring Stephen to what he has been telling himself he needs
most, Stephen has learned during his time with Bloom that there is
something he needs more. He needs to think of Bloom as more than a
go-between to the woman who may launch him into his brilliant career, needs to think of Bloom as more, even, than the prototype for the
"hero" (16: 1643) of a famous book he wants to imagine he could write.
"You wouldn't think he had it in him yet you would" (16: 1478). Just
as Stephen's thoughts are momentarily directed toward and surpassed
by Bloom's unwriteable face, so too are the words of *Ulysses* that inscribe Bloom directed toward an otherness that surpasses them in the
way the born surpass the unborn or the merely written. Bloom, Stephen, Molly, Ned Lambert, and other unborn characters in *Ulysses*
interest me only if I already take an interest in persons who have been
born and who keep surprising my readings of their appearances, acts,
and words. Stephen will no more father Bloom than James Joyce has
fathered those of us who read *Ulysses*. Unlike characters in books, readers, like writers, are not written into being. They are born.

Though it might have, Stephen's insult has not necessarily cancelled his sexual transaction with Molly by way of Bloom. After he rejects Bloom's offer to spend the night, he reconfirms his willingness to instruct Molly in Italian, "place the residence of the instructed" (17: 962–63), time, we can be sure, when Bloom is not home. Stephen may or may not be back. Bloom thinks he will not, though the off-chance that he might makes it worth mentioning to Molly. But whatever happens, and despite the fact that Stephen could have done so far more directly, Stephen has done something. He has urged Bloom to recognize that the man who lays down his wife for a friend is less than a friend since to pander is to reduce all parties involved to passive ciphers in a selfsame plan. This one act of Stephen's may have pointed him toward a gap in those plans for himself that so far have not gotten him started toward becoming the person he might be. That may seem too much to ask of so small a thing. But I believe with Bloom that "an opening was all was wanted" (16: 1658), and I believe that "a step in the required direction it was" (16: 1843). "You move a motion? Steve boy, you're going it some" (14: 1528).

3.

J A M E S   J O Y C E

"Ireland, Parnell Said . . . "

SUCCEEDING

by the the time his "retreating feet" (17: 1243)
walk him out of *Ulysses*, Stephen has not played at having begun to
write either of the two books in which he is a character. If he is to begin
to do the writing he wants very much to do, writing that in his own
terms would qualify him as father, he must therefore do what no character can: he must become the person who wrote *A Portrait of the Artist
as a Young Man* and *Ulysses*, he must become that single one of Ireland's
sons named James Joyce.

The line I will follow in these pages describes what Stephen wants
to do as it emerges in the light of what Joyce did. I can imagine a
connection between Stephen and the mature James Joyce that goes
something like this: when Stephen walks away from Bloom's house he
stops playing the would-be-writer and begins to be James Joyce in 1904,
begins ten years later to write a book in which Stephen walks away from
Bloom's house. With the completed *Ulysses* available to me, I can write
a simple retrospective according to which Stephen traded being Stephen for being a success. According to this view, Stephen will succeed
because he is well-connected. Though his need to grow requires time
and is therefore at odds with Jamesy's timeless being, Stephen's timely
connection with James Joyce testifies that *Ulysses*-Jamesy is itself the
fulfillment of Stephen's need. To view Ulysses this way is to read it as
an enclosure within which its spiritual sons (but not also its daughters)
are pleased to keep making fine adjustments of its earlier readings without ever being moved by it to answer any person's call.

What such a view conveniently ignores are the terms against which
Stephen's future successes must be gauged. *Ulysses* makes it clear that
Stephen will become a successful writer only if his writing succeeds
politically—succeeds, that is, in the sense of continuing a political suc-
cession, of following from. . . . Though it is precisely his Irishness that
Stephen feels he must escape if he is to mature as a writer, his matura-

tion will have to wait upon his hearing a general but nonetheless compelling call—a call to which *Ulysses* will be his very specific answer. The polis into which he did not choose to be "born" calls Stephen to be *for* its people. To be for them is among other things to be subject to what they themselves need. To be for them is to be called to a weal so public that private well-being by itself is deprivation.

Just as it is a call that antedates Stephen's "birth," so too does it antedate the unchosen birth of James Joyce, the writer Stephen is to become. Stephen is not necessarily a portrait of the way Joyce "really" was in 1904. But insofar as it connects with Joyce at all—as it does for me and for other readers of *A Portrait* and *Ulysses*—Stephen's character is necessarily infiltrated by connections Joyce felt called upon to make in writing it. The most formidable of these is Joyce's connection with Charles Stewart Parnell, that one of Ireland's sons whom Joyce recognizes as having most successfully met his obligation to the community of persons Joyce knew best. I read Stephen Dedalus as a connecting middle term between Parnell and Joyce. While Stephen's connection with Joyce summons him away from "1904" along a course toward and into 1921, that very course is one that Stephen and Joyce were obliged to follow because of Joyce's connection with Parnell. It is a course that will transform Stephen not only into the writer of *Ulysses*-Jamesy but also, and however incredibly, into Parnell "reborn," a "rebirth" wishfully and sentimentally foretold in Joe Hynes's elegy for Parnell in "Ivy Day in the Committee Room."

> *They had their way: they laid him low.*
> *But Erin, list, his spirit may*
> *Rise, like the Phoenix from the flames.*   (D, 135)

Stephen is this "Phoenix," for it is from nothing other than Parnell's death in 1891 that Stephen takes his birth as a character.

"ONLY NAMES"

In one of his earliest crises of conscience, Stephen is walking through the streets of Cork with his natural father when he is nearly overcome with the fear that "by his monstrous way of life" he was rendering himself "dumb and insensible" to the "real world" (*P*, 92). Because he intuits that language alone will help him maintain a relationship with the world, he forces himself "to interpret the letters of the signboards of the shops." Needing to test whether or not this interpreting proceeds from himself, he thinks two sentences with himself as grammatical subject. "—I am Stephen Dedalus. I am walking beside my father whose name is Simon Dedalus." But as he goes on, as he tries to locate himself within the "real world," the words that are his means for doing so begin to deny him the provenance of the first-person pronoun. "We are in Cork, in Ireland. Cork is a city. Our room is in the Victoria Hotel. Victoria and Stephen and Simon. Simon and Stephen and Victoria. Names." Throughout his life, the word "Stephen" had seemed to him to have been properly his. But instead of retaining its privilege as a word with which to begin a proposition, "Stephen" is now merely one among other names, two syllables sandwiched between conjunctions that could extend the series of names indefinitely, each additional name dislodging "Stephen" or the "I" that stands for "Stephen" just that much more from any pretensions it might have to origin or centrality.

If "Stephen" has become just another name, he suspects, it may be that he himself, the supposed referent of that name, no longer exists. Had he ever existed, he wonders, or had there always been "only names"? First-person pronoun yields to third-person as he tries to reconstruct a past that might enable him to identify a point in time before he had "wandered out of existence" (*P*, 93), before he had been lost to the world into which, with his birth, he had been *placed outside*, been made to *ex-ist*. Whatever the boy's name, "a little boy had been taught geography by an old woman who kept two brushes in her wardrobe," one of them for someone named Parnell. This boy had then been sent away to school. From his bed in the infirmary there, he had constructed a dreamlike story, his fever impairing his capacity to distinguish fancy from fact. After he had imagined himself dead and laid out on the "catafalque," "a tiny light twinkled at the pierhead where the ship was entering" and he had heard Brother Michael say "—He is dead. We saw him lying upon the catafalque" (*P*, 27). If the word "catafalque" had led Stephen to think that his own death was being announced, the next words he had heard had brought him out of his confusion: "—Parnell! Parnell! He is dead!" And as he walks past the shops trying to remember what has happened to him in his one life, Stephen manages to remind himself that "he had not died then. Parnell had died" (*P*, 93).

BABY TUCKOO'S BIRTH

But while Parnell alone had died, not the boy, it was his fevered dream in the infirmary that had marked the boy's "passing out of existence" (*P*, 93). Prior to that dream and the coincident news of Parnell's death, the boy had existed within "the limits of reality" (*P*, 92), limits that had preserved him as a visible body in time and space. Temporarily stripped of those limits by the dream and by hearing that Parnell was dead, Stephen became estranged from a world to which his subsequent return is strange. As it was "strange" for him to think of the boy "being lost and forgotten somewhere in the universe," so too was it "strange to see his small body appear again for a moment: a little boy in a grey belted suit" (P, 93). Through the alliance of memory and language, Stephen extends what he is able to "see" of the boy's now-invisible body. "His hands," he remembers, "were in his sidepockets and his trousers were tucked in at the knees by elastic bands" (P, 93).

When I read Stephen as a character on his way to becoming the person who wrote first A *Portrait* and then *Ulysses*, I read his construction of the "little boy" as the first in what was to become the long series of predications that are now Stephen's character. As I read it, Stephen will later remember about this little boy that he had once been "baby tuckoo," that "once upon a time" a little boy's father had told him a story about something baby tuckoo himself had lived and could therefore strangely make "appear again for a moment" (P, 93) on the road near Betty Byrne's. "Once upon a time and a very good time it was," A *Portrait* begins,

> there was a moocow coming down along the road and this moocow that was coming down along the road met a nicens little boy named baby tuckoo. . . .
>
> His father told him that story: his father looked at him through a glass: he had a hairy face.
>
> He was baby tuckoo. The moocow came down the road where Betty Byrne lived: she sold lemon platt.
>
> > O, the wild rose blossoms
> > On the little green place.
>
> He sang that song. That was his song.
>
> > O, the green wothe botheth.   (P, 7)

Among other factors that make them what they are, these words are governed by the young child's need to locate the moocow and by his trouble with consonants. And so there is a sense in which they are *Stephen's* words, are as much his, say, as his having sung "*wothe botheth*" had made the song "his song." But in a way that is more important still, the passage as a whole is Stephen's once he himself is recognized as connecting with the writer who decided that A *Portrait* should begin with just these words. Having suffered the misapprehension that, like Parnell's, his allotted time in space was gone forever, Stephen's remedy had been to make himself "appear again" by predicating this and that about the "little boy." Parnell's death is signal in Stephen's beginning to construct a third-person character from whom he would not distinguish himself as his fear that he was dead had compelled him to distinguish himself from the dead Parnell. Because until then it had never occurred to Stephen to make himself a character in a story, all of the writing that constitutes Stephen Dedalus in *A Portrait* and *Ulysses* can be read as having its inception in Parnell's death.

Stephen's connection with James Joyce makes it possible to view Stephen in retrospect as a character who might grow up and eventually write books that include a character with his own name. And yet within those books, Stephen never again comes as close to being the predicator of the character named Stephen Dedalus as in that moment when he remembers that he himself "had not died then," that it had been Parnell who had died and who could not now or ever make himself "appear again" as Stephen finds that he can make the little boy appear. If in "1904" Stephen could have written baby tuckoo's first memories and begun to follow them by writing the very pages that make Stephen the character he is, it is not in Stephen's mind to do so. In "1904" he is not imagining himself as a character in something he might write. It is only because James Joyce has written him that Stephen's making himself "appear again for a moment" can be read as self-generating. The character whose "birth" is coincident with Parnell's death would have been stillborn if it were not for a certain writer.

PARNELL'S "REBIRTH"

Stephen has had two "births." Only because he is "born" to himself as a character about whom certain things are predicable does he connect with the writer who gives "birth" to him in the predications of *A Portrait* and *Ulysses*. Because it occurs to Stephen to predicate certain things about a character named Stephen Dedalus, Stephen connects with James Joyce. Because it might not have occurred to Stephen to do such predicating if it had not been for Parnell's death, Stephen connects with Parnell. Lacking his connections with either of two people who were born, Stephen would not *be*. For Stephen to play at having had the one birth that any character plays at having had, two people had to have been born not just in play.

When Stephen is born to himself as a character, Parnell was only just then out of time. Though Joyce was obviously not out of time when he gave "birth" to Stephen's character, he was necessarily out of that particular time in his own past which he in some measure tries to make "appear again" by writing Stephen. Nine years after the birth that Stephen plays at having had, Parnell dies. More than twenty years after Parnell's death, Joyce makes some aspects of his own seemingly dead past "appear again," in Stephen, out of Parnell's ashes. Parnell is "reborn" in Stephen Dedalus. But this "rebirth" would be unrecognizable if Stephen were not also and simultaneously Joyce's victory over the "death" of his own past.

What Joyce wants to believe he has won back from his past is the chance to "appear again" for Ireland. It is only by "appearing" there that he can once again be a public thing for the aspiring re-public within which he, like Parnell, was no longer to be seen. Only if he "appears" for it may the community from which he had disappeared pass judgment on his service. Only insofar as he "appears again" for Ireland is James Joyce answerable for the words he left Ireland in order to write.

MURPHY

Not that within those words he has not supplied reasons enough for having left. Many of Joyce's characters are unjust, foolish, and devoted to their own ruin. As he understood them, his countrymen had indeed laid Parnell low. Whatever else might be said for and not against it, the Ireland that *Dubliners*, *A Portrait*, and *Ulysses* point to is an Ireland from which it would be prudent to disappear in favor of the relative privacy of exile. And yet while Joyce knew that expatriation had been the only acceptable course for his life, *Ulysses* is his way back home. While he was writing it, he obviously could not come back to Ireland and be twenty-two in 1904, the year he emigrated to the continent. What he could and did do was to write a book in which he spirits himself back to Dublin "1904" in the disguise of D. B. Murphy.

The evidence for connecting Murphy with Joyce is of two sorts. The first implicates Joyce's biography only insofar as *Ulysses* itself does. Just as the line "*Trieste-Zurich-Paris*, 1914–1921" (18: 1610–11) offers the information that James Joyce spent seven years writing a narrative that for June 16, 1904, alone brings him back to Ireland, so too does Murphy turn out to be a "doughty narrator" (16: 570) "of the here today and gone tomorrow type" (16: 1223–24) who says he has been away from Ireland "for seven years" (16: 421). Like Joyce, Murphy had disembarked for part of that time in a place called "Trieste" (16: 576). Tattooed on Murphy's chest along with the portrait of the artist is "the figure 16" (16: 675)—a figure that, on the night of the sixteenth day of the month in the sixteenth chapter of the book, he opens his shirt for all to see.[1]

The second kind of evidence becomes evidence only when it is brought together with biographical information recoverable from writ-

ing other than *Ulysses*. By the time Murphy speaks again after an eigh-
teen-page silence, Bloom had nearly forgotten him.

> —Give us a squint at that literature, grandfather, the ancient mari-
> ner put in, manifesting some natural impatience.
> —And welcome, answered the elderly party thus addressed. The
> sailor lugged out from a case he had a pair of greenish goggles which
> he very slowly hooked over his nose and both ears.
> —Are you bad in the eyes? the sympathetic personage like the
> townclerk queried.
> —Why, answered the seafarer with the tartan beard, who seem-
> ingly was a bit of a literary cove in his own small way, staring out of
> seagreen portholes as you might well describe them as, I uses gog-
> gles reading. (16: 1669–78)

A reader who knows no more about Joyce than that he had serious
trouble with his eyes might read this passage as a clincher, for it is in
the context of such trouble that Bloom himself comes closest to recognizing Murphy's stature in the world of books.

Through figures of speech, Bloom inadvertently replaces "Jamesy"
with "Murphy" as the name of the intelligence that narrates *Ulysses* as
a whole. Sleep, for Bloom, is "the arms of Morpheus" (16: 947–48).
When he changes it to "the arms of Murphy" (16: 1727), he has provided only half a clue to the narrator-general's name, for that half-clue
must be paired with his reading of Murphy as "Sinbad" (16: 858).
When it happens that Bloom's litany to "Sinbad the Sailor" (17: 2322)
takes him off to sleep at the end of chapter 17, he is literally "wrapped
in the arms of Murphy" in that he has consigned to the narrating Murphy the last of his seemingly autonomous thoughts.

It is quite all right with Jamesy that Bloom imply this transfer, since
Bloom's epithet for sleep is of course not Bloom's at all but rather
Jamesy's own. The words of chapter 16 are Jamesy's all-knowing disclosure of the words Bloom would write (but has not written) if he were to
act on his wish to become a prize-winning author for *Titbits* by penning
his experiences, let us say, in a cabman's shelter. Within this disclosure, Bloom reads Murphy as an "ancient mariner who sailed the ocean
seas to draw the long bow" (16: 844), to tell the tall tale: as the ancient
mariner of the "Rime" is to Coleridge, so is Murphy—and not
Jamesy—to James Joyce. Jamesy's bid to an impersonal place within the
compound reality *Ulysses*-Jamesy is thereby reinforced. As Joyce is to
Coleridge and Murphy to the ancient mariner, so is the "chronicle"
Ulysses-Jamesy to the "Rime" itself. When Murphy replaces Jamesy as
the name of the narrator, Jamesy is purified of those personal aspects
inherent in any name that so much as *sounds* as if it refers to a person.

Through Bloom's agency, therefore, "Jamesy" is the name for all that is impersonal in the narrator of *Ulysses*, "Murphy" for all that is personal. I believe the two names are interchangeable at every point within the narrative. Jamesy has Murphy always at hand to relieve him of any sullying traces of the personal, traces that, because they have the character Murphy as their auspice, can be read as having an acceptable place. As it is not with Jamesy, who does not so much as substitute for a person, it is all right with Murphy that his connection with James Joyce be read.

WHOPPERS

Though Bloom doubts that the stories Murphy tells are "genuine" (16: 822), he concedes that "the lies a fellow told about himself couldn't probably hold a proverbial candle to the wholesale whoppers other fellows coined about him" (16: 845–47). A few months before beginning to write the chapter in which Murphy figures, Joyce wrote to his brother and asked him to "contradict" the stories that were circulating about him—that he was the founder of dada, a cocaine addict, and "a violent bolshevik propagandist," that he was writing *Ulysses* in conformity with "a prearranged pro-German code."[2] One story had it that he had made his last trip to Dublin as a spy for the Austrian Foreign Office. It may have been this one that got him into the spirit of the thing, for after he had written a chapter in which Murphy is a successful disguise for a man whose business is reported to be espionage, Joyce no longer wanted to silence the "whoppers" about himself: "a nice collection could be made of the legends about me,"[3] he wrote to Harriet Shaw Weaver in prefacing for her his collection of them. Is it on a mission of reconnaisance that D. B. Murphy, a/k/a James Joyce, leaves the cabman's shelter and walks to the left very nearly but not altogether out of Bloom's view? After some minutes, Bloom "could by straining just perceive him . . . gaping up at the piers and girders of the Loop line rather out of his depth as of course it was all radically altered since his last visit and greatly improved" (16: 932–35).

Or it may be that if Murphy is in Dublin to glean what one thing or another looks like, he is on a mission not for Austria but rather (and only vicariously) for someone who again and again needed to check the details he was writing against a city he had convinced himself was absolutely closed to him. Joyce had decided that in chapter 17 his protagonist would find himself keyless. Wanting neither to face Molly just now nor to have her face Stephen at less than her best, Bloom "climbed over the area railings" at number 7 Eccles Street, "grasped two points at the lower union of rails and stiles, lowered his body gradually by its length of five feet nine inches and a half" (17: 84–87), and thereby established a relationship with a part of the world that Joyce very much needed to but believed he could not go see for himself. How much of Dublin would there be between the bottom of Bloom's soles and the pavement below? So much that the character named Bloom would not use this particular "stratagem" for getting in?

Whereas the impersonal Jamesy would of course know the answer as he knows all things, it is a different matter for the person named James Joyce. "Is it possible," he wrote his Aunt Josephine, "for an ordinary person to climb over the area railings of no 7 Eccles Street, either from the path or the steps, lower himself down from the lowest part of the railings till his feet are within 2 feet or 3 of the ground and drop unhurt?"[4] His aunt was not always quick to do the legwork and then reply. He needed to know from her what objects Bloom might have been able to make out in the twilight. More than a month after his first request for that information, he wrote her to ask "whether there are trees (and of what kind) behind the Star of the Sea church in Sandymount visible from the shore."[5] Both impatient and persuaded that the help he needed would not come in time, Joyce concealed his own less-than-perfect memory by having the confusion be Bloom's. "Were those nightclouds there all the time?" Bloom wonders. "Looks like a phantom ship. No. Wait. Trees are they? An optical illusion. Mirage. Land of the setting sun this. Homerule sun setting in the southeast. My native land, goodnight" (13: 1077–80).

SOUNDING THE LIE OF THE LAND

Because he substitutes for Joyce's wish to expedite the writing of *Ulysses*, because he is Joyce's playful portrait of himself as foreign spy, Murphy connects with Joyce in a way that is personal and largely buoyant. Part of the disguise's buoyancy is how unlike Joyce it is. Murphy is so unlike Joyce, in fact, that it may be argued that he is not a disguise for Joyce since Joyce was free to write Murphy in such a way that the connection between the two could not be missed. But while the counterargument that a disguise must be a good one if it is to work strikes me as specious, I will resort to it if only because the evidence for connecting Murphy with Joyce seems both unignorable and comic in a way that is perfectly in keeping with *Ulysses* as a whole. If for the seven years it took him to write *Ulysses* Joyce was figuratively "all at sea" (16: 380), it is as funny to imagine him literally spending most of that time on a boat as imagining him having Murphy's interests and manners of speech.

There are other elements in the connection that are more personal still if somewhat less fun. Murphy dramatizes Joyce's almost solemn desire that *Ulysses* be read as the most political of books. Insofar as this desire infiltrates *Ulysses* itself, Murphy is an exhibit of Joyce's restlessness to be for a community of people.

Italo Svevo has written that Joyce said to him, "It is dangerous to leave one's country, but still more dangerous to go back to it, for then your fellow-countrymen, if they can, will drive a knife into your heart."[6] Joyce's biographers report that after he left it in 1912 he never returned to Ireland. In a note he appended to the proofs of Herbert Gorman's *James Joyce*, he explained why. His "vivid memory of the incident at Castlecomer when quicklime was flung into the eyes of their dying leader, Parnell" was reason enough for him to stay away: he didn't want "a similar unfortunate occurrence to interfere with the composition of the book" he was writing.[7] "One morning you would open the paper, the cabman affirmed, and read: *Return of Parnell*" (16: 1297–98). "Highly unlikely," Bloom thinks, "and, even supposing, he thought return highly inadvisable, all things considered" (16: 1310–12). For "as regards return," "you were a lucky dog if they didn't set the terrier at you directly you got back" (16: 1339–40). "A more prudent course" would be "to sound the lie of the land first" (16: 1349–51). Proceeding with the imposture of "let X equal my right name" (16: 1636) and in disguise, "D. B. Murphy" (16: 452), as an alias for Parnell, or for Joyce, or for both at once, may be sounding the lie of the land.

Were either to return, Parnell might need such prudence. But would Joyce? "Highly unlikely." Joyce's written words were not so incendiary that the Irish would have mobilized to silence him if he had given them the chance. But while he must have known that his impact on them hardly compared with Parnell's, Joyce declares himself answerable for the comparison not only in his note to Gorman's biography but also through Murphy's relationship to the character named Stephen Dedalus.

WHAT STEPHEN IS CHARGED WITH

When Shakespeare wrote *Hamlet*, Stephen had said, "he was and felt himself the father of all his race" (9: 868–69). Stephen wants to write something that will qualify him as just such a father, but he is currently suffering "the inevitable procrastination which often tripped up a too much fêted prince of good fellows" (16: 1858–59). Stephen's reading of *Hamlet* is his way of prodding himself out of the role of the would-be-writer-son and into that of the writer-father. Murphy updates the analogies in Stephen's reading. As King Hamlet is to the prince, the disguised but mature James Joyce is to Stephen. The son in *Ulysses* cannot be expected to hear his father's charge to him. The charge is that Stephen write *Ulysses*, the written words of *Ulysses* are themselves that charge, a charge so updated that its words were not readable until Stephen had stopped being Stephen and had spent seventeen years being the person who has written *Ulysses*. Bloom thinks that however "inadvisable" it would be for you to return to Ireland if you were Parnell, "you had to come back. That haunting sense kind of drew you. To show the understudy in the title role how to" (16: 1331–33). To show him "how to," the father must return from 1921 with what in 1904 has not yet been made to appear. Returning to Ireland both as Parnell and as Joyce, Murphy is that "father of all his race" whom Stephen has charged himself to become.

Between the hours of one and two in the morning on June 17, 1904, Murphy augurs that Stephen can no more fail to become the James Joyce of *Ulysses* than *Ulysses* can now be said never to have been written. In "a retrospective sort of arrangement" (11:798), "a host of things and coincidences" (16: 826) declare that Murphy is at once both Stephen Dedalus and James Joyce, "the son consubstantial with the father" (9: 481) but in an altogether different way than Stephen imagines when he speaks that phrase. "—Curious coincidence" (16: 414), Bloom remarks after Murphy had "singled out" Stephen "for attention in particular" (16: 368), had asked Stephen his name and if he knew someone named Simon Dedalus, an "all Irish" (16: 383) sharpshooter who was touring the world ten years before with Hengler's Royal Circus. There are other coincidences. "Kinch, the knifeblade" (1: 55), Mulligan says, is the name that best fits Stephen's character: "quite in keeping with his character," Murphy produces "a dangerouslooking claspknife" (16: 578–79). During the years in which he has become father, Murphy has improved slightly on the son's pointed negligence in cleaning and clothing their one body. "—The unclean bard makes a point of washing once a month" (1: 475), Mulligan says of Stephen; "I must get a wash tomorrow or next day" (16: 670–71), says Murphy. Stephen would look much better if he would wear the trousers Mulligan offers him, which he refuses: "Them are his trousers I've on me" (16: 655), Murphy says of this ex-friend Antonio, who has left him on his "*ownio*" (16: 703) just as the "gay betrayer" (1: 405) Mulligan has now left Stephen.

Stephen had foretold his meeting with Murphy.

—As we, or mother Dana, weave and unweave our bodies, Stephen said, from day to day, their molecules shuttled to and fro, so does the artist weave and unweave his image. And as the mole on my right breast is where it was when I was born, though all my body has been woven of new stuff time after time, so through the ghost of the unquiet father the image of the unliving son looks forth. In the intense instant of imagination, when the mind, Shelley says, is a fading coal, that which I was is that which I am and that which in possibility I may come to be. So in the future, the sister of the past, I may see myself as I sit here now but by reflection from that which then I shall be. (9: 376–85)

In 1904, Murphy is the ghost of the unquiet father insofar as he turns up in the action of *Ulysses* seventeen years before the James Joyce of *Ulysses* could have. The image of the unliving son looks forth through Murphy insofar as Murphy promises that the Stephen of *Ulysses* will in seventeen years be written. It is only as words that Stephen lives. When he was at last constituted as words, when he was written, that which Stephen was became that which he is, his imagined body having been woven of new word-stuff time after time during the succession of days that separated character-as-writer-to-be from writer. In 1921, in a book that plays at being 1904, Stephen plays at wanting to become the father of his race by wanting to write the "postcreation" that is *Ulysses*. Insofar as the writer of *Ulysses* is that which in possibility Stephen plays at wanting to become, James Joyce knows word for word what Stephen's future holds. Stephen's ship will come in. For by the time he is Stephen it already has.

STEPHEN'S SHIP

In the clear light of meridian, on the strand, Stephen picks "dry snot" (3: 500) from his nostril and deposits it carefully on a ledge of rock. Worrying that someone "behind" (3: 502) him may have spotted him doing this, he turns to look and sees "a threemaster, her sails brailed up on the crosstrees, homing, upstream, silently moving, a silent ship" (3: 504–5), bringing the ghostly Murphy home to what Stephen plays at wanting to begin to write in ten years. "Ten years," Mulligan says of Stephen that afternoon.

He is going to write something in ten years.
—Seems a long way off, Haines said, thoughtfully lifting his spoon. Still, I shouldn't wonder if he did after all.
He tasted a spoonful from the creamy cone of his cup.
—This is real Irish cream I take it, he said with forbearance. I don't want to be imposed on.
Elijah, skiff, light crumpled throwaway, sailed eastward by flanks of ships and trawlers, amid an archipelago of corks, beyond new

Wapping street past Benson's ferry, and by the threemasted schoo-
ner *Rosevean* from Bridgwater with bricks. (10: 1089–99)

The words "*Rosevean* from Bridgwater with bricks" make this first appearance in what may be read as one of Jamesy's past-tense sentences.
Later, the same words become the signature of James Joyce. "—We
come up this morning eleven o'clock," says Murphy. "The threemaster
Rosevean from Bridgwater with bricks. I shipped to get over" (16: 450–
51). The signature implies that *Ulysses* has realized what the son plays
at hoping for in 1904. Though Stephen might not have, though the
ship of his hopes for himself might well have perished by that time,
Ulysses implies that Stephen is substituting for a person who will begin
to write *Ulysses* in ten years. Not until Joyce-Stephen-Murphy has written it can the character who plays the artist as a young man look over
his shoulder and see that "homing" ship from whose foredeck all his
thoughts and actions are inscribed. Once *Ulysses* is written, Stephen
will have acceded to that very place within the father-son-ghost trinity
he plays at wanting.

"*Von der Sirenen Listigkeit / Tun die Poeten dichten*" (16: 1815–16),
Stephen sings for Bloom toward the end of the sixteenth chapter.
"From the Sirens' craftiness / Poets make poems." Not surprisingly, the
words of the song accord closely with Stephen's reading of Shakespeare
and therefore with the scenario for himself that he will later have to
revise: fated to fall to the mortal nature that calls to him in a feminine
voice, the writer aspires to inscribe his immortal freedom within the
heart of what has bound him over to destruction. What is surprising,
on the other hand, is the suggestion implicit in Stephen's misremem-
bering of one of the subsequent lines. In the song itself, the sailors are
lured into the sea and then lulled to sleep by the sweetness of the Sirens' singing, "The ship is brought into misfortune / And all becomes
evil."[8] But instead of "*das Schiff in Unglück bringt,*" Stephen sings "*Und
alle Schiffe brücken*" (16: 1884), all ships are bridged; between these
ships, as between Stephen and Bloom and maybe other mortals who
talk to one another in the sea of the world, the links that preserve life
are surprisingly in place and doing their work. One of these links is a
book that Stephen will mature to write. Like the *Rosevean*, *Ulysses* is
the vehicle for Stephen's uninsurable voyaging as a writer. Like the ship
in Stephen's altered version of the song he sings for Bloom, *Ulysses* has
been brought to safe harbor without Stephen knowing that it has.

Nor is this Stephen's only accidental transposing from a meaning of
ruin to one of both promise and well-being. Just before he had begun
singing, he had described for Bloom "exquisite variations . . . on an air
Youth here has End by Jans Pieter Sweelinck" (16: 1810–11). Whereas

Sweelinck's song means unequivocally that the youth "must perish / In Death's conflict and struggle," Stephen's rendering of the title can as readily mean that from this point foward, maturation has begun.

RESPONSIBILITY

That Murphy-Joyce comes back to Ireland does not in itself prove that Joyce thought Ireland worth coming back to. There may have been scores to settle there, or his days elsewhere just tedious enough that even the bad old haunts would have offered an amusing break.

But between the leaving and the coming back there is usually time to weigh and be affected by the irreversible consequences of having left. "And then coming back was the worst thing you ever did because it went without saying you would feel out of place as things always moved with the times" (16: 1401–3). By staying away, you do not have to face how out of place you feel and may the more easily delude yourself into thinking that you are absolved. To "appear again" (P, 93), on the other hand, is to respond, to promise to do for . . . , even if only for yourself as a break from boredom, even if in revenge for wrongs suffered, but also possibly in atonement for obligations unmet, for responsibilities that are nonetheless yours for having left. Bloom tells Stephen that every country, "our own distressful included, has the government it deserves" (16: 1097–98). But if the Irish have earned their own distress, each who has stayed and earned it has at the very least and however tacitly declared himself answerable for Ireland. James Joyce the émigré can make no such declaration. On the eve of his "homecoming" after seven years away, Murphy-Joyce is "palpably a bit peeved" (16: 1012–13) if not also shamed by the keeper's advice to every Irishman: "stay in the land of your birth and work for Ireland and live for Ireland. Ireland, Parnell said, could not spare a single one of her sons" (16: 1007–9).

And yet if Ireland has had to do without James Joyce, it has also had to do without Parnell. If Joyce violated Parnell's axiom by leaving Ireland, Parnell himself had violated it by having died.

> —Let us go round by the chief's grave, Hynes said. We have time.
> —Let us, Mr Power said. They turned to the right, following their slow thoughts. With awe Mr Power's blank voice spoke:
> —Some say he is not in that grave at all. That the coffin was filled with stones. That one day he will come again. Hynes shook his head.
> —Parnell will never come again, he said. He's there, all that was mortal of him. Peace to his ashes. (6: 919–27)

If Joyce cannot revoke his own expatriation, neither can Parnell return from the grave to lead his disappointing brother "out of the house of commons by the arm" (8: 518–19). Hynes's words in Glasneven Cemetery apply only to "all that was mortal" of Parnell, not to "his spirit." But with the access of years since he wrote his elegy, Hynes has become much less ready to imagine that Parnell's spirit will "rise." Requiescats are settlements with the dead.

AVERTING LAST TERMS

"Once you are dead you are dead" (6: 677). Thereafter, you may not intervene willingly in the affairs of the living. It is possible, if unlikely, though, that you may serve them still. If they bring you forward into their time by remembering what you did and said, you may be made to "appear again for a moment" (*P*, 93) as if in answer to their call. Your example might be just unsettling enough to remind them that "room for improvement all round there certainly is" (16: 1096) and that the little they can do to help reduce that room is worth doing. But while to that degree you may remain responsive and even responsible for the living, whether or not they remember you is beyond your power to will. "People talk about you a bit: forget you," Bloom thinks about the dead. "Even Parnell. Ivy day dying out" (6: 853–55).

Joyce is to Parnell as expatriation is to death. Once you have left Ireland never to return, you have left Ireland never to return. Joyce's having left Ireland forever so that he could become a writer was effectively the "death" of his power to intervene willingly in the affairs of the Irish. Though it was not also necessarily the "death" of his responsibility for them, his responsibility for them survives only insofar as what he wrote is read.

Connected with each, Stephen connects Parnell and Joyce. Whenever Parnell "appears again" for memory, his death is not the last term in a sequence that ends with his being forever "lost and forgotten somewhere in the universe" (*P*, 93). Whenever Joyce's version of his own past "appears again" as Stephen Dedalus for a reader of A *Portrait* and *Ulysses*, Joyce's expatriation is not the last term in a sequence that ends with his being forever "lost and forgotten" in that part of the universe called Ireland. Death and expatriation may but need not be last terms in a sequence that is responsibility itself. Joyce wants to believe of his relationship with Ireland that the only sequence that matters is a sequence that proceeds uninterruptedly from Parnell to Stephen-as-James-Joyce-at-age-nine. Only if the Stephen who then goes on to write *Ulysses* is an unworthy successor to Parnell has James Joyce defected and failed Ireland.

"LET US CHANGE THE SUBJECT"

As Joyce dicloses them in *Ulysses*, his hopes as one of Ireland's indispensible sons are a revision of Stephen's hopes for himself as the father of his race. If the mature James Joyce has succeeded Parnell, as he hopes to have done, he has done so along a line that can be charted through Stephen's still-to-be-revised assessments of importance and belonging to and work.

"I call that patriotism," Bloom tells Stephen. "*Ubi patria . . . vita bene*. Where you can live well, the sense is, if you work" (16: 1138–40). When Stephen says "—Count me out" (16: 1148), Bloom understands him to be saying he will not work. "—I mean, of course, the other hastened to affirm, work in the widest possible sense. Also literary labour not merely for the kudos of the thing" (16: 1152–53). As a member of Stephen's political community, Bloom is willing to compare different and perhaps even incomparable kinds of work, the coefficient for his comparisons being the interests of the community itself.

> You have every bit as much right to live by your pen in pursuit of your philosophy as the peasant has. What? You both belong to Ireland, the brain and the brawn. Each is equally important.
> —You suspect, Stephen retorted with a sort of a half laugh, that I may be important because I belong to the *faubourg Saint Patrice* called Ireland for short.
> —I would go a step farther, Mr Bloom insinuated.
> —But I suspect, Stephen interrupted, that Ireland must be important because it belongs to me.
> —What belongs, queried Mr Bloom bending, fancying he was perhaps under some misapprehension. Excuse me. Unfortunately, I didn't catch the latter portion. What was it you . . . ?
> Stephen, patently crosstempered, repeated and shoved aside his mug of coffee or whatever you like to call it none too politely, adding:
> —We can't change the country. Let us change the subject. (16: 1157–71)

Though he is simply if "none too politely" letting Bloom know that he has heard enough from him about Ireland, Stephen's "let us change the subject" is an especially loaded sentence. Ireland belongs to him, he thinks, because he will discover important things to say about it, because the words he goes on to write about the Irish will make them "subject" to what he would forever have them be. The Irish will be important, Stephen thinks, only when he has worked such changes on them in his writing that they become unchangeably his—something he is sure they will never be so long as he belongs in any way to them.[9] Rather than being for them, rather than belonging to them in such a way that he might be changed by them insofar as he is subject to their call, Stephen characterizes himself as the one who will do the calling. "You have spoken of the past and its phantoms," he had said. "Why think of them? If I call them into life across the waters of Lethe will not the poor ghosts troop to my call? Who supposes it? I, Bous Stephanoumenos, bullockbefriending bard, am lord and giver of their life" (14: 1112–16). No longer subject to one another in community, subject only to Stephen, those who have been born must remain "poor ghosts" until Stephen lends them changeless importance by writing them into being.

And he will write them according to that scenario for his own success that he mistakenly believes he has at last hit upon with his reading of Shakespeare. The differences between Stephen's and Joyce's respective exemplars pivot around the word "subject." Whereas Joyce's Parnell had worked toward a community within which its subjects might have a more adequate if always necessarily imperfect relationship with their world, Stephen's Shakespeare meets himself in all other people and then subjects them to the perfection of his own image. With Shakespeare as his model, Stephen plans to write a "postcreation" that will perfect the merely created world by liberating each soul from its unchosen birth within a race or nation. The only call Stephen proposes to answer is the call to replace Ireland as well as all other inconstant communities with "the word that shall not pass away" and shall be his.

A child is conceived. With his birth, as Stephen says, he "brings pain, divides affection, increases care. He is a new male: his growth is his father's decline, his youth his father's envy, his friend his father's enemy" (9: 855–57). Stephen means to engender no such alien but rather and only such sons as he will write into being either as characters that substitute for persons within the story he writes or as readers who hear their father's word in the one way it is meant and are therefore of one substance with it forever. Written, these sons will be of a country so perfect that any "room for improvement" will already have been eliminated through the perfecting of his word. "Because it was a task for a superior intelligence to substitute other more acceptable phenomena in place of the less acceptable phenomena to be removed," Stephen's superior intelligence will have empowered him to father timeless-because-substance-filled characters and readers in place of persons who are born to die.

"SILENCE, EXILE, AND CUNNING"

There is such a thing as time because persons who are born to die usually find from moment to moment that they are not ready to.[10] "It's the moment you feel," Bloom thinks about any person who is dying. "Must be damned unpleasant. Can't believe it at first. Mistake must be: someone else. Try the house opposite. Wait, I wanted to. I haven't yet. Then darkened deathchamber" (6: 843–46). Because death must be damned unpleasant and because it takes time, Stephen proposes to write a "postcreation" within which timeless characters and readers are substituted for persons who have time. Death may thereby be not so much postponed, as it is by persons who have time, but rather forsworn, abjured, given the lie to, as one wants to give the lie to any unpleasant thing to which one finds oneself subject. Without having asked him if he wanted to be born to die, Stephen's natural progenitors "clasped and sundered, did the coupler's will." Without having asked him if he wanted to belong to it, the community into which he was born obliged him to be for its people. "A redress God grant" (14: 214). Meaning to awaken from what he believes are its nightmarish errors, Stephen forswears the time he has been made subject to. He refuses to serve. This refusal is a refusal to remain in time—a refusal to remain, that is, in the spatial sense, as if to remain in time were also to remain at home.

"Silence, exile, and cunning" (*P*, 247) is Stephen's formula, not Joyce's. Had it been Joyce's, he would have been much less eager to suggest that the time it will take Stephen to become the James Joyce of *Ulysses* is time that succeeds without interruption from Joyce's own unchosen and undeclinable responsbility for a people he had only seemed to have left. Had Joyce found that the completedness of what he has written was exactly what he wanted, the writing itself would imply that the person who had once been subject to time and home had been consummately absorbed and transported. *Ulysses* would read as if it were a confirmed exile's luscious recompense for having had to suffer exactly those spatial and temporal determinations Stephen wants desperately to escape. Because *Ulysses* does not read that way to me at all, I have deliberately skirted phrases in which Joyce's "prescience" about Stephen's "future" blends suspiciously into claims about the future he foresees for himself, a future from which he seems to be looking back on history as if from a point outside it. Because these claims may be read as saying that Joyce wrote *Ulysses* so that he too, with Jamesy, might be out of time, I must take them up now. If James Joyce wrote

Ulysses so that he might be with Jamesy, then Joyce is not to be distinguished from Stephen's "artist" who, "like the God of the creation, remains within or behind or beyond or above his handiwork, invisible, refined out of existence, indifferent, paring his fingernails" (*P*, 215).

BLOOM AS UNWITTING ELIJAH

Like the God of the Old Testament, James Joyce has sent into the handiwork of *Ulysses* a prophet who quietly proclaims that Stephen will become the savior of his people by writing *Ulysses*. "Behold I will send you Elijah," read the last words of Malachi, the last prefiguring book of the Bible, "before the coming of the great and dreadful day of the Lord: And he shall turn the heart of the fathers to the children, and the heart of the children to their fathers, lest I come and smite the earth with a curse." Malachi Mulligan's last words in direct discourse call Haines's attention to Parnell's brother and report Stephen's plan to write something in ten years: later in this same section of the tenth chapter, Stephen's incoming ship is passed by "Elijah, skiff," the "light crumpled throwaway" (10: 1096) that "ben Bloom Elijah" (12: 1916) had dropped into the Liffey two chapters before.

Hallucination is Bloom's only access to his role as seer. In Nighttown, after John Howard Parnell has introduced him as "successor to my famous brother!" (15: 1514), Bloom tells the masses that they "shall ere long enter into the golden city which is to be, the new Bloomusalem in the Nova Hibernia of the future" (15: 1543–45). A Voice asks him if he is "the Messiah ben Joseph or ben David" (15: 1834). Though Bloom answers "darkly," he has already been shouted down by The Mob—"Lynch him! Roast him! He's as bad as Parnell was" (15: 1762)—and so he is therefore the Messiah ben Joseph who will be killed by the enemies of Israel after heralding the new world. While Bloom does not know that is what he is doing, and whatever else his relationship with Ireland implies, he has been cast as oracle to the Advent of the Messiah ben David—Stephen-Dedalus-as-James-Joyce-at-age-twenty-two—who, once he has written *Ulysses*, will be the agent of Ireland's rebirth.

Since Joyce himself is manipulating so immodest a claim, the prophecy is understandably offhand, vague, very nearly ignorable. If it were any more direct than it is it could be read as being shamelessly absurd. To be aware, as Bloom is, that Stephen is "far and away the pick of the bunch" (16: 1477–78) is hardly to equate him with "Erin's uncrowned king" (16: 1496). Only as an unspoken parenthesis to something he is saying does it occur to Bloom that his companion resembles Parnell. "A more prudent course, as Bloom said to the not over effusive, in fact like the distinguished personage under discussion beside him, would have been to sound the lie of the land first" (16: 1349–51). Stephen is "like" Parnell in that he is "not over effusive." But what Bloom is intending as resemblance turns out to be grammatical identity. The "personage . . . beside" Bloom is Stephen, the "personage under discussion beside him" Parnell, Stephen and Parnell forced through Bloom's inadvertent truncation into the one "personage." Just as involuntary is Bloom's yoking of Stephen and Parnell within a single, repeated phrase: Stephen can serve Ireland through "literary labour, not merely for the kudos of the thing" (16: 1153), but for a decent wage; Parnell, "a gentleman born," worked for his country "more for the kudos of the thing than anything else" (16: 1518–20).

Bloom's forecast is the quieter for being slightly misleading. Because he is equally oblivious to his role as prophet and as "hero" in a book, he at first directs Stephen toward a course of action that would preclude that book's being written: he tells Stephen that he should support himself as a journalist. When it comes to him that Stephen might find such writing a compromise of his interests, he hatches his "utopian plan" for Stephen's "vocal career." If he could find the right "backerup"—"a big *if* however" (16: 1856–57)—Stephen could become the darling of Dublin concertgoers, he could command "a stiff figure" (16: 1855) for each of his few performances and therefore "have heaps of time to practise literature in his spare moments when desirous of so doing" (16: 1860–61).

HAVING NEVER REALLY LEFT

In contrast to Bloom, Joyce himself can only be on the mark as he frames what lies ahead for Stephen over the next seventeen years. Much of this "foresight" about what Stephen will do as a writer is of course mere hindsight about what he himself had done. Insofar as Stephen is a portrait of himself at age twenty-two, Joyce knows that Stephen will begin to write *Ulysses* "in ten years" and that he will complete it seven years after that. Joyce also knows at least one thing that will happen to Stephen *after Ulysses* is written: when Stephen thinks the words "Shakespeare and company" (9: 729), he has had the uncanny good luck of hitting upon the name of *Ulysses'* publisher.

But Joyce does not stop there. *Ulysses* implies a future for Stephen that does not stop with what by 1921 was Joyce's past. While Joyce was still writing it, he was assured that *Ulysses* would be published, and by whom: what he could only predict, on the other hand, was how *Ulysses* would be received over the long haul. He is therefore hinting at his own and not just Stephen's future when he hints that *Ulysses* will turn out to be a classic. "Our national epic has yet to be written" (9: 309), Stephen hears someone say in the national epic Stephen himself will write. "The most beautiful book that has come out of our country in my time. One thinks of Homer" (9: 1164–65), says Mulligan, innocently presaging that Stephen will provide this most beautiful book with the Homeric bearing of *Ulysses*.

Quiet or not, therefore, the proclamation stands: *Ulysses* is what Ireland has been waiting for. Joyce means more by this claim than that *Ulysses* will be showered with adulation, some of it trickling down to the Ireland *Ulysses* is ostensibly "about." He is claiming more, even, than that Ireland will ultimately welcome the book to her bosom as if welcoming the return of a loved if vagabond son. More boastfully still, and as if immune to the indeterminacies that threaten mere prediction, Joyce is claiming that *Ulysses* is already a political and not just a literary success.

What intrigues me most about Joyce's claim is that it declares him subject both to Jamesy's timelessness and to time. Only if it succeeds politically has Joyce continued to serve Ireland with no time out. But since he is claiming both that *Ulysses* is already that service and that it succeeds only later when its readers find that it serves, Joyce has taken such radical liberties with the chronological relationship of present to future that he can "appear" only to have been out of time and not in it. In the one sequence of consequence for Ireland, Joyce's claim goes, his own expatriation is preceded and not followed by the reception of *Ulysses* as the "national epic." Since leaving Ireland was what he had to do to write the national epic, James Joyce had never really left!

TWO PHRASES

Stephen, too, never leaves. By the time Joyce has paid service to Ireland by writing *Ulysses*, Stephen's "*non serviam*" (15: 4228) has not yet led him off to permanent exile on the Continent. It never does. *Ulysses* ends before it can. Unlike James Joyce, Stephen does not have to leave Ireland in order to become Parnell "reborn." To be the agent of Ireland's rebirth in the tradition of Parnell, all Stephen has to do is to be written exactly as he is. It does not matter if the young man who must himself do this writing seems in "1904" to be a political cripple. For the "appearance" of his crippling egocentrism is at most peripheral within the "national epic" a matured Stephen will already have written by 1921. While Stephen can only "read the skies" (9: 939) to discover whether or not his still-unwritten art will make him a worthy successor to "Saxon Shakespeare" (9: 44), Joyce has already written in both *A Portrait* and *Ulysses* that Stephen's spiritual line of descent is through Ireland's Parnell. As that line cannot fail Stephen, so too has Stephen

not failed to follow it. Having by 1921 already heard and then responded to Bloom's instruction and to the inaudible directives person-
ified in the paternal ghost who calls himself D. B. Murphy, Stephen
will have become the writer-father of *Ulysses*.

Stephen therefore dramatizes Joyce's dependence on the writtenness
that is Jamesy's very being. I read Murphy as James Joyce's "return in
space through irreversible time" (17: 2026–27). That space, as I have
insisted throughout, is Jamesy's. It is the space and spacing of the
printed page, of the written words without which Murphy could not be
read. Because Jamesy's space is a presencing, a presented presence, an
eternal now, it eludes time's irreversibility, it allows James Joyce to return from 1921 to 1904 with what should be enough to put Stephen's
tormenting self-doubt to rest if only he could do what no mere person
can, which is to read a book he has not yet written but will write.
Across the "reversible space" (17: 2026) of page 509, Stephen speaks
with D. B. Murphy, who is at once Stephen's future self and the rebirth
of Parnell.

In Stephen's timeless character as it coalesces with the oafishly disguised but paternal Murphy, Joyce has written what is not possible in
time: the coalescence, beyond time, of Parnell and Joyce, two sons of
Ireland who, because they were born to be for persons and to die, were
subject to time. With his death in 1891, the mortal Parnell was no
longer able to will the regeneration of Ireland's naturally born sons and
daughters. With his expatriation in 1904, the mortal James Joyce was
no longer able both to stay in the land of his birth and to do the writing
he felt called upon to do. But whereas Parnell and Joyce were through
working for Ireland, the never-to-be-biologically-born, never-to-die
Stephen has by "1904" not yet even begun the phoenixlike revitaliza-
tion of Parnell's immortal legacy within the hearts of those who cannot
fail to be served by the immortal and national epic Stephen cannot fail
to write. Because Stephen has not yet begun to write it so that it may
serve, *Ulysses* is the "Nova Hibernia of the future." But that future has
already arrived since its past-tense sentences are as incontrovertibly
present from page to page as is Jamesy himself.

Two phrases: *Ulysses* is already the Nova Hibernia of the future;
"room for improvement all round there certainly is." Since both are
incontrovertibly present, both phrases must and do maintain a parity.
As their reader, though, I find myself wanting one of the two to yield
to the other if only in the interests of sense. If the Nova Hibernia of
the future has arrived for good and all, then room for improvement all
round there certainly is not. Jamesy would have it be a standoff between the two phrases. If it is to happen at all, one of the two must be
made to give way. It can be made to do so only by a reader who has
time: and Jamesy is perfectly indifferent to such a beast.

USE

As I read *Ulysses*, Joyce would have the first of these phrases yield to the second, would have it that way because he wants *Ulysses* to be more than his "usylessly unreadable Blue Book of Eccles" (*FW*, 179). As I said earlier, I think Joyce believes that *Ulysses* is readable only if it manages at the same time to be useful. How it might turn out to be that, he knows, is none of his business. His part in it was over when, as a condition of his making *Ulysses* public, he determined that he had used up all "room for improvement" within the book. Thereafter, only time would tell whether or not *Ulysses* would perform the miracle of helping the Irish improve their country.

Between his death and 1904, time had told that Parnell had to be remembered since he could not be replaced.[11] "Parnell," Bloom remembers. "Arthur Griffith is a squareheaded fellow but he has no go in him for the mob" (8: 462–63). "You must have a certain fascination" (8: 462) to command at Westminster a Home Rule Party of eighty-five as Parnell had done. To remember Parnell is not to require that "improvement" come in the exact form it had promised to: to remember him is instead to pursue Ireland's self-determination through altogether different means.[12] "So anyhow when I got back they were at it ding-dong, John Wyse saying it was Bloom gave the ideas for Sinn Fein to Griffith to put in his paper all kinds of jerrymandering, packed juries and swindling the taxes off of the government and appointing consuls all over the world to walk about selling Irish industries" (12: 1573–77). And just as 1904 calls not for parliamentarians but for canny separatists, later times will call for other persons still.

If *Ulysses* is to be of use to the Irish, it must help its readers identify room for improvement and then make beneficial changes within a continuing succession of Irelands. Just as those changes will vary according to the Ireland of the time, so too will they vary in communities other than Ireland. Because there is room for improvement not only in Ireland but all round, in any community, what that improvement will be and how it can best be effected must remain as far outside Joyce's ken as how *Ulysses* will be read. Joyce's most important difference from Stephen is this: he accepts, as Stephen does not, that what his book comes to is for persons other than himself to say. Jamesy's authorial imperiousness is paradoxically what Stephen must be purged of if, years after 1904, he is to mature and write both Jamesy and *Ulysses*. Joyce's construction of Jamesy is at once precisely the written transcendence of biology and time that Stephen seeks and the unrelenting critique of that transcendence that I have described. For Joyce to level such a critique both at Stephen's immature aspirations and at Jamesy may seem to imply that Joyce is somehow "beyond" Jamesy himself and thereby the more imperious of the two. But as the constructor of Jamesy, Joyce is not so much beyond Jamesy (who, in his omniscience, is above and beyond all things) as other than Jamesy insofar as Joyce is a person who was born to time and Jamesy is a series of timeless phrases. While Joyce did what he could to be the least forgiving reader of the phrases he wrote, while the quality of *Ulysses* depends in large measure on the degree to which he scrutinized its phrases as if with an intelligence altogether different from his own, he knew that he could not come to his book as if he were a person other than himself.

So why does he claim, in however furtive a way, that *Ulysses* is just what the country needs? If he is to be distinguished from Jamesy and the immature Stephen because he turns his words loose on the vicissitudes of time, if he is much the less imperious and appropriative than Jamesy or Stephen, why does he allow Stephen to be recognized as the redeemer, *Ulysses* as redemption? If I am right that Joyce is declaring himself subject to the "impredictable" (17: 465), if he is saying he can know neither how *Ulysses* will be read nor how it will serve, why not cut his losses, why not at the very least divide what he cannot know instead of going double or nothing? Why urge its readers to compare with work Parnell had done the work *Ulysses* may never do? Why not settle for the much safer bet that *Ulysses* will succeed as art?

Why if not *preposterously* to be turning backside to the front in carnivalesque exposure? The writer in the person could have no assurance that what he had stopped writing in 1921 would be for other people. Perhaps he had done no more in writing *Ulysses* than to present his "royal Irish arse" (7: 991)—an "arse" that could be kissed or not (as by now it has been many times), but which for being kissed could hardly be of use. By referring to *Ulysses* as the Nova Hibernia of the future, Joyce poses as having gotten so far ahead of himself that he is removed forever from the people who, however they can, have time to change whatever country they have time to change. He wants to face these people and be for them. But because he knows his only access to them is through a timeless book, he suspects he may be turned the wrong way. Only readers of *Ulysses* can turn the person in the writer back around so that strangely, responsibly, he may "appear" for them again and be of their time.

Being for Justice

G. J. Watson writes that "*Ulysses*, like all great books, perpetually renews itself in the circumstances of different times; and it is hard not to look again at the book with fresh interest—and respect—in the context of the last fifteen or so bloody years in Ireland."[13] Watson reads *Ulysses* as Joyce's "massive attempt to deconstruct the mythology of Romantic Ireland" with its emphasis on legend, "blood sacrifice," "the cult of the peasant and a corresponding hatred of the commercial and urban."[14] Having argued that *Ulysses'* pluralistic form is itself a critique of "the monocular vision of the sacred march of Irish history endemic in the nationalist imagination," Watson asks "What was Joyce *for?* What were his positives?" but quickly appeals to Stephen's invisible, above-it-all artist as evidence that the questions may be "inappropriate."[15] I feel the questions would be appropriate even if Joyce had not challenged me to ask and answer them through his blatant comparison of *Ulysses* and the political achievements of Parnell. If I am to accept that challenge, I must not let Joyce remain invisible for me but must instead allow him to "appear" to the degree that I recognize *Ulysses* as his case.

It runs through Bloom's mind about Murphy, who "of course had his own say to say" (16: 901–2), that "it was his own case he told, as people often did about others" (16: 836–37). When James Joyce allows himself to be recognized in Murphy, he asks to be recognized as someone who throughout *Ulysses* is telling his own case. I read his case no less personally because Joyce presents it in the third person instead of the first. He is not using the third to conceal that the case is his own, as Bloom's phrases imply. I will be saying why I think Joyce's case demands a third-person presentation. But suppose that I am wrong; suppose that Joyce wants nothing more than for a reader to penetrate through third-person disguise to first-person genuineness. Once I had done that, how would I be any closer to his case than I would be in reading his letters? Why not spare myself the trouble of translating third to first by going directly to the undisguised and untranslated first-person source?

"Since I came here," Joyce wrote to Pound from Trieste during his last months of work on *Ulysses*,

> I have not exchanged 100 words with anybody. I spend the greater part of my time sprawled across two beds surrounded by mountains of notes. I leave the house at 12:22 and walk the same distance along the same streets buy the Daily Mail which my brother and wife read and return. Idem in the evening. I was once inveigled into a theatre. I was once invited to a public dinner, as professor of the Scuola Superiore here, and next day received from them a request to subscribe 20,000 or 10,000 or even 5000 lire of Italian war loan.[16]

In this letter, Joyce's case in the first person is a series of grievances about what it is costing him to be writing his case in the third. He needs to be living a far more varied life and could stop writing *Ulysses* to that end. Were he not to complete *Ulysses*, on the other hand, there would be a much greater cost than that of his insipid daily rounds: not to finish writing his case in the third person would mean that he would never again face the persons on whom he had turned his back. "His advice to every Irishman was: stay in the land of your birth and work for Ireland and live for Ireland. Ireland, Parnell said, could not spare a single one of her sons."

MY INDICTMENT OF HIM

Because he had turned it on his people, James Joyce had turned his back as well on all persons who are of a people, which all persons are. Presenting his case in the first person serves him well enough with specified second persons, with Martha Fleischmann, Frank Budgen, Harriet Shaw Weaver, Ezra Pound. But it is the nature of James Joyce's case that he needs responses from persons he does not know, since it was on these persons, and not to his acquaintances and friends, that he had turned his back.

While he was writing *Ulysses*, which is to say before his case could be heard, each of these strangers was a third person for James Joyce. He needed to be heard, and it is second persons only who hear. But while their hearing and responding to his case would change them from third to second persons for him, he could not assume that even one among them would respond. Given what he needed, it would not be enough for him either to indict or to pardon himself for having left his people. Whereas what he needed was to be turned around by any other person's judgment of him, the most that self-indictment or self-pardon could do would be to leave him answerable only to himself. "His advice to every Irishman" is delivered in the cabman's shelter by Skin-the-Goat, "assuming he was he" (16: 985). Assuming he was not he, not Skin-the-Goat at all, not a character merely substituting for a person but rather a person, James Joyce, I can translate "his advice" into thinly disguised self-indictment. Or I can translate it into self-pardoning sarcasm directed at any person silly enough to indict James Joyce for having left Ireland. If I translate it in either of these two ways I do nothing more than overhear James Joyce's conversation with himself.

I do not translate it. Instead, I read it that Joyce presents "his advice" in a third person that is genuine insofar as it is not disguising a more genuine first. I read it as advice that might come from any third person, the merits of which I can judge for myself and then apply to any third person, James Joyce included. Because I want justice and because justice requires that a person face and be for other persons, I judge that "his advice" is worth applying. When I apply it to James Joyce, I make him a second person for me by indicting him for the injustice of having left his people. From his side of our unspoken encounter, I, who had formerly been a third person, am now facing him as a second. I have heard what he had to say. He has begun to have a case with me. I have begun to respond.

MITIGATION

As I read *Ulysses*, James Joyce's case is this: the injustice of his having turned his back is mitigated by the degree to which *Ulysses* is for justice. *Ulysses* in itself is neither just nor unjust. Its characters merely substitute for persons; there is no substitute for birth, and justice requires persons who were born. But its being neither just nor unjust does not preclude its being for justice. It is for justice only insofar as persons judge it to be so.[17] I will say why it is my judgment that *Ulysses* is for justice.

Joyce's characterizations of Stephen and of D. B. Murphy are third-person tellings of what I referred to above as Joyce's narrower case. By relegating his narrower case to a third-person telling, Joyce served his wider case, which is to be for justice. It was to the end of being "with any as any with any" that he settled on the third person in telling the cases of many Dubliners, James Joyce among them.

From *A Portrait* to *Ulysses*, there is an obvious shift away from Stephen's first-person-like centrality toward his taking, along with Murphy, a much less prominent place among others. While *A Portrait* mostly tells in the third person the case of the person for whom Stephen substitutes, Stephen himself is the whole story throughout—so much so, even, that there is no inconsistency when, in the last pages of the book, first-person entries from Stephen's journal replace third-person narrative about Stephen. Through his interior monologues, Stephen brings with him into *Ulysses* something of this same first-person perspective. But *Ulysses* does not stay with Stephen as *A Portrait* does, nor is it Stephen alone whose thoughts are presented in the first person, twelve other characters being accorded that privilege along with him. After his last interior monologue less than a third of the way through *Ulysses*, Stephen's case is told exclusively in the third person.

Third person or not, Stephen's discernible connections with James Joyce encourage me to translate third- into first-person tellings of Joyce's narrower case. The most up-to-date telling of that case, though, is not Stephen: it is instead D. B. Murphy. Only because it is told in the third person by a character named Leopold Bloom does Stephen unknowingly meet his own future face to face, the juncture of Stephen's and Murphy's cases eliding a seventeen-year span within James Joyce's narrower case. While it is of course Joyce himself who has written Bloom's phrases, I find that even my subtlest translation from

Bloom's third-person Stephen and Murphy into first-person Joyce is a distortion and betrayal not only of Joyce's wider case but of his narrower case as well. What I am saying is that Stephen and Murphy retain at least something of their third-person status for me. I judge that *Ulysses* is for justice to the degree that Joyce's narrower and wider cases merge as he goes about telling his own narrower case as one case among others.

THE CASE OF RICHARD BEST

A third-person telling of many cases, one's own narrower case among them, is only potentially for justice: whether or not it is for justice depends on how one tells all the cases. Another person whose case you tell might not want you to have told his case for him. If your telling of it differs so much from what his would be that he judges yours unjust, it will be incidental to him that along with his case you have also told your own narrower case in the third person. It is my judgment, as I have said, that *Ulysses* is for justice. I also judge that *Ulysses* is not for justice in every case. Richard Best's grammatical parity with Stephen and with Murphy meant little or nothing to him when interviewers from the BBC sought him out so that they could extract a person from the equivocal character named Richard Best. "What makes you come to me?" Best wanted to know, understandably not wanting to be recognized in the ridiculous character in *Ulysses* to whom Joyce had affixed Best's name.[18]

Best has a case with me. It is a case against James Joyce, whose injustice in this case is not mitigated by his having anticipated that Best would have a case against him.

> BEST
> That is my name, Richard, don't you know. I hope you are going to say a good word for Richard, don't you know, for my sake.
>
> > (laughter)
>
> . . . . . .
>
> I hope Edmund is going to catch it. I don't want Richard, my name. . . .
>
> > (laughter)
>
> QUAKERLYSTER
> (*a tempo*) But he that filches from me my good name. . . .
>
> > (9: 902–19)

There can be defamation of character only if the defamer presents himself as superior to the defamed. It is Stephen whom Best playfully warns not to defame him, and Stephen and Best are two characters each of which connects with one person who was born. Because each is presented in the third person, each faces and is answerable to the other "as any with any." But that third-person presentation has not stopped James Joyce from pulling rank. The person named Best could easily have been spared the shame of any connection with the character: but it did not matter enough to Joyce to spare him, Joyce's own narrower case as teller of *Ulysses* taking precedence. Joyce is not for justice in telling Best's case because he tells it from a position above Best, a position that he presents as coming first to Best's lowly third.

ANSWERING FOR ALL CHARACTERS

Out of mean-spiritedness or sheer whim, Joyce has filched Best's good name by substituting for the person not so much a character as a caricature. To filch is to steal something of small value. For someone who wants justice, a person's good name is of large value. In filching Best's good name, Joyce unjustly trivialized the value of any person's good name.

Most characters in *Ulysses* are unlike Richard Best in that they connect with no one person who was born. Because in making such characters he filches no one person's name, the bad names he gives to such characters hurt no one person. And yet while this ensures that he will not have to answer to me for pulling rank, I must hold him answerable for these characters nonetheless: for if I do not, I am left having to concede that such characters cannot be for justice, a concession that applies not only to Joyce's characters but also to those I make.

Substituting characters for persons is something I do more and less justly from case to case. I do your case justice only when the way I tell it to myself or someone else does not preclude my responding justly to your call. You may be someone I do not like, someone I do not want to respond to. If only to myself, I give you a worse name than I give persons to whom I respond with some justice. Subject to the unpleasant feeling that I am defaming you, I want to hide from my responsibility as the defamer. One effective way to hide is to sentimentalize by forgetting the connection between character and person. When I manage to forget it, the person becomes for me a character that is unconnected to you, one person who was born. Having forgotten, having taken the product so far as to have unjustly nullified its connection with the person, I can remember the justice I want only by reversing my forgetting, by working my way back out of sentimentality from character toward person. Joyce's characters are useful to me in this remembering only if I hold him answerable for them all. Whether mine or Joyce's—and whatever their discernible connections with persons—characters can be for justice only if in making them their maker is for justice.

Because justice is a situation in which every person has a case with every person other than himself, a character cannot be for justice if it substitutes for a person too reprehensible or too idealized to have a case with its maker. It is not at all that I must characterize in the same way every person who has a case with me, for no two persons who have a case with me turn out to be the same character. It is not even that each character must have an acceptable balance of redeeming traits. It is instead a matter of characterizing a person justly enough so that he has a case. Because I am likelier to give her tacit or explicit case a hearing if it interests me, "justly enough" is measurable more by my interest in the person than by anything else, that interest manifesting itself in the character. If I am to judge that Joyce's characters are for justice, I must judge whether or not the bad names he gives some of them proceed from his having turned a deaf ear to the persons whose cases they tell. Unless a reader does so, a character that connects with no one person has no one to answer for it against the writer's possibly unjust telling of its case. I answer for all of Joyce's characters through my judgment of what he has told about them in *Ulysses*.

It is not a simple judgment. As substitutes for persons, most of whom are less than saints, characters substitute for persons who themselves have much to answer for to other persons with whom they interact. Only if he holds each of his characters answerable to every other can Joyce himself be for justice in telling the cases of many Dubliners, his own case among them "as any with any." How a character comes off in *Ulysses* is almost always inseparable from that character's entanglements. In holding Joyce answerable for his characters, I must hold the persons for whom they substitute answerable to other persons, some but not all of whom are substituted for within *Ulysses* by other characters still, each character substituting for a person who is called by other persons and must answer.

"HOLD HIM NOW"

   —Hello, Simon, Father Cowley said. How are things?
   —Hello, Bob, old man, Mr Dedalus answered, stopping.
   They clasped hands loudly outside Reddy and Daughter's. Father Cowley brushed his moustache often downward with a scooping hand.
   —What's the best news? Mr Dedalus said.
   —Why then not much, Father Cowley said. I'm barricaded up,

Simon, with two men prowling around the house trying to effect an entrance.

—Jolly, Mr Dedalus said. Who is it?

—O, Father Cowley said. A certain gombeen man of our acquaintance.

—With a broken back, is it? Mr Dedalus asked.

—The same, Simon, Father Cowley answered. Reuben of that ilk. I'm just waiting for Ben Dollard. He's going to say a word to long John to get him to take those two men off. All I want is a little time.

He looked with vague hope up and down the quay, a big apple bulging in his neck.

—I know, Mr Dedalus said, nodding. Poor old bockedy Ben! He's always doing a good turn for someone. Hold hard!

He put on his glasses and gazed towards the metal bridge an instant.

—Here he is, by God, he said, arse and pockets.

Ben Dollard's loose blue cutaway and square hat above large slops crossed the quay in full gait from the metal bridge. He came towards them at an amble, scratching actively behind his coattails.

As he came near Mr Dedalus greeted:

—Hold that fellow with the bad trousers.

—Hold him now, Ben Dollard said.

Mr Dedalus eyed with cold wandering scorn various points of Ben Dollard's figure. Then, turning to Father Cowley with a nod, he muttered sneeringly:

—That's a pretty garment, isn't it, for a summer's day?

—Why, God eternally curse your soul, Ben Dollard growled furiously, I threw out more clothes in my time than you ever saw.

He stood beside them beaming, on them first and on his roomy clothes from points of which Mr Dedalus flicked fluff, saying:

—They were made for a man in his health, Ben, anyhow.

—Bad luck to the jewman that made them, Ben Dollard said. Thanks be to God he's not paid yet. (10: 882–917)

In telling the cases of the persons Dedalus, Cowley, and Ben Dollard substitute for, Joyce also tells the cases of persons who have cases against them. It is a long list, a list not limited to financial creditors. Cowley and Dollard are answerable, respectively, to Reuben J. Dodd and an unnamed Jewish tailor. But Cowley, Dollard, and Dedalus are all three answerable to any Jew for the joy they take in any Jew's misfortune. The list goes on. It has been years since Dedalus has managed to provide for his family. He has just refused to answer his daughter's charge that he is withholding from her, and therefore from the whole brood of hungry Dedaluses, money that she is sure he will later drink away. Cowley says he wants only a little time before he has to answer for his loan, then looks with "vague hope" for some impossible deliverance from that failure to repay it that his stalling betrays. Cowley also fails to answer those persons he would otherwise be serving if he had kept his former office as their priest, the moustache he sports a continuing reminder that he has failed. Ben Dollard's "big's ship's chandler's business" (11: 1012–13) having "failed to the tune of ten thousand pounds" (11: 1014) and leaving debts to many persons in its wake, he has fallen on times so lean that he can afford neither to pay for the suit of clothes he is wearing nor to eat enough to fill it. The good turn he is always doing for someone is done always at someone else's expense, that other someone probably often an outsider, often a Jew.

Or am I missing the point? Is Joyce really holding these characters answerable? Or is he focusing in another direction altogether? Since each of the three substitutes for a person who is insolvent, should I not see that Joyce addresses them as the oppressed but not also as oppressive? W. J. McCormack reads *Ulysses'* characters as victims of what he calls the "colonial nexus,"[19] a morally bankrupt economy within which "language is increasingly removed from the individual's control."[20] Through "the infinite reproduction of any one element in any possible context," language tends toward cliché. Cliché, McCormack writes, "encapsulates not so much the exhaustion of language" as "its consumption on a scale and in a system deserving to be termed consumerism."[21] For Mary King, too, *Ulysses* is a world in which "relations between man and man, between man and nature and between man and woman in a commodity economy, where those in power seek to fill people's lives with things, inevitably 'assumes the fantastic form of a relation between things.' "[22] Because they are so thoroughly colonized that their words and even they themselves have become commodities, how can I claim that the persons for whom Cowley, Dedalus, and Dollard substitute are answerable for their differing inabilities to answer? Is Joyce not insisting that it is only England and capital that must answer?

I think not. If *Ulysses* is Joyce's "effort against the pressures which turn human beings into clichés," as McCormack says, Joyce consistently calls my attention to "pressures" imposed not only by institutions but by persons as well.[23] *Ulysses* reminds me throughout that I myself am colonizing whenever I determine that certain persons are not answerable because a facelessly colonizing force had gotten to them before I did.[24] Had Joyce not consistently resisted making that determination himself, his characters would indeed have been clichés. He best counters those pressures that threaten to level all distinctions between persons by tirelessly distinguishing any one of his characters from all the rest. What is most remarkable for me in the passage I have just quoted is the intimacy between Dedalus and Dollard, an intimacy that turns upon each character's bringing to their encounter the very specific traits by which each can be recognized throughout *Ulysses*. Rather than avoid the all-too-evident subject of Dollard's indigence as if it were unspeakable, Dedalus openly chides him with it. Rather than be hurt by the chiding, Dollard acknowledges the affection in it, returns the affection in kind by pretending to be piqued. It is "on them first," on Dedalus and Cowley, that Dollard beams. And it is in response to Dollard's undisguised pleasure in them that Dedalus drops his game of chiding and commemorates a happier time.

But notice that Joyce is no readier to offer the charm of their insiders' exchanges as a saving grace than he is to excuse them on the ground that they are pawns to intolerably oppressive forces. Damned by what satisfies them in their likenesses, Dollard and Dedalus answer only to those in their circle and only in ways that restrict them all the more to the paralytic courses they are on. Nothing in whatever else Joyce tells about them diminishes his indictments of Cowley, Dedalus, and Dollard as slothful, self-pitying bigots. And yet his interest in nuances that exceed even as they reinforce those indictments persuades me that the persons for whom Dedalus and Dollard substitute each have a case with James Joyce. Nor are they exceptions in this respect, Joyce showing comparable or even keener interest in Mulligan, Haines, Deasy, M'Coy, Martin Cunningham, Jack Power, Joe Hynes, John O'Connell, Ned Lambert, Professor MacHugh, J. J. O'Molloy, Myles Crawford, Josie Breen, Nosey Flynn, Davy Byrne, John Eglinton, Mr. Lyster, Blazes Boylan, Dilly Dedalus, Tom Kernan, Almidano Artifoni, Jimmy Henry, Lenehan, Master Patrick Aloysius Dignam, Richie Goulding, the barfly, John Wyse Nolan, the citizen, Gerty MacDowell, Edy Boardman, Cissy Caffrey, Dixon, Bannon, Zoe Higgins, Lipoti Virag, Bella Cohen, Corny Kelleher, Corley, and Skin-the-Goat.

Joyce is more interested still, of course, in Bloom, in Molly, and in Stephen. I have addressed Stephen as a substitute for a person whose forthcoming success, if it is that, waits exactly on his success in letting other persons have cases with him. It happens that the most prominent among those are the persons for whom Molly and Bloom substitute. If he himself is to substitute for the person who matures to write *Ulysses*, it is Molly and Bloom whose cases Stephen must mature to tell. And only if those cases are for it can James Joyce be for justice.

Molly and Bloom

Just as Stephen is a third-person telling of Joyce's narrower case, Molly and Bloom are the most prominent telling of his wider one. It can be argued that the story of Bloom and Molly is not wide at all since they are characters substituting for persons who are married to one another, marriage being an extremely constricted relationship that may turn out to have been making its exit from cultural history as early as the twentieth century. But their story remains wide for me nevertheless. Whatever comes of marriage as an institution, each person in history will still be subject to a world with other persons in it, one person among those others becoming the person to whom he or she is closest: what it would take not to be subject to any one closest relationship, obviously, would be a totalitarianism within which such closeness would have been eradicated.

More than any other that I have read, Bloom and Molly's story is for justice. Both substitute for persons who acknowledge and forget their debts. The burden to forget is greater with Bloom than it is with Molly. Bloom substitutes for Molly a character that protects him from having to hear Molly's case. He never hears it. I hear it only after he is asleep and then only by way of an intelligence that differs from mine as radically as certain knowledge differs from judgment, and imperson from person. My delay in hearing her case evokes my separateness and duties as a person in a world filled with second and third persons. Just as you are a third person for me until I face you and let you have a case, so too Molly does not substitute for a second person with me until the final chapter of *Ulysses*, when at last she has her say. Having heard her case, I want her to have a case with Bloom. My wanting as much is for justice to the degree that it evokes Joyce's wanting you to have a case with me. If I am to respond to Joyce's case, I must be as clear as I can be about how it might apply to yours. To that end I must follow in some detail the story of Bloom's and Molly's entanglement.

A SUPPRESSED PRONOUN

June 1904. Ten and a half years before, Bloom's and Molly's infant son Rudy died. Bloom has not ejaculated in Molly's vagina since that time. He comes no closer to interpreting his abstinence with her than when he thinks: "Twentyeight I was. She twentythree. When we left Lombard street west something changed. Could never like it again after Rudy" (8: 608–10).

Which of them could never like it again? Molly, since she is the nearer antecedent to the unstated pronoun? Her monologue reveals not only that she still likes it very much with Boylan but that she would like it even more with Bloom. That she feels this way Bloom knows only too well. So is it Bloom himself and not Molly who could never like it again? No. It is clear from everything he thinks about her body and his attraction to it that he both could and would like "complete

carnal intercourse" (17: 2278) with her. He is therefore as unlikely a
subject for the fragment as is Molly. Were Bloom to begin the phrase
with either "she" or "I," or even "we," he would be forced to confront
the phrase's inaccuracy as an explanation of what has gone wrong sexually between Molly and himself. He suppresses the pronoun to save
the explanation: saved, it saves him from having to remember that he
owes Molly a good turn in bed.

Bloom's sexual debt to Molly is one he wants to forget because he is
afraid to discharge it. More than ten years after the irreversible events
of Rudy's conception, birth, and death, Bloom continues to fear complete carnal intercourse with Molly because it could be followed by the
conception, birth, and death of another child.[25] His fear is not specifically that time moves in circles and that history will repeat itself. Time
that moves straight and unpredictably ahead is more than enough to
frighten him into not starting anything the consequences of which he
could not bear.

If they talk to another about it at all, Bloom and Molly do not talk
clearly about what each needs in their sexual life together. Bloom needs
Molly sexually. What he thinks he needs more is to protect himself
from his fear. The prophylactic he carries would offer him reasonable
protection: out of respect for what he assumes is her readiness to observe the church's injunction against contraceptives, he does not propose its use. Whether or not they have talked about his withdrawing
from her vagina before he ejaculates, that is what he does, and what
she expects him to do.[26] While each knows intimately some aspects of
the other's case, Bloom does not state his case to Molly just as she does
not state hers to him. Hers is that each incomplete act of lovemaking
with Bloom is one more "limitation of fertility" (17: 2274), these accumulating "inhibitions of [her] conjugal rights" (17: 2271) enlarging
a need that neither Boylan nor Stephen nor any sexual partner other
than Bloom can begin to meet.

Though implicit only and therefore easier to forget, Molly's call to
Bloom is a call he knows he has time to answer in its present form until
four o'clock that afternoon, when Boylan calls. He knows that what he
must do before four, what Molly needs him to do, is simply to go home.
It would take that little to spoil Boylan's and Molly's tryst. If he spoiled
it, he could handle her covert or maybe even overt displeasure. What
he could not handle, though, would be the new adhesiveness of his
debt to her. Because by going home he would be denying her Boylan,
whom he is otherwise agreeing she may substitute for himself as her
sexual partner, he would be declaring himself ready to be responsible to
her sexually, ready to start something with her that has been stopped
for more than ten years. Afraid to start it, afraid of the time in which

it might still be started, Bloom takes refuge in his version of his and Molly's troubles in bed. One phrase in that version, "could never like it again," puts him relatively at rest by implying that it is already too late to do what he must.

"VORREI E NON VORREI"

For what might otherwise be his response to Molly, Bloom substitutes a story about why it is too late to respond. He has come to rely on that story to the degree that it has kept things stopped between them. Keeping them stopped has been and remains the chief project of his will. A person wills something not when he says "yes" to it and then proceeds to do it but rather before he does it, while there is still time to say "no" to it as well as "yes."[27] Merely saying "yes" is not to act out of what that "yes" affirms. It is instead to postpone the act itself, perhaps but not necessarily forever. The power commanded by the will is extinguished when willing itself gives way to an act. Unlike the will, which fluctuates between the possibilities of doing a thing and not doing it, a "thing done" has consequences that the willer himself is powerless to command. Bloom could reverse Rudy's death as well as every unhappy thing that has followed from it if he could cancel the act of lovemaking during which Rudy was conceived. He obviously cannot cancel that act. What he has done and can continue to do is to say "no" to those possible acts of lovemaking with Molly that their long-standing mutual need, as well as his recent jealousy of Boylan, impel him to say "yes" to.

"*Vorrei e non vorrei*," I would like to and I would not like to: Bloom remembers and misremembers this phrase eight times.[28] He knows that Molly will sing it as part of the musical program she and Boylan are planning to take on tour. The phrase is an apt one for Molly, Bloom knows, insofar as she would both like to make love with the Don Giovanni-like Boylan and would not like to. But Bloom knows too that it is also apt for him. He would and would not like to have complete carnal intercourse with Molly, to conceive another child with her. He would like to push Boylan out of her life but at the same time would not like to, so that Boylan can continue to protect him from what he fears.

Molly's sexual satisfaction and Bloom's own, Molly's sexual fidelity to him, her possible impregnation by him with a child who would be as healthy as their daughter, even the resumption of "complete mental intercourse" (17: 2285) between Molly and himself—these would be the positive consequences of Bloom's abandoning his will to his sexual appetite for Molly, of his going ahead and acting on what he would like. But knowing that it could fall the wrong way, he holds onto what he has, to what he thinks he might lose to despair were he to lose another child: that capacity simultaneously to will and to nill which allows him to feel he is in control of what happens.

"Gob, he's a prudent member and no mistake" (12: 437), the barfly says of Bloom, his colloquialisms reverberating with sexual puns that characterize Bloom exactly. Bloom makes no mistake with his male member because his cautiousness is willful. Unwatched, his desire for Molly and hers for him could surprise him, undo his prudence, and lead to a mistake. Saying "no" to desire once and for all is not enough in itself to ward off such surprise. Saying "yes" to desire as well as "no" is the more prudent course. Bloom says "yes" to desire by admitting instances of it into his thinking. Once they are thought, and without his ever having to issue them a final "no," which might lead to his losing track of them and his subsequently being surprised, he keeps them suspended within the dialectic of his "yes-" and "no-" saying will.

AGITATION AND REPOSE

Bloom gives desire a place in his thoughts by willfully staying on the lookout for titillation. In chapter 5 he remembers the girl settling her garter three days ago in the Eustace street hallway (5: 133–34), and the next-door girl earlier that morning at Dlugacz's butchershop (5: 47). He tells himself to "Watch! Watch! Silk flash rich stockings white. Watch!" (5: 130) as a woman climbs up into an outsider in front of the Grosvenor. Even when they are prompted by women other than Molly, Bloom's sexually provocative memories and perceptions are only relatively safe. In contrast to his imperative to himself about Molly in chapter 4—"Be near her ample bedwarmed flesh. Yes, yes"(4: 238–39)—they are visual, not tactile, and it is obviously his proximity to Molly's flesh that puts him most at risk. But since titillating perceptions are possible only because of a physical distance that the desiring observer desires to close, they have their danger too. Unless Bloom's will successfully absorbs these provocations, they may move him to close the physical distance between himself and Molly.

Agitating him to move, all instances of desire are paired within Bloom's will with thoughts of the repose that would follow his having closed with Molly. "With will will" he "withstand, withsay" (14: 311–12) that repose. He withstands and withsays it by equating repose and satisfaction with nothing less absolute and negative than death. In this equation, Rudy's death completed the most satisfying, most reposeful part of Bloom's and Molly's personal history. If satisfying himself with Molly by acting out of his sexual desire for her is death, his willful equation has it, then unsatisfied agitation is life. Against the indivisible losses time has brought him and might bring him still, the dialectic of agitation and repose offers him its protection from moment to moment.

It is a dialectic rehearsed again and again in chapter 5. While he is being stimulated by the prospect of Martha's letter and by the letter itself, he is aware that he will have to be attending soon to the depressing business of Dignam's funeral. He watches the woman climbing up into the outsider while M'Coy recounts his having learned of Dignam's death and then goes on to say that he might miss the funeral if he and the coroner have to look at the body of the "drowning case at Sandycove" (5: 170–71). Bloom has the fantasy that a flower in a woman's letter to her lover might be "a poison bouquet to strike him down" (5: 262). Inside All Hallows Church, which he thinks of as a "nice discreet place to be next some girl" (5: 340–41), he sees the communion as "eating bits of a corpse" (5: 352). From the chemist he orders a lotion for Molly's skin that will make her all the more attractive to him and thinks of "chloroform," an "overdose of laudanum" (5: 481–82).

KEEPING IT UP

Stimulants and depressants, irritation and satisfaction, agitation and repose. As instances in one or the other of these three pairs align for Bloom with life and death, they align too with a second dialectic: West and East. The pin Martha has used to affix a flower to her letter becomes the pin in a song he had heard two prostitutes singing, and then the crown of thorns, the cross, and the I.N.R.I., "iron nails ran in" (5: 374), of Catholicism. As irritants that extend even to the "punish me, please" (5: 426) of confession, these contrast for him with the "heathen Chinee" (5: 327) preferring their opium to the eucharist, with Buddha lying reposefully on his side, with the "fleshpots of Egypt" (5: 548) and the mosque of the baths where Bloom foresees himself masturbating. He has never been outside of Ireland: but because he is a Jew he thinks of the East as his spiritual home. Molly was born in Gibraltar and therefore has her bonds with the East as well. The East, for Bloom, is that distant past that preceded their own lives. It is also the past they lived together prior to Rudy's death. In chapter 4, remembering "pleasant evenings we had then" and "Molly in Citron's basketchair" (4: 206–7), Bloom thinks of "Spain, Gibraltar, Mediterranean, the Levant. Crates lined up on the quayside at Jaffa, chap ticking them off in a book" (4: 211–13). But as a cloud covers the sun, he changes his version of the East so that it substitutes for a fruitfulness used up and dead to him forever. "No, not like that. A barren land, bare waste" (4: 219).

"Dead: an old woman's: the grey sunken cunt of the world" (4: 227–28).

Bloom feels that to be satisfied sexually is to die not just in the Elizabethan sense but also in the way his memory of Rudy's death enforces. Outside the house, away from Molly, this memory is understandably less binding. "Are you not happy in your home you poor little naughty boy?" Martha asks him in her letter, "I do wish I could do something for you" (5: 246–47). Except for Molly, Bloom has not had sexual intercourse with any woman who is not a professional. Martha clearly is not a professional, and her letter tells him that she wants him sexually. While his letters to her manage to elicit the response he wants only because they imply that he is saying "yes" to sex with her, he says to himself about it that he is "not having any" (5: 271). By itself, though, that resolution does not quell his sexual interest in Martha. Agitated nearly to the limits of the will, he tries first to soothe what she has aroused in him by thinking "cigar has a cooling effect. Narcotic" (5: 272), and that thought is in turn just balancing enough to let him think that he will "go further" (5: 272) with the prurience in his next letter to her. "Try it anyhow. A bit at a time" (5: 274). Provoked by her letter to translate her into one of the "two sluts that night in the Coombe" (5: 279) whom he had heard singing

> *O, Mairy lost the pin of her drawers.*
> *She didn't know what to do*
> *To keep it up,*
> *To keep it up.* (5: 281–84)

he then translates the "sluts" into a picture he had seen of Mary and Martha, the sisters of Lazarus. It is only within that Eastern context with its geographical remoteness and its completedness-as-past that he lets himself imagine forgetting to say "no." "Just loll there: quiet dusk: let everything rip. Forget. . . . Then a sigh: silence. Long long long rest" (5: 293–99).

All of this is of course only and very safely in his mind. In the implicit comparison he makes with his friend Dignam, who is about to be lowered to his long rest in accordance with the "law of falling bodies" (5: 44–45) and the Catholic rites of burial, Bloom's mental activity lets him feel that he is indeed getting somewhere. When it is in league with a will that imposes its constraints on action, thinking supplies the illusion that the will gets things done. It is an illusion the will promotes so that it does not give itself away as dilatory. Preserving the will's jurisdiction is the same as "keeping it up." Knowing what to do "to keep it up," Bloom suspends the desire that would otherwise move him to act. To keep his desire suspended takes time, just as it takes time to act out of his desire for Molly and hers for him. Keeping it up is obviously much the safer expenditure of time, since to keep it up precludes the risk of conception, birth, and death. Keeping it up is to appropriate for the will that time in which something intolerable might happen. Bloom's thinking about desire is his willful effort to feel himself in command of what happens in time.

"CAN'T BRING BACK TIME"

Getting it up, then giving way and getting it off, then resting for awhile, or doing something else, not thinking about it, forgetting, finding sometime later that it is up again, and so on—Bloom diverts the natural intermittence of such a sequence into the much more appropriative back-and-forth movements of the will. Leaving home at ten in the morning, he makes it his will's job to keep him away from home until it is too late to stop Molly from having her romp in bed with Boylan sometime after four. Two of the six hours he spends mostly by himself. Between ten and eleven and then again between one and two, his sexual responsibility to Molly is especially prominent because few other responses are summoned from him. With increased cause and opportunity, his will works all the harder to keep him from going home. During the first of these two hours, he thinks repeatedly about the ups and downs of sexual agitation and repose. During the second, he thinks repeatedly of food.

The eighth is the only chapter that begins inside Bloom's head: "Pineapple rock, lemon platt, butter scotch" (8: 1). With food on his mind from the outset, and without the narrative ever leaving him, there are over two hundred references to food and drink before Bloom manages to order himself a glass of burgundy and a cheese sandwich. He thinks about the sixpenny lunch at Rowe's, and that the eightpenny at the Burton is better. He stalls and stalls, keeps telling himself he is hungry and that he must eat. Imagining the ecstasies of lovers in "deep summer fields, tangled pressed grass, in trickling hallways of tenements, along sofas, creaking beds" (8: 642–44), he opens the door of the Burton, sees "the animals feed" (8: 651–52), is repulsed, backs out the door, and thinks a "light snack" at Davy Byrne's would be a "stopgap" (8: 698), something to keep him going.

Maybe he simply is not hungry. It could be that his attention to food during the hour comes only from that practical strain in him which tells him that, hungry or not, he must nourish his body. I believe it is more that he thinks again and again of food so that he can say "no" to it again and again. As his continuing to say both "yes" and "no" to sex is, his thinking of food to say "no" to it is Bloom's resistance to the time it takes for bad things to happen. Remembering his life with Molly before Rudy was born, he thinks "I was happier then. Or was that I? Or am I now I? . . . Can't bring back time. Like holding water in your hand" (8: 608–11). He cannot bring back time, but he can at least resist beginning those acts that his appetites for food and sex make him want to begin. Such resistance helps him feel he is clearer about who he is—he is the one doing the resisting—while to go ahead and eat or to make imprudent love with Molly would be to dissolve his will into the "stream of life" (8: 95) in which Dignam is "carted off" while Mina Purefoy waits in pain to have "a child tugged out of her" (8: 479–80). When he sees one of Dedalus's fifteen children outside Dillon's auction rooms and assumes that she "must be selling off some old furniture" (8: 28) to get money for food, he thinks "increase and multiply. Did you ever hear such an idea? Eat you out of house and home" (8: 33–34).

PROGENY AS WASTE

Having told himself he must eat, he can hold out against eating only so long. He holds out longer than he might by conflating his separate appetites for food and for sex. Each time he fails to distinguish between the two he superimposes on the thought of eating all the injunctions that have enforced his ten-year sexual fast with Molly. As the associations become more current they become more unpleasant, thereby emphasizing that his enjoyment of food, like his enjoyment of sex, is a thing of the past. From a time before Rudy was born he remembers frying up some lap of mutton as he watched Molly in the bedroom "unclamping the busk of her stays" (8: 196–97). He remembers Josie Powell as a "rhubarb tart with liberal fillings, rich fruit interior" (8: 273). At Davy Byrne's he thinks of "fizz and Red bank oysters. Effect on the sexual. Aphrodis. He [Boylan] was in the Red Bank this morning" (8: 865–67). As he tries to decide what to eat, he thinks of a Limerick about the Reverend MacTrigger, whose "parts of honour" (8: 746) increase the sexual potency of a cannibal chief. He is able to come up with the punch line only after he has dressed his sandwich with mustard and had Nosey Flynn ask him the critical question about Molly's singing tour. "Who's getting it up? . . . Isn't Blazes Boylan mixed up in it?" (8: 773–88). "Yes," Bloom allows after considerable delay, "He's the organiser in point of fact" (8: 797). Bloom eats the sandwich. But by letting his willful distaste for sex infiltrate what might otherwise be a gusto for food, he manages not to like what he is eating even as he eats. Whereas the first phrase about him in chapter 4 discloses that he "ate with relish the inner organs of beasts and fowls," now, at lunchtime, he eats "his strips of sandwich, fresh clean bread, with relish of disgust" (8: 818–19).

Because his thoughts about food and sex collapse into one another, Bloom thinks of the progeny that come from lovemaking not as persons the body engenders so that they might live but rather as what the body passes and disposes of as vile. The stillborn, for Bloom, are "trouble for nothing" (8: 389–90), waste, as Rudy is waste. With a whole "cityful passing away, other cityful coming, passing away too" (8: 484), the wooden counter in Davy Byrne's appeals to him because, like the statues of naked goddesses its curves remind him of, it has been made to last. Unlike the women who arouse him sexually, the statues in the library's museum do not—he is sure of it, though he will check—have anuses.

HOME

Metabolism is in itself a threat for Bloom. Just as he has time to eat and digest, so too does he have time for his prudence with Molly to be overcome either by his sexual appetite for her or by his duty to satisfy hers for him.[29] Fearful of a time in which he might make a mistake simply because bodies do what they do when they have time, he thinks his way past the procreative and alimentary acts to their residue. Thoughts of corpses and feces do little to recommend making love or eating. While he thinks these thoughts because they buttress his prudence, they also offer him the welcome illusion of a point outside his body and therefore outside of time. From such a willed point, Bloom could go back as if in memory through his already completed life with Molly, could go back through it and be assured that they never conceived a third child. Or from such a point he could antedate the need for that assurance by going back to a time before they had conceived a second and then not do what has been done.

Knowing that he cannot go back in either of these two ways because a point outside of time is not available to him, he thinks of what he cannot undo and what he still can do as the same. Were he to think of the two as different, he might "go back" (not as if in memory but) home. Unwilling to go home, he refuses to think of the two as different. "Useless to go back. Had to be" (8: 633). What has happened "had to be" in that it cannot now be undone. But while it is therefore "useless to go back" in memory to a time before it was done, Molly's adultery is something that has not happened yet and that Bloom alone can keep from happening. By telling himself it is useless to go back both in memory and home, by refusing to distinguish between the two so that he may spare himself the risks attendant on his doing what he must, he is a party to Molly's forthcoming adultery and answerable to her for it.

"QUIET KEEP QUIET RELIEF"

What has happened already, of course, is Molly and Boylan's assignation two weeks ago, which Bloom himself had been there for. "She was humming. The young May moon she's beaming, love. He other side of her. Elbow, arm. He. Glowworm's la-amp is gleaming, love, Touch. Fingers. Asking. Answer. Yes" (8: 589–91). Feeling his jealousy bring him dangerously close to the thought of going home, Bloom orders himself to "stop. Stop," and follows that imperative by thinking of the present as the past. "If it was it was. Must" (8: 592). Two weeks earlier, Molly had implicitly agreed to make love with Boylan. That was then, this is now, and Bloom willfully ignores the distinction. Ignoring it entails an ambiguous "must." "Must" what? "Must let her have Boylan," probably—a thought that substitutes safely for the far too risky "must let her have me."

But just as "must let her have me" is an obligation that will adhere to Bloom even after Molly's adultery, it adheres now and will not soon go away. Because a simple acknowledgment of it could at any time start him on a course back to Molly, he commands himself to acknowledge anything else. Dublin is what is at hand. "With ha quiet keep quiet relief his eyes took note this is the street here middle of the day of Bob Doran's bottle shoulders" (8: 594–95). The turmoil around him substitutes handily for the turmoil his jealousy has thrown him into: to "quiet" both at least momentarily, it is enough to do some specific predicating about his location in time. What "this is," he establishes with some difficulty, is "the street." If he is to restore his composure he will have to be more precise. After he slips back into a less particularizing "here," he recoups somewhat by remembering that it is the "middle of the day" and then abruptly has his precision in two proper nouns, he has recognized someone, Bob Doran, a drunk whose short biography he reads in the "bottle shoulders."

For as long as Doran is visible to him, Bloom follows him with his eyes and thoughts. "Relief," for now, is whatever he can say to himself that stops him from thinking about going home. Simple coherence is his will's ally, the articulations between one safe thought and the next sustaining him throughout much of the time he has to kill before Boylan calls on Molly at four. Though the intimacy with which he knows Dublin keeps him generally undisturbed, Dublin itself does not turn out to be perfectly shock-free. In Kildare Street at the end of the chapter, his heart and thinking are sent into paroxysms when he recognizes not just any Dubliner but Blazes Boylan. To quell the disturbance, Bloom appeals first to what he can make cohere within his surroundings. "Handsome building" (8: 1174), he tells himself about the National Museum on his hurried way inside where he knows the "cold statues" will help him feel "safe" (8: 1176–77).

WHY A NIGHT ON THE TOWN?

Rather than avoid Boylan two hours later at the Ormond Hotel, Bloom decides to spy on him. He does so because the danger, by now, has nearly passed. If Boylan leaves the Ormond, Bloom assumes, it is at last and by the clock "too late" to stop Molly from becoming an adulteress. Having carried him safely through a time in which the peril of answering her call has been its most extreme, Bloom's will can rest, its backs and forths giving place to a sadness that does not come and go, throughout the hour of four, but rather stays.[30]

He understands very clearly that he is not to catch Molly with Boylan. Quite aside from the unseemly embarrassment of it, catching them would be both foolish and an act of bad faith since he could easily have prevented their lovemaking before it started. And to catch them would of course leave Bloom all the more immediately in Molly's debt. He would in that case be denying her Boylan as a substitute for himself: was he prepared, she might ask him if only implicitly, to resume his former place as her sexual partner?

But if he must not catch them and therefore cannot go home for several hours, why wait more than ten? Partly to delay the awkwardness of their having to face one another after what has happened: the longer he stays out, the more occasion he gives her either to be asleep or to feign sleep. And partly because he is occupied during these ten hours with persons other than Molly. For as long as his will had been working overtime to keep him safely on the streets and away from home until after four o'clock, Molly had been his preoccupation if only because he had strained so to forget her. That straining temporarily behind him, he can now attend less dividedly to Martha Clifford by way of the post, to the crowd at Barney Kiernan's, to the widow Dignam, to Gerty MacDowell, and, most of all, to "Stephen Dedalus, professor and author" (17: 2270). Bloom stays out partly because he is busy being for people, his various responses to them offering him prolonged if temporary respite from the weight of Molly's call.

There is another possible explanation for his staying out. He has been aware for the past nine months that Molly consistently wants to know what he has been up to. Has her unusual afternoon and evening rendered her less concerned than usual about how he has spent his day and night? Though he thinks she will probably grill him, she has not done that yet and he cannot be sure she will. The longer he stays out, the more cause he gives her to be curious, the more he will learn about the temperature with her by her indifference or her response. Unfeigned coolness from her will mean he is less obliged; warmth, that nothing much has changed.

"ANTAGONISTIC SENTIMENTS"

Until he goes to sleep, he conducts himself as if he suspects that nothing much has changed. Overlooking his debt to Molly is now less frenzied than it had been during the morning and early afternoon, but it remains a project for him still. Anticipating that Boylan may not please Molly for very long and that he himself might therefore soon be back on call, Bloom begins to play the cuckold-panderer in a story according to which Stephen and not Boylan will be his substitute as Molly's sexual partner. After Stephen leaves, he indulges himself with the idea of Flowerville, a fantasy about his and Molly's future that conveniently avoids the question of whether they will resume their lovemaking, and conceive a child.

That question arises for him only when he toys with an only slightly less fantastic idea: leaving home.

What considerations rendered departure not irrational?

The parties concerned, uniting, had increased and multiplied, which being done, offspring produced and educed to maturity, the parties, if not disunited were obliged to reunite for increase and multiplication, which was absurd, to form by reunion the original couple of uniting parties, which was impossible. (17: 1962–67)

Molly and Bloom are not disunited as long as Bloom does not depart. As long as he remains, though, he and Molly are obliged to reunite for increase and multiplication. It is his acknowledgment of this duty that prompts his not irrational but wildly contorted excuse for running away. He reasons that it is absurd for the not disunited to reunite, impossible for the not reunited to reunite by returning to the time before their original union produced their one surviving and now mature offspring. What he and Molly were obliged to do, he tells himself, they have done. It is Milly's turn now, not Molly's, not his.

But remember what this very reasoning obliges him to do. If he stays with Molly—and the signs are that he will—then he is obliged to reunite sexually with her for increase and multiplication. Molly's call to him, he supposes, will be no less binding than before. He can counteract and withstand its force only if he keeps his will in working order. For Bloom as he climbs in bed next to her, Boylan's imprint on the sheet elicits the "antagonistic sentiments" of "envy, jealousy, abnegation, equanimity" (17: 2154–55). Because envy and jealousy threaten his continuing prudence, he suspends them between the poles of his wanting and not wanting to answer Molly's call. Suspended, they are then diffused: neither is so strong, he finds, as the tempering sentiment with which it is paired. To himself he justifies his all-too-balanced feelings. Then he lets their antagonisms converge, satisfied, at Molly's rump. Unlike the twin poles of his will, her "posterior female hemispheres" are "insusceptible . . . of contrarieties" (17: 2232–35). As she interrogates him, he feels "a limitation of activity, mental and corporal, inasmuch as complete mental intercourse between" (17: 2284–86) Molly and himself has not taken place since Milly had her first period nine months ago. He declines to be answerable to Molly for Martha, for his run-in with the citizen, for Gerty, and for Nighttown. He composes himself for sleep and goes to sleep.

MOLLY AWAKE

What Bloom rests from when "he rests" (17: 2320) is the hard work of keeping his marriage under control. On a day when that control or the marriage itself might have begun to dissolve irrecoverably, he has withstood those of his antagonistic sentiments that most threatened the status quo. One jolt or another during the past eighteen hours might have shaken him from his willful prudence, but none has. So Molly is now an adulteress, he thinks. He can take it. Boylan, after all, is only the most recent in a long list of men whom he has suspected. And is adultery any more outrageous than marriage itself? If she has violated him by committing adultery, he tells himself, he had violated her by denying her his husbandly duty. "He's a safe man" (8: 982), Bloom is. On this first day of her sexual infidelity, and with his full knowledge of how she meant to spend her afternoon, Bloom has made it all the way to sleep without conceding much that is new to Molly's need for him.

But there are of course two in any marriage, not just one, and Molly is not asleep yet, as her chapter is about to disclose. Not until I have read what Molly herself thinks do I know how accurately Bloom is reading her. Her chapter confirms what he suspects: that her having taken another man to bed with her today for the first time means neither that she would allow that other man to impregnate her nor that she is any less inclined to have another child by Bloom. Molly: "Supposing I risked having another not off him though still if he was married Im sure hed have a fine strong child but I don't know Poldy has more spunk in him yes thatd be awfully jolly" (18: 166–68). Her chapter makes it clear that Bloom is right to intuit that her newly launched affair has not reduced her need for him and that he therefore cannot let down his guard. But if the affair has not changed her in that way, it may have changed her in some other that may in turn lead to changes in their marriage. If there were no room in it for one of the partners to act differently than the other has come to expect, marriage would be even more outrageous than it is. When I read Molly's chapter, I have a preview of what may turn out to be a series of quiet surprises that Molly visits upon Bloom, a series that could alter for the better the course their marriage has been on.

"WAS IT HIM MANAGED IT"

Molly's sexual time with Boylan today has been more than good. "I was coming for about 5 minutes with my legs round him I had to hug him after O Lord I wanted to shout out all sorts of things fuck or shit or anything at all" (18: 587–89). She's arranged to see Boylan again in four days and she "cant wait" (18: 595). But for all the pleasure she has taken in it already and all she looks forward to taking, she thinks about having consummated her first extramartial affair as if she has lost something she longs for even as she understands that it had to go: "Anyhow its done now once and for all" (18: 100). Deprived once and for all of her sexual fidelity to Bloom, she may be much readier than she has been to make him answer for his part in her infidelity. "With him so cold never embracing me except sometimes when hes asleep" (18: 1400–1401), she decides, "its all his own fault if I am an adulteress" (18: 1516).

She may also be more aware of his complicity in her unfaithfulness. With Milly living at home and often there, Molly could hardly begin a sexual relationship with Boylan. But it was Bloom and not Molly who determined that Milly should move a safe sixty miles away to Mullingar and take up work as a photographer's assistant. "Such an idea for him to send the girl down there" (18: 1004–5), Molly thinks, bewildered that Bloom would let their fourteen-year-old daughter be out in the world on her own. Then Molly solves the riddle. Bloom had gotten Milly out of the house "on account of me and Boylan thats why he did it Im certain the way he plots and plans everything" (18: 1007–9). She wonders about her singing tour with Boylan if it had not been Bloom himself who set it up: "Was it him managed it this time I wouldnt put it past him like he got me on to sing in the Stabat Mater" (18: 379–80).

While she is sure that he is behind her affair with Boylan, she is less sure what he has in mind for her with Stephen. "What is he driving at now showing him my photo," she puzzles. "I wonder he didnt make him a present of it altogether and me too" (18: 1302–5). She thinks that what he is driving at is to offer her to one or another able-bodied male—a prospect that disturbs her less because it means he is treating her as chattel than that he is wanting someone else to be answerable to her in his stead. Her hold on Bloom, she knows, is nothing other than his acknowledgment that he is beholden to her. Is it because he regards his debt to her as a thing of the past that he now does mostly as he pleases? For nine months now she has sensed that he is less firmly in her grasp than he used to be. She wants to regain and maybe even tighten that grasp not because she misses the exhilarations of her former power but rather because she misses him, the man whose duty toward her she still wants after ten less than satisfying years.

HER POSSESSIVENESS

Bloom's recent adventures are intolerable to Molly in direct proportion to her ignorance of them. They can be combatted only when she is more sure of what they are. "Lord knows what he does that I dont know" (18: 1430–31). "2 oclock well thats a nice hour of the night for him to be coming home at to anybody" (18: 1232–33). His last orgasm with her was two weeks ago: "because he couldnt possibly do without it that long" (18: 76), she is sure "he came somewhere" (18: 34) today or tonight, suspects that "its some little bitch hes got in with" (18: 1256), "the hotel story he made up a pack of lies to hide it" (18: 37). If it turned out that he was involved with Josie Powell Breen, whom he told her he had run into and who used to be and probably still is sweet on him, Molly would know what to do. "Id just go to her and ask her do you love him and look her square in the eyes she couldnt fool me" (18: 193–94), nor would it be long before Molly had it her way.

Even when unstated, Molly's claim to Bloom says "he's mine" to rivals, "you're mine" to Bloom. He resists making a comparable claim to her, as I have said, by literally not getting caught with his pants down. So that the most threatening of his feelings will not surprise and overpower him, he consistently pairs each with its "antagonistic sentiment," holds it in suspense between the poles of "yes" and "no," and thereby diffuses in it what might otherwise move him to act. Bloom's feelings for Molly are no less intense than hers for him. But he willfully short-circuits the response-promoting connection between his feelings for her and his claim to her. Molly is his, he understands, only if he responds to what she needs from him, only if he acts as if she is his. To claim her even tacitly would be to promise that he is for her, for what she needs from him. He relinquishes that claim, leaves it to Molly to claim him with so much strength that the bond between them will hold. Were he himself to wander "selfcompelled, to the extreme limit of his cometary orbit, beyond the fixed stars and variable suns," Bloom imagines, "he would hear and somehow reluctantly, suncompelled, obey the summons of recall" (17: 2013–18). That summons is not merely still or never to come. It is ongoing. It inheres in Molly's claim to him.

THE COMPROMISE

To Bloom's ears, Molly's claim to him is decidedly ongoing. It is also commanding and gruff. In the fourth chapter she tells him to "hurry up with that tea" (4: 263), but first to "scald the teapot" (4: 270). He does both things and is rewarded with complaint. What he does not hear from her but surely senses is that she delights in his answering her most mundane of calls, delights in it less because he is someone she can boss around than because his obsequiousness has become the readiest way for him to show her his care, for her to feel cared for by him. "I love to hear him falling up the stairs of a morning with the cups rattling on the tray" (18: 933–34). How to sort out Molly's joy in being catered to from her affection for her husband and their daily life? She has learned over the years both to accept and to covet what Bloom gives: if less than his full sexual services, then his domestic service and occasional sums of money, most of it spent on keeping her attractive to him. "Ill tell him I want to buy underclothes then if he gives me that well he wont be too bad" (18: 1523–24).

It will be a test. For him not to consent would mean that he has it in mind to change the terms of their silent, long-standing compromise. She has more evidence than she wants that he may be thinking he can offer her another man not only as his sexual replacement but in place of gifts and his subservience as well. "Yes because he never did a thing like that before as ask to get his breakfast in bed with a couple of eggs" (18: 1–2). Though she has tolerated his fear of conceiving another child, she will not abide his slipping off under cover of it to some other woman and possibly out of her life. His recent attentions to their physically mature daughter have left Molly feeling supplanted by another generation of childbearers and therefore all the more vulnerable to rejection. "I suppose he thinks Im finished out and laid on the shelf well Im not no nor anything like it well see well see" (18: 1021–23), which of course we will not since the narrative plays out before Molly has a chance to say so much as "boo" to him again.

"MAKE HIM WANT ME THATS THE ONLY WAY"

What she does have a chance to do is to plan seducing him. "I know what Ill do" (18: 1506), she thinks as she begins rehearsing the approach she will take with him tomorrow morning. The contest of wills has for years been going Bloom's way, not hers. But for all that, she is not intimidated, is confident that she is more than his match. She wanted him to propose to her sixteen years ago, she remembers, "because I saw he understood or felt what a woman is and I knew I could always get round him" (18: 1578–80). Always is always, and Molly is still very much in the game. No less heartbroken than Bloom over Rudy's death but less paralyzed by it, she has stayed alert to Bloom's needs, has actively coaxed him into expressing his hyper-prudent readiness to meet hers. From his side of the marriage, he has done just enough to keep her in the game, his docile attentions reassuring her steadily if scantily that there is still time. I do not think Molly is overrating her influence with Bloom. Having gone along for ten years with their less than satisfying compromise, she has been biding her time. With the compromise itself no longer firm, she thinks it may now be time to turn the game her way.

She will win tomorrow if her seduction of him secures three things. Money for lingerie is the first and least crucial. More important to her is whatever she can extract from him about the liaison she thinks he may have struck with another woman. "Ill put on my best shift and drawers let him have a good eyeful out of that to make his micky stand for him" (18: 1508–10). If he wants the satisfaction of hearing that she has cuckolded him, she will give him that. Out of the knowledge of him that she alone has, she will indulge each of his sexual eccentricities. At the height of his excitement, she thinks, "Ill do the indifferent 1 or 2 questions Ill know by the answers when hes like that he cant keep a thing back" (18: 1529–30). Bloom and Molly have not had "complete mental intercourse" during the nine months since Milly's first period. Candor is essential to their reducing the estrangement between them. If she can get him to level with her about his goings-on, they may begin to close another, older distance as well.

For if she is right, if "when hes like that he cant keep a thing back," Bloom's prudence is in more immediate jeopardy than it has ever been. Confronted with her zeal to have him, a zeal intensified by her feelings about the events of the past day, he may be no more able to withhold semen from her vagina than candid answers from her ears. This third thing she is after, "complete carnal intercourse" with Bloom, is of course the most difficult to win because her wanting it inspires his sternest defense. The resources she intends to draw on for winning are the same as victory itself: for Molly, it is at once both means and end to prove so irresistible that Bloom lets "everything rip" (5: 294), his prolonged fear of impregnating her giving way at last.

Her plan for seducing him is graphically comprehensive, but it is also incomplete. She has never set out to do this before, or never with such purpose. How should she go about it with so much at stake? What is there in his current advantage over her that she would be smartest to change? Since "he thinks nothing can happen without him knowing" (18: 281–82), he probably assumes that she will "tour the chief towns" (6: 217) with Boylan while he is away in County Clare, that she will then drop Boylan for Stephen and otherwise do little that he himself is not cognizant of and does not sanction. She does not want his sanction, wants even less to be as transparent as he seems to think she is. Would she not be more desirable to him if he were less sure of her? How can she make it harder for him to take her for granted?

Only as she is contriving the most heated moments of their next sexual encounter does she hit on the angle that she is sure will work. "Ill tighten my bottom well and let out a few smutty words smellrump or lick my shit or the first mad thing comes into my head then Ill suggest about yes O wait now sonny my turn is coming Ill be quite gay and friendly over it" (18: 1530–33). She will not risk betraying all at once the fierceness with which she is now wanting him to let himself go with her. What she will do instead is to begin eroding his confidence that he knows everything about her. If she can give him occasion to feel that he knows less about her than he wants to, it is likely that his possessiveness of her will begin to match hers for him. "Ill wipe him off me just like a business his omission then Ill go out Ill have him eying up at the ceiling where is she gone now make him want me thats the only way" (18: 1538–40).

AGAINST HIS WILL

From its first word, Molly's monologue is driven by her need to assess what has happened to her today. A lot has. Starting her affair with Boylan gave her plenty to think about. Bloom has given her even more. He stayed out half the night, lied to her about what he had been doing, seemed bent on supplying her with a lover eleven years her junior, on having her begin to show him the daily courtesies he had been showing her. Enough has changed for Molly in the past ten hours that tomorrow does not look like just another day. With her marriage in the balance, she has to be as clear as she can be about what to do next. It is the middle of the night. She knows she should not be awake this late, that sleep is integral to any plan since to be at her best with Bloom in the morning it will help to be well-rested. But not until she resolves that she must make him want her does she let herself try to "doze off" (18: 1545).

Because each wants the other, I want Molly to move Bloom out of his self-protective rut and back to her. Against his desire for her, Bloom has defended himself so unfailingly for so long that Molly will have to take him against his will. She knows that she will have to persevere. Her perseverance may or may not be enough. He avoids impregnating her by keeping between his body and hers a distance that from day to day frustrates them both. I want her to seduce him not so they will conceive another child but so that neither is denied the other's full response to his and her respective needs. More than Bloom needs the guarantee that he will never again impregnate Molly, he needs to touch her when he wants to: "Looking at me, the sheet up to her eyes, Spanish, smelling herself, when I was fixing the links in my cuffs" (5: 494–95).[31] More than Molly needs to be pregnant, she needs her husband to put his arms around her: "A woman wants to be embraced 20 times a day almost" (18: 1407–8), as Bloom, who understands or feels "what a woman is," knows very well. As they talk in bed before he falls asleep, Molly feels "a limitation of fertility" not only because Bloom refuses to fertilize her egg but also because fertility is itself the limit she feels. It is nothing other than her capacity to be fertilized that renders her off-limits to Bloom's embraces.

THE NEW

For more than ten years, Bloom has been telling himself a story in which his character and Molly's collide at the unutterable question of whether they should have a third child. Sensitive to his inordinate grief over Rudy's death, Molly knew from the start how Bloom's story ends. "I suppose I oughtnt to have buried him in that little woolly jacket I knitted crying as I was but give it to some poor child but I knew well Id never have another" (18: 1448–50), and by the time *Ulysses* ends she has not, *Ulysses* and the story Bloom tells about the Blooms being in that respect the same. Throughout his various revisions of it, the most recent of which include Boylan and Stephen as her lovers, Molly has stayed in character within Bloom's story. It has been easier for her to do so because his story has room within it for the two of them to be in love. Not once in all the thinking he does about her infidelity does Bloom pretend that Molly might not love him. But neither does he let it occur to him that she does. Molly reads his story about them as a love story, wants it to have a similar emphasis for him. "Is she in love with the first fellow all the time?" (4: 355–56), she asks Bloom about a book he had brought her to read. Protecting himself against the suggestiveness of her question, he answers curtly that he "never read it."[32]

"The new I want" (13: 1104), Bloom thinks after masturbating. As he tells them to himself, though, his and Molly's characters are locked in the same old story and so there's "nothing new under the sun " (13: 1104–5). Nothing, that is, except the story Molly has begun only tonight to tell herself about the two of them. Not until she decides that she must make him want her does Molly stop reading Bloom's story and start constructing her own. *Ulysses* makes room for her story as well as for his. "Ill just give him one more chance" (18: 1497–98), she thinks before *Ulysses* ends. If it is to be his last chance, she had better make it a good one, not just another episode in Bloom's old story. "I cant help it if Im young still can I" (18: 1398–99), she reasons, almost apologizing for no longer taking her cues from him. Reminded by her day that by seducing him she can do something with her youth that she has not yet done, she tells herself that her character and Bloom's are about to enact a story in which "the old love is the new" (18: 1291).

When the story he tells himself throughout his waking hours is overtaken by sleep, Bloom begins to be a new character, a character whose dangers and possibilities are enlarged by the new story someone is telling herself about him. One way or the other, renewal is on its way for Bloom: "Yes because a woman whatever she does she knows where to stop" (18: 1438–39), and Molly has at last had more than enough of Bloom's story. "O thanks be to the great God I got somebody to give me what I badly wanted to put some heart up into me" (18: 732–33). Until tonight, it had been narrowly acceptable to her that Bloom not respond directly and fully to her needs. She had remained for him a character that he managed to keep at a safe distance and still keep. Until tonight. For instead of placating her, as Bloom had thought it might, Molly's having gotten what she badly wanted has primed her to want more. She acknowledges that she wants to be embraced again and again "no matter by who . . . if the fellow you want isnt there" (18: 1408–10): "suppose I never came back" (18: 373), she speculates about going on the road with Boylan. Bloom is sure that she will not run off with the "worst man in Dublin" (6: 202), and he is probably right. But if Molly stays with the story she has begun to tell herself, one of two things will happen. Either she will leave Bloom—in which case he will

decidedly be a new character—or he will be a new character by beginning to meet her needs more satisfyingly than he has for years.

I feel that Bloom would prefer "the latter, by the line of least resistance" (17: 1957). It will never come to that for him, though, unless
the new Molly is both tenacious and patient with her plan. She will be
neither unless she continues to want Bloom and to sense that he wants
her. What has been a mutual interest between them may not hold. If
it does not, one of them will leave and not come back: if it does hold,
each will learn things about the other's character that will change for
the better their respective stories about themselves and one another.

NEXTS

What comes next for Molly and Bloom there is no one to say. There
are no "nexts" for them because, as substitutes for persons and not persons, they have been out of time all along.

Unlike Bloom and Molly but like James Joyce and you, I do not
substitute for a person. If I did, I would not have time to read or write.
Because they are timeless substitutes for persons and not persons, there
has never been a time when Bloom and Molly needed something from
me, not even the time it takes to read *Ulysses*. Because he took the
time to write a book that turns out to be for me, James Joyce needed
something from me in time, something that includes you.

Over the thirty years that I have been reading Bloom's and Molly's
story, it has implicated me in a series of "nexts" that make an issue of
justice. From "Mr Leopold Bloom ate with relish" through Molly's final
"Yes," each part of speech is so imbued with what Joyce needs to be
heard as having said about justice that in any next moment of reading
Ulysses I am likely to be distracted, involuntarily called away from
something Joyce has said for me to what I must say or do for you. At
the same time that their story's claim to my attention has me reading
it, I may be reminded by that story and in spite of myself that you have
much the more compelling claim. If I refuse to heed its reminder then
I am Bloom refusing to heed Molly. Quite independently of my sex and
yours, and although you are not my lover, I cannot at the same time
heed Bloom's willful refusal of Molly's claim to him and refuse your
claim to me.

More forcefully than any other story in it—and there are many—
Bloom's and Molly's story reminds me that *Ulysses* as a whole is over
and done with. It also reminds me that as such, as over and done with,
its claim to my attention is unjustly strong because of its resemblance
to persons' claims to me. Because my responses to *Ulysses* are not over
and done with but ongoing, I am free to sentimentalize by mistaking

my ongoing responses to it as my ongoing responses to persons. But *Ulysses* is refractory to sentimentalizing. *Ulysses* reminds me that whereas it is complete and forever present, what I must do for persons is messily fragmented, always in another time. While I have time to do it, I will obviously have to do what I must do in another time than the present. To the degree that it sends me away from the cases it has told and into those that I myself have left to tell, James Joyce's *Ulysses* is for justice.

Introduction

1. The recording was made in 1924. It was released only in 1961 by Rhein-Verlag under the title *James Joyce Spricht*. Except for a few relatively minor changes, the passage Joyce recorded appears in *Ulysses*, ed. Hans Walter Gabler (New York: Random House, 1986) (7: 827–69). All quotations from *Ulysses* are from this edition, and parenthetical references in the text are to chapter and line number.

2. Because the word "need" is central to my interests in the pages below, I must acknowledge Jean Baudrillard's critique of it. For Baudrillard, "needs are strictly specified in advance in relation to *finite* objects. There is only need for *this* or *that* object." *Selected Writings*, ed. Mark Poster (Stanford, Calif.: Stanford University Press, 1988), p. 41. A "system of objects" operates and "imposes its own coherence and thus acquires the capacity to fashion an entire society" (pp. 14–15). "Because *the structure of the sign is at the very heart of the commodity form* . . . , its very form establishes it as a total medium, as a *system of communication* administering all social exchange" (p. 79.). Within this sign-exchanging medium, "purchasing and consumption must have the same value as any *human* relation" (p. 14). Signification "is the locus of an elemental objectification that reverberates through the amplified systems of signs. . . . All the repressive and reductive strategies of power systems are already present in the internal logic of the sign" (p. 92). In the pages that follow, I will be supposing that the signs through which persons' needs are responded to will not in all cases have been appropriated to what Baudrillard calls "*the commodity form*": in those cases in which the signs have been so appropriated, the responses carried by those signs cannot be just. I understand "need" as the need that Baudrillard himself is responding to by way of his own writing: "we *need*," he insists, "a critique of signifier fetishism" (p. 63, my emphasis).

3. George Meredith, *The Ordeal of Richard Feverel* (New York: Scribner's, 1917), p. 180.

4. I apply the definition of the sentimentalist to MacHugh and his listeners despite the fact that it is one of their number, Stephen, who has "cribbed" it. In Stephen's use of the definition, the sentimentalist is of course Mulligan, whom Stephen is accusing of trying to freeload.

5. "No blame attached to anyone": James Joyce, *Dubliners* (New York: Viking Press, 1958), p. 115. Subsequent references to this work in the text will be identified with *D* and a page number. While my use of the word "case" has obvious connections with its uses in forensics, law, medicine, psychoanalysis, and philosophy (I am thinking here of the standard "just in case," as in "just in case I am a

person writing these phrases and not a brain in a vat"), the focus I would like for it is closer to the colloquial sense in which someone might say about someone else, "His is an interesting case."

6. Bloom to Stephen in the cabman's shelter: "It's all very fine to boast of mutual superiority but what about mutual equality" (16: 1098–99).

7. It is not far into *Ulysses* that a question of this kind is asked by the first character named. "Why don't you trust me more?" Mulligan asks Stephen. "What have you up your nose against me?" "Cough it up. I'm quite frank with you" (1: 161–62, 179–80).

8. Emmanuel Levinas describes the "locus of justice" as a "terrain common to me and the others where I am counted among them, that is, where subjectivity is a citizen." *Otherwise than Being*, trans. Alphonso Lingis (The Hague: Martinus Nijhoff, 1981), p. 160.

9. Don Gifford with Robert J. Seidman, *Notes for Joyce: An Annotation of James Joyce's* Ulysses (New York: E. P. Dutton and Co., Inc., 1974), p. 118.

10. Stephen thinks of *"Isis Unveiled"* (9: 279). H. P. Blavatsky, *Isis Unveiled* (1877; reprint, Pasadena, Calif.: Theosophical University Press, 1972), vol. 1, p. 179.

11. Hugh Kenner, *Joyce's Voices* (Berkeley: University of California Press, 1978), p. 75.

12. Hugh Kenner, *Ulysses* (London: Allen and Unwin, 1980), p. 63.

13. David Hayman, Ulysses: *The Mechanics of Meaning* (Englewood Cliffs, N.J.: Prentice-Hall, 1970), p. 84.

14. Ulysses: *The Mechanics of Meaning*, rev. ed. (Madison: University of Wisconsin Press, 1982), p. 123.

15. Karen Lawrence, *The Odyssey of Style in* Ulysses (Princeton: Princeton University Press, 1981), p. 60.

16. Ibid., p. 67.

17. What I mean by a "line" in this sense is a sequence of phrases that refers to one or another of the three elements within *Ulysses* that I am proposing to describe.

18. A. Walton Litz, *The Art of James Joyce: Method and Design in* Ulysses *and* Finnegans Wake (New York: Oxford University Press, 1961), and Michael Groden, *Ulysses in Progress* (Princeton: Princeton University Press, 1977), attend directly to the history of Joyce's work on the book.

19. Fritz Senn, *Joyce's Dislocations*, ed. John Paul Riquelme (Baltimore: Johns Hopkins University Press, 1984), p. 71.

20. Ibid., p. 66.

21. Patrick McGee, *Paperspace* (Lincoln: University of Nebraska Press, 1988), p. 175.

22. Julia Kristeva, "Joyce 'The Gracehoper,' or the Return of Orpheus," in *James Joyce: The Augmented Ninth*, ed. Bernard Benstock (Syracuse: Syracuse University Press, 1988), p. 180.

23. Jean-Michel Rabaté, "A Portrait of the Artist as a Bogeyman," in B. Benstock, *James Joyce*, p. 110.

24. Vicki Mahaffey, *Reauthorizing Joyce* (New York: Cambridge University Press, 1988), p. 60.

25. Ibid., p. 61.

26. Fredric Jameson, " 'Ulysses' in History," in *James Joyce and Modern Literature*, ed. W. J. McCormack and Alistair Stead (London: Routledge and Kegan Paul, 1982), p. 139.

27. Ibid., p. 139.

28. Ibid., p. 140.

29. Ibid., p. 127.

30. Shari Benstock, "City Spaces and Women's Places in Joyce's Dublin," in B. Benstock, *James Joyce*, p. 296.

31. Jacques Derrida, "Ulysses Gramophone," in B. Benstock, *James Joyce*, p. 58.

32. Ibid., p. 62.

33. Ibid., p. 60.

34. Ibid., p. 54.

35. Ibid., pp. 61, 63, 65.

36. Ibid., p. 63.

37. Ibid., p. 62.

38. Ibid., p. 58.

39. James Joyce, *Finnegans Wake* (New York: Viking Press, 1959), p. 179. Subsequent references to this work in the text will be identified with *FW* and a page number.

40. How I read them is informed by what has registered with me in my encounters with other persons, whether those encounters are face to face or by way of written language. Two writers other than Joyce who have been especially formative for me are Emmanuel Levinas and Jean-François Lyotard. While it would be an altogether separate project to do as little as to summarize my debt to Levinas and Lyotard, I will refer to their work repeatedly in these notes.

41. Lyotard on "specular representation: a sick person does not get well by looking in the mirror." *The Differend*, trans. Georges Van Den Abbeele (Minneapolis: University of Minnesota Press, 1988), p. 152. Also, "the examination of phrases . . . cannot take the place of politics" (p. 158).

42. "The differend is the unstable state and instant of language wherein something which must be put into phrases cannot yet be." "In the differend, something 'asks' to be put into phrases and suffers from the wrong of not being able to be put into phrases right away." *Ibid.*, p. 13. What I am calling the "tacit" is this "something" that " 'asks' to be put into phrases and suffers" less from the "wrong" of its not yet being phraseable than from the consequent prolongation of the need that renders it a "something" to be asked.

43. "The Other, in the hands of forces that break him, exposed to powers, remains unforeseeable, that is, transcendent." Emmanuel Levinas, *Totality and Infinity*, trans. Alphonso Lingis (Pittsburgh: Duquesne University Press, 1969), p. 225. "The silence that surrounds the phrase: *Auschwitz was the extermination camp . . .* is the sign that something remains to be phrased which is not." Lyotard, *Differend*, p. 57.

44. "Reason," writes Levinas, "conducts a monologue." "A reason cannot be other for a reason." *Totality and Infinity*, p. 72.

45. "What have I done to be from the start in debt?" Levinas, *Otherwise than Being*, p. 87. The answer: I have started.

46. "In the proximity of the other, all the others than the other obsess me, and

already this obsession cries out for justice." *Ibid.*, p. 158. "Language . . . refuses the clandestinity of love, where it loses its frankness and meaning and turns into laughter and cooing. The third party looks at me in the eyes of the Other—language is justice." Levinas, *Totality and Infinity*, p. 213. "Justice remains justice only in a society where there is no distance between those close and those far off, but in which there also remains the impossibility of passing by the closest." Levinas, *Otherwise than Being*, p. 159.

47. "He who speaks to me and across the words proposes himself to me retains the fundamental foreignness of the Other who judges me; our relations are never reversible." Levinas, *Totality and Infinity*, p. 101.

48. "All ideology in the strongest sense, including the most exclusive forms of ruling-class consciousness just as much as that of oppositional or oppressed classes—is in its very nature Utopian." Fredric Jameson, *The Political Unconscious* (Ithaca: Cornell University Press, 1981), p. 289. Because ideology is utopian, justice refuses to be ideological.

49. According to Levinas, the impulse to say or do something is itself "the surplus of responsibility," "a responsibility with regard to men we do not even know." *Otherwise than Being*, p. 100. "Under accusation by everyone, the responsibility for everyone goes to the point of substitution. A subject is a hostage" in that it is obliged to substitute itself *for* the other. "Everything is from the start in the accusative. Such is the exceptional condition or unconditionality of the self, the signification of the pronoun *self* for which our Latin grammars themselves know no nominative form" (p. 112).

50. "In discourse the divergence that inevitably opens between the Other as my theme and the Other as my interlocutor, emancipated from the theme that seemed a moment to hold him, forthwith contests the meaning I ascribe to my interlocutor." Levinas, *Totality and Infinity*, p. 195.

51. "The subject is the more responsible the more it answers for, as though the distance between it and the other increased in the measure that proximity was increased." "Proximity is my approaching of the other, the fact that the proximity of the same and the other is never close enough. The summoned one is the ego—me. I repel and send away the neighbor through my very identity, my occupying the arena of being; I then have always to reestablish peace." Levinas, *Otherwise than Being*, pp. 139–40, 137.

52. Richard Ellmann, *James Joyce* (New York: Oxford University Press, 1982), pp. 374–75.

53. *Letters of James Joyce*, vol. 1, ed. Stuart Gilbert (New York: Viking Press, 1957), p. 168.

54. Ibid., p. 171.

Chapter 1. Jamesy

1. James Joyce, *A Portrait of the Artist as a Young Man* (New York: Viking Press, 1964), p. 16. Subsequent references to this work in the text will be identified with *P* and a page number.

2. Gifford and Seidman, *Notes for Joyce*, p. 140.

3. See Hugh Kenner, "The Rhetoric of Silence," *James Joyce Quarterly* 14 (Summer, 1977): 382–94.

4. "There's a friend of yours gone by, Dedalus" (6: 41).

5. Clive Hart, "Wandering Rocks," in *James Joyce's* Ulysses, ed. Clive Hart and David Hayman (Berkeley: University of California Press, 1974), pp. 197–98.

6. Robert Martin Adams, *Surface and Symbol* (New York: Oxford University Press, 1962), p. 218.

7. Hugh Kenner has caught Jamesy in the act of allowing Bloom to suppress from his budget for the day (17: 1455) "the eleven shillings he left behind in the whorehouse" (*Joyce's Voices*, p. 88). My claim is that Jamesy knows not only about the eleven shillings and their suppression but also that a person of Kenner's acumen would hold him answerable for having let the "falsified" budget pass.

8. According to Kenner's Uncle Charles Principle, "*the narrative idiom need not be the narrator's*" but may instead be that of the character the narrative describes. See *Joyce's Voices*, pp. 15–38.

9. Shari and Bernard Benstock on *Ulysses*: "One must assume that the work itself presents a certain 'reality' consistent in its effort to render the city in as many forms and from as many perspectives as possible, and it is to that reality the reader must attend in an effort to distinguish the personal subjectivity of characters' impressions from the models of physical phenomena present everywhere in the text." "The Benstock Principle," in *The Seventh of Joyce*, ed. Bernard Benstock (Bloomington: Indiana University Press, 1982), p. 16.

10. They become countable thanks to Shari and Bernard Benstock's *Who's He When He's at Home* (Urbana: University of Illinois Press, 1980).

11. Ellmann, *James Joyce*, pp. 374–75.

12. David Hayman observes that the headlines are disruptive only of space, the temporal context of the chapter remaining "continuous." *Ulysses*, p. 95.

13. Gifford and Seidman identify Hynes's "Jimmy Johnson" as "the Reverend James Johnson (fl. 1870–1900), a Scot Presbyterian, who styled himself 'The Apostle of Truth.' " *Notes for Joyce*, p. 284. It must be only coincidence that "so help you Jimmy Johnson" can also be read as invoking that Jimmy who was the son of John Joyce.

14. In reading *Ulysses*, Shari and Bernard Benstock write, "The possibility that one voice subsumes all voices, all stylistic and linguistic permutations, becomes conceptually difficult to manage: after all, narrators (even reliable ones) are known by their consistencies—and here is a narrative that seems to rest on inconsistency." "Benstock Principle," p. 12.

15. Hugh Kenner describes an "impersonator" in *Ulysses'* narrative but limits it to what he takes to be the second narrator's "impersonation of a Dublin barfly" in chapter 12. *Joyce's Voices*, p. 77.

16. It is precisely the five chapters in the middle, chapters 10 through 14, that S. L. Goldberg finds most wanting. See *The Classical Temper* (New York: Barnes and Noble, 1961), pp. 280–88.

17. Hugh Kenner counts only one, the barfly. I am assuming that the barfly qualifies with Kenner while my other two guest-narrators do not because the barfly's is the only narrative of the three in the first person.

18. David Hayman on chapter 16: "It is a mind with its defenses up and not

down, one which has turned suddenly public in the manner of a conventional and self-deceiving narrator." *Ulysses*, p. 102.

19. "Amid the book's general movement from the clear to the opaque and from the specific to the general, character is the closest thing to a constant." James H. Maddox, Jr., *Joyce's* Ulysses *and the Assault upon Character* (New Brunswick, N.J.: Rutgers University Press, 1978), p. 16.

20. "We may reach a standpoint so removed from the perspective of human life that all we can do is to observe: nothing seems to have value of the kind it appears to have from inside, and all we can see is human desires, human striving—human *valuing*, as an activity or condition. . . . From far enough outside my birth seems accidental, my life pointless, and my death insignificant, but from inside my never having been born seems nearly unimaginable, my life monstrously important, and my death catastrophic. Though the two viewpoints clearly belong to one person— these problems wouldn't arise if they didn't—they function independently enough so that each can come as something of a surprise to the other, like an identity that has been temporarily forgotten." Thomas Nagel, *The View from Nowhere* (New York: Oxford University Press, 1986), p. 209. As I describe them, Jamesy's disclosures proceed exclusively from what Nagel calls the "outside" point of view. What Jamesy knows, he knows from "a standpoint so removed" from any person's that his only "problem" is how to feign being subject to any person's two points of view.

21. Hart, "Wandering Rocks," p. 191.

22. That Jamesy so much as poses at remembering what he has said is a change from chapter 10, and one that calls more attention to his impersonating. Even in the onelegged sailor's second appearance in chapter 10, Karen Lawrence points out, he remains "a" and not "the" onelegged sailor (10: 228). "The repetition is strange because there is no acknowledgment in the narrative that the sailor is the *same* one in both descriptions. The narrative inability to progress from the indefinite to the definite article illustrates a strange failing in the 'narrative memory.' " *Odyssey of Style*, p. 84.

23. This definition is from the *Oxford English Dictionary* (New York: Oxford University Press, 1971).

24. "By exposing an impromptu eruption of folly, the speaker *imposes* on it a sort of sanity and order and *asserts*, for the benefit of his silent audience, the priorities of order." David Hayman, "Cyclops," in Hart and Hayman, *James Joyce's* Ulysses, p. 260.

25. A "kind of talk," any kind of talk, is what Lyotard refers to as a "genre of discourse": "a phrase that comes along is put into play within a conflict between genres of discourse. This conflict is a differend, since the success (or the validation) proper to one genre is not the one proper to the others." *Differend*, p. 136.

26. "To the question, Why are there men rather than man? Kant would have answered: In order that they may talk to one another." Hannah Arendt, *Lectures in Kant's Political Philosophy*, ed. Ronald Beiner (Chicago: University of Chicago Press, 1982), p. 40.

27. "An institution takes shape, removed from public places. In its heart, the stakes are not that of vanquishing but of coming to an agreement." Lyotard, *Differend*, p. 23.

28. "I am sitting with a philosopher in the garden; he says again and again 'I know that that's a tree,' pointing to a tree that is near us. Someone else arrives and hears this, and I tell him: 'This fellow isn't insane. We are only doing philosophy.' " Ludwig Wittgenstein, *On Certainty*, trans. Denis Paul and G.E.M. Anscombe (New York: Harper Torch Books, 1972), p. 61e.

29. "Almost every possible person has not been born and never will be." Nagel, *View from Nowhere*, p. 211.

30. "*L'aiuola che ci fa tanto feroci*," Dante, *Paradiso*, 22:151 (trans. Laurence Binyon).

Chapter 2. Stephen

1. Karen Lawrence, "Paternity, the Legal Fiction," in *Joyce's* Ulysses: *The Larger Perspective*, ed. Robert D. Newman and Weldon Thornton (Newark: University of Delaware Press, 1987), p. 90.

2. Mahaffey, *Reauthorizing Joyce*, p. 46.

3. Ibid., p. 46.

4. Lawrence, "Paternity," p. 95.

5. "Power is passed 'from only begetter to only begotten,' without the love of opposition represented by biological reproduction." Mahaffey, *Reauthorizing Joyce*, p. 48.

6. Since paternity "can never be proven by the evidence of the senses," Jean-Michel Rabaté writes, it "rests upon the superior truth of a purely 'apostolic succession,' " which "bars the way to a feminine identification of an offspring and opens up the realm of the Symbolic—therefore, of literature." "Paternity, Thy Name Is Joy," in B. Benstock, *James Joyce*, p. 221.

7. "Self-sending barely allows a detour via the virgin mother when the father imagines sending himself, getting high on, the seed of the consubstantial son." Derrida, "Ulysses Gramophone," p. 67.

8. Maud Ellmann describes the navel as the scar "where the mother's namelessness engraves itself upon the flesh before the father ever carved his signature." "Polytropic Man: Paternity, Identity, and Naming in *The Odyssey* and *A Portrait of the Artist as a Young Man*," in *James Joyce: New Perspectives*, ed. Colin MacCabe (Bloomington: Indiana University Press, 1982), p. 96. While Ellmann insists that Stephen is forced to confront a world in which "the phallus has surrendered to the omphalos," she does not entertain the possibility that the father's very capacity to "sign" his name is a biologically "necessary" dispensation granted him by the mother and not something he manages to do on his own.

9. The theory is Peter J. Wilson's in *Man, the Promising Primate* (New Haven: Yale University Press, 1980).

10. Wilson examines Wittgenstein's use of this term and goes on to argue that "kinship . . . provides the major metaphor by which a relatedness between different phenomena can be grasped and communicated." See *ibid.*, pp. 163–69.

11. On the strand, Stephen thinks "you will not be master of others or their slave" (3: 295–96), one of several instances in *Ulysses* in which his impatience with

his dialectic breaks through and points him toward a less neatly circumscribed perspective on his world.

12. See Hannah Arendt, *The Human Condition* (New York: Anchor, 1958), p. 182.

13. Gifford and Seidman, *Notes for Joyce*, p. 44.

14. "Stephen's weakness is not that he is bookish but that he is so excessively bookish." Maddox, *Joyce's Ulysses*, p. 5.

15. See Michael Patrick Gillespie on Stephen's interest in Goulding and Egan. "Redrawing the Artist as a Young Man," in Newman and Thornton, *Joyce's Ulysses*, p. 131.

16. For Hugh Kenner's reading of what occurred, see his *Ulysses*, pp. 115–16.

17. These words are in part Bloom's application of the "spellingbee conundrum," "embarra two ars is it? double ess ment of a harassed pedlar while gauging au the symmetry" (7: 167–68).

18. Colin MacCabe writes that by the end of the ninth chapter, when Stephen and Bloom meet briefly at the library, "Stephen is still unable to accept the chance encounters which will remake him through a series of accidents." "The Voice of Esau: Stephen in the Library," in MacCabe, *James Joyce*, p. 115. I am suggesting that Stephen is moving, however slightly, in the direction of just such acceptance by the end of chapter 16.

19. "Brother Michael," *P*, 23; "his father," *P*, 65; "the dean of studies," *P*, 184.

20. "—Mrs Bloom, my wife the *prima donna* Madam Marion Tweedy, Bloom indicated. Taken a few years since. In or about ninety six" (16: 1437–38). Molly was born in 1870.

Chapter 3. James Joyce

Parts of this chapter first appeared in *Southwest Review* 71, no.2 (Spring, 1986): 150–69.

1. "In a chapter concerned with mysterious disguises and the possibility of revelation, perhaps Murphy's most significant act is the baring of his chest. He draws aside his shirt and thereby reveals one of the classic means of establishing identity, a tattoo." Maddox, *Joyce's Ulysses*, p. 159. Because the tattoo is a portrait of its artist as a young man, Maddox reads the "young man's sideface looking frowningly rather" (16: 675–76) as Stephen. When Murphy then pulls the skin beneath the tattoo, the same face's frown gives way to a "forced smiling" (16: 687)—the phrase that for Maddox best characterizes the life and times of Leopold Bloom. Only the writer could reveal that within his autobiographical portrait Bloom had "displaced" Stephen. Maddox therefore concludes that "Murphy is a witty portrait of the artist as James Joyce" (p. 160).

2. See Ellmann, *James Joyce*, p. 509.

3. Gilbert, *Letters of James Joyce*, vol. 1, p. 165.

4. Ibid., p. 175.

5. Ibid., p. 135.

6. Quoted in Ellmann, *James Joyce*, p. 291.

7. Ibid., p. 338.

8. Gifford and Seidman, *Notes for Joyce*, p. 459.

9. Hans Jonas describes "an emotional relation comparable to love on the part of the political individual toward the community whose destiny he wishes to guide to the best." Such an individual is "descended" from that community "and through it has become what he is; he is thus, indeed, not the father, but a 'son' of his people and country (also class, etc.) and thereby in a kind of sibling relation to all the others—present, future, even past—with whom he shares this bond." *The Imperative of Responsibility*, trans. Hans Jonas with David Herr (Chicago: University of Chicago Press, 1984), p. 104.

10. Levinas defines time as "the postponement of death in a mortal will." *Totality and Infinity*, p. 232.

11. For a summary of these years, see Edward Norman, *A History of Modern Ireland* (Baltimore: Pelican Books, 1973), pp. 221–44.

12. Dominic Manganiello traces Joyce's political interests and allegiances during the thirty years between Parnell's death and the completion of *Ulysses*. See his *Joyce's Politics* (London: Routledge and Kegan Paul, 1980), pp. 98–174.

13. G. J. Watson, "The Politics of *Ulysses*," in Newman and Thornton, *Joyce's Ulysses*, p. 41.

14. Ibid., p. 41.

15. Ibid., p. 56.

16. *Letters of James Joyce*, vol. 2, ed. Richard Ellmann (New York: Viking Press, 1966), p. 468.

17. *Ulysses* may not seem to be for justice to a person who looks to it for a specific program for justice. *Ulysses* urges that every case be heard and responded to justly: beyond that, it advances no program for identifying injustice, nor could it be for justice if it did. "Injustice cannot be detected by any constant signs; on the contrary, to have recourse to the constancy of would-be clear signs, to the articles of the code, to established institutions, recourse to the *letter* as that which allows the just to be separated from the unjust—that is unjust." Lyotard, "Levinas' Logic," trans. Ian McLeod, in *The Lyotard Reader*, ed. Andrew Benjamin (Cambridge, Mass.: Basil Blackwell, 1989), p. 286.

18. Ellmann, *James Joyce*, pp. 363–64.

19. W. J. McCormack, "James Joyce, Cliché, and the Irish Language," in B. Benstock, *James Joyce*, p. 329.

20. Ibid., p. 327.

21. Ibid., p. 331.

22. Mary King, "*Ulysses*: The Dissolution of Identity and the Appropriation of the Human World," in B. Benstock, *James Joyce*, p. 342. The phrases she quotes are from *Capital*.

23. McCormack, "Irish Language," p. 335.

24. "Suppose I am the semaphore man guiding planes in to land. The language I use is entirely determined by forms and conventions; but do I then have no control over it, could I not be responsible for wishing or intending and thus causing a plane to crash?" Christopher Butler, "Joyce and the Displaced Author," in McCormack and Stead, *James Joyce and Modern Literature*, p. 69.

25. "The central trauma of Bloom's life," according to James H. Maddox, Jr., is

that "his love of Molly lured him on to the catastrophe of his son's death and the sorrowful aftermath of the subsequent years." Because of his "deep-seated fears of suffering the death of another child," "the idea of renewed sex with Molly constitutes the true zone of disaster in Bloom's mind." *Joyce's Ulysses*, pp. 70, 61, 71.

26. "He couldnt possibly do without it that long so he must do it somewhere and the last time he came on my bottom when was it" (18: 76–77).

27. See Hannah Arendt, *The Life of the Mind*, vol. 2, *Willing* (New York: Harcourt Brace Jovanovich, 1978), pp. 69–70, 102, 130.

28. "Voglio e non vorrei" (4: 327). Bloom subsequently corrects himself: "*Voglio e non vorrei*. No. *Vorrei e non*" (6: 238).

29. "For Bloom, to look forward to the future is to be reminded of the past—the death of his son Rudy. Cut off from continuity with either past or future, Bloom is unable to participate in the very process of Nature to which he gives intellectual and emotional assent." Maddox, *Joyce's Ulysses*, p. 56.

30. "Very sad thing. But had to be" (11: 1121).

31. It is in this same paragraph that Bloom decides he will masturbate before Dignam's funeral. "Also I think I. Yes I. Do it in the bath. Curious longing I" (5: 503–4). Five hours later, he has not masturbated, and he thinks: "Her eyes over the sheet. Yashmak. Find the way in. A cave. No admittance except on business" (11: 943–44).

32. "Never read it. Do you want another?" (4: 357). Bloom is asking if she wants another book, obviously, but as a response to Molly's question it implies "Do you want another fellow?"

INDEX

ULYSSES AND JUSTICE

James McMichael

"The overall argument of this book is
original, forceful, and significant; it
promises to play an important part in
the reevaluation of Joyce's relationship
to his readers that began a few years
ago. Moreover, McMichael's account
of the differences between Stephen
Dedalus and James Joyce is better than
anything I have read on the subject,
and his analysis of Bloom's relationship to Molly is equally fine."
—*Vicki Mahaffey*,
University of Pennsylvania

For James McMichael, Joyce's *Ulysses*
invites the wide range of interpretations
it has received: what it also does is to prod
its interpreters to put the book to some
just use. If *Ulysses* were more conventional than it is, McMichael claims, its
readers could set more comfortable limits
for themselves in their responses to it,
limits that did not extend beyond *Ulysses*
into their dealings with persons in the
world. But what happens instead is that
the singularly unconventional narrative
structure of *Ulysses* keeps reminding them
that the story they are being told about
any of the characters is the same kind of
story they tell themselves whenever they
think about a person. It reminds them
that every person needs to be responded